D1256079

THE SATIRES
OF LUDOVICO ARIOSTO

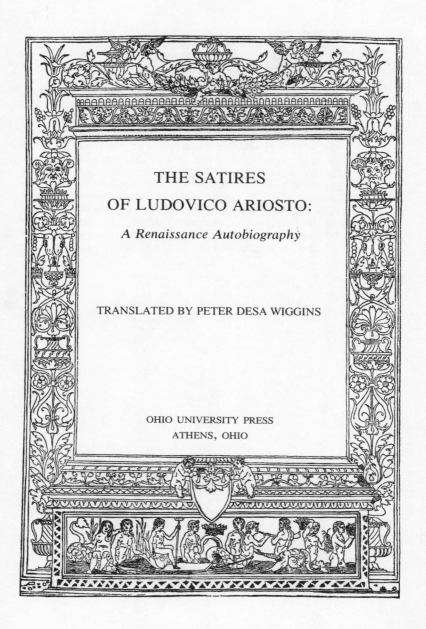

THE SATIRES
OF LUDOVICO ARIOSTO:

A Renaissance Autobiography

TRANSLATED BY PETER DESA WIGGINS

OHIO UNIVERSITY PRESS
ATHENS, OHIO

ACKNOWLEDGMENTS

I owe particular gratitude to Professor Maurice J. Valency, "*che ragion vuol ch'io sempre benedica*," for having directed my attention to Ariosto's *Satires* and for having guided me patiently through the many difficult stages toward the completion of this project. Otherwise my range of debts is great. Mario Corona, my first instructor of Italian at Columbia College, deserves some credit for this book. Had he not imparted his love of Italy and things Italian to all of us in his class so well and so powerfully, I wonder if I would ever have gone on to read Ariosto. Equally strong is my sense of gratitude to those who have given me most recently the benefit of their criticism and experience. Professors Thomas G. Bergin, James J. Mirollo, and Joseph Tusiani were particularly gracious with their time and encouragement. For having made possible the publication of this book with a generous subsidy, the Committee for Faculty Research of the College of William and Mary also deserves many thanks. Lastly, the bilingual format of this edition of Ariosto's *Satires* was facilitated by the generosity of Riccardo Ricciardi Editore who granted me permission to use their excellent text of the original edited by Cesare Segre.

For Maureen

CONTENTS

INTRODUCTION

THE REPUTATION OF THE *SATIRES*

The *Satires*, overshadowed as they have always been by the *Orlando Furioso*, have never received, until recently, the quality of critical attention they deserve considering their central position among Ariosto's works. They were composed at odd moments during the years 1517 through 1525, when Ariosto was in his forties. He had been practising the art of poetry for more than twenty years. As a young man, during the decade from 1493 to 1503, between the termination of his legal studies and his conversion to writing poetry in the vernacular, Ariosto composed most of the poems which comprise his *Lirica Latina*. It was not a first-rate collection by the standards of his time, but it was promising enough to have gained for him, long before its posthumous publication, the respect of Pietro Bembo.[1] Although no dates can be attributed to the vast majority of the vernacular lyrics comprising the *Canzoniere*, it is safe to assume that many of them were written between the summer of 1513, when Ariosto first sensed that Alessandra Benucci might return his love, and the autumn of 1517, when he wrote his first satire after having refused to follow Cardinal Ippolito d'Este to Hungary.

In any case, Ariosto's lyric poetry, though extremely influential throughout the sixteenth century, is unimportant by comparison with the *Orlando Furioso*. This was first published in forty cantos in 1516, a year before the poet began to work on the *Satires*. The *Orlando* received a second edition in 1521, with only minor changes and additions, and a third edition in 1532, this time with six new cantos and an extensive revision. The *Satires* also underwent a thorough revision after the last in the group was completed. Although the "*limae labor*" devoted to the *Satires* cannot be compared with the intensive work of polishing, correcting, and amplifying which Ariosto devoted to the third edition of the *Orlando Furioso*, it must have been carried on, albeit sporadically, at the same time. Ariosto gave the *Satires* their present form just when he was striving most conscientiously to bring elegance and harmony to his work. We should look for beauties in the *Satires* which only a great poet in his maturity can produce.

In addition to his accomplishments in the lyric and romance forms, Ariosto had, by 1517, established himself as Italy's leading dramatist. His first comedy, *La Cassaria*, was performed in its prose version at the Ducal Theater in Ferrara on 5 March 1508. His second comedy, *I Suppositi*, translated into English in 1566 by George Gascoigne as *The Supposes*, was performed in Ferrara on 6 February of the following year. Ariosto's reputation as a dramatist and as an expert on all matters involving the staging of plays grew throughout his life, and the comedies he completed, four in number with the *Lena* and *Il Negromante*, served as models for his successors.[2] As in his satires he turned to Horace's *Satires* and *Epistles* for models, he imitated Plautus and Terence in his comedies. However, the same freshness and concern with contemporary life apparent in the *Satires* also permeate the comedies, and especially the *Lena* and *Il Negromante*. In fact, the prologues to the comedies exhibit in their wit, irony, and references to everyday life a strong predilection on their author's part for formal satire.

The *Satires* have not been accorded the unanimous acclaim of Italian critics and literary historians that their place in the Ariosto canon seems to demand. They have been both praised and maligned, but rarely in either case has there been a critical statement that illuminates our understanding of them as poetry. In his introductory *Discorso sopra la materia della satira* accompanying the *Sette libri di Satire* published in 1563, Francesco Sansovino grants Ariosto a place next to Horace in his esteem. He declares that satire calls for the naked truth, plain and simple, so much so that Horace among the Latins and Ariosto among the moderns wrote in such a low style that there is not the slightest difference between their verse and prose. A twentieth-century reader might turn pale at this statement, but Sansovino only meant, with the characteristic sixteenth-century confusion of *satura* with *satyros*, that Ariosto had captured perfectly that "*humili sermone*" which Horace considered appropriate to the satyr play. Sansovino accords Ariosto the highest praise of all in his little anthology of satire, the first in any vernacular, because Ariosto understood the spirit of

Horace well enough to recreate in Italian the form and content of Horatian satire. In the preface to his own three contributions, Sansovino admits that it was Ariosto's example that first encouraged him to write satires.

Others besides Sansovino recognized Ariosto as the father of classical satire in the vernacular and the perfect imitator of Horace. The trouble with sixteenth-century comments on the *Satires* is precisely that the commentators to a man stress the perfection of Ariosto's imitation and say nothing about what characterizes the work as his own. In the *Vita di Horatio* prefacing his translation of Horace's *Satires* and *Epistles,* Lodovico Dolce cites Quintilian's judgment that Horace wrote in a clear and simple style and that he reproved the wicked by laughing at their vices. "In these respects, as in many others," adds Dolce, "Ludovico Ariosto has followed marvelously in Horace's footsteps."[3] In the *argomento* to the seventh epistle of Book I, he notes that "this is the epistle that was so gracefully imitated by Ariosto in one of his satires."[4]

Perhaps Ariosto's earliest recognition as the foremost Italian satirist came from his younger contemporary, also a writer of satires, Luigi Alamanni. In the conclusion to his third satire, which must have been written sometime between 1523 and 1528, Alamanni boasts with characteristically cloying elegance,

> Nè l'Ariosto ancor di me si lagne,
> Il Ferrarese mio chiaro e gentile,
> Ch'oggi con lui cantando m'accompagne,
> Nè'l mio basso saper si prenda a vile
> Chè fors'ancor (s'io non l'estimo indarno)
> Girando il verno in più cortese aprile,
> Non havrà a schivo il Po, le rive d'Arno.

Nor indeed should Ariosto complain of me, my illustrious and noble Ferrarese, that today I join with him in singing, nor should he scorn my humble knowledge, for perhaps even yet (if I am not mistaken) when winter turns into more gracious April, the Po will not hold in disdain the shores of the Arno.

By 1523 Alamanni had found his way to France after having been exiled from Florence because of his participation in the conspiracy of 1522 against Cardinal Guilio de' Medici. While writing his own satires in France, he probably recollected having read, prior to his exile, copies of Ariosto's first three satires. There is also the possibility that he had copies sent to him in France. His friend and fellow conspirator, Zanobi Buondelmonte, had fled from Florence in 1522 to Garfagnana, where he knew that the commissioner, Ludovico Ariosto, would shelter him. In any case, some of Ariosto's satires were known to at least one literary figure at the French court long before their posthumous publication in 1534.

Clearly Alamanni considered Ariosto his major rival in the genre of satire and hoped that his own satires would equal those of the master. Even in his own century, he never won the acclaim he thought should be his. In the famous dialogue on the Italian language entitled the *Ercolano,* Benedetto Varchi declares through his surrogate that Ariosto's satires are very beautiful and fulfill all the requirements appropriate to satire. When asked about Alamanni's, he replies laconically, "Too beautiful."[5] Alamanni's satires are indeed too ostentatiously elegant, florid in their rhetoric, and tedious in content. Frequently they give the impression that their author was merely practising *amplificatio,* and they lack entirely the direct, natural tone of conversation common to Horace and Ariosto. The subtle concealment of art seems to have been beyond Alamanni's talent.

For the next significant mention of Ariosto's *Satires,* after Varchi, one must look all the way to the early eighteenth century and the second book of Vincenzo Gravina's *Ragion poetica.* Gravina declares that Ariosto is not only excellent in the epic and comedy, but also in satire, because of his nearness to Horace, who knew better than any of the Latins how to preserve the figure of comedy in his satires. Gravina goes on to praise Ariosto for the immense variety of subjects he deals with and for the naturalness and beauty of his style. He concludes that, by comparison with Ariosto, no other satirist in Italian, however learned, is worthy of mention.[6]

The first important appraisal of the Satires in the nineteenth century appears in the essay entitled "*Sui poemi narrativi e romanzeschi italiani*" written in 1819 by the romantic poet Ugo Foscolo. Here the *Satires* are said to deserve a place near those of Horace, because they express strong and noble sentiments tempered by the benign disposition of their author. In an elegant style, Foscolo says, Ariosto displays a profound understanding of human nature, and frankness in revealing to us his own character and his private life. The *Satires* are "veritable jewels of art." These merits, he concludes significantly, contribute to give the *Satires* the character of modern works.[7]

It should not surprise us that Foscolo was tempted on account of the *Satires* to claim Ariosto as a fellow romantic. No doubt, Ariosto chose the Horatian model for the very reason that it gave him the opportunity to express private feelings more or less candidly in the first person, though not with the frankness Foscolo had in mind, and not certainly in the spirit of the confessional. Foscolo failed understandably to take into consideration a practice very popular among writers of the Renaissance. Dante, Petrarch, and Boccaccio had firmly established in literary tradition the poet's creation for himself of an ideal autobiography, a blend of actual fact and studied fiction designed to form a picture of the poet, not as he actually was, but as he wished posterity to remember him. Ariosto would never have dreamt of writing confessions in the manner of Rousseau.

In the opening of the chapter on the *Orlando Furioso* in his *Storia della letteratura italiana*, first published in 1870-71, De Sanctis, repeating Foscolo's mistake, draws a biographical sketch of Ariosto based very largely on passages quoted from the *Satires*. According to De Sanctis, Ariosto reveals himself just as he is, simply and naturally, in the *Satires*. They represent an honest release of certain resentments that had built up over many years. The result, says De Sanctis, is that we are presented with a comical figure of a man—a lazy, cultured bourgeois, all wrapped up in his little private vexations, literary concerns, and love-affairs. Although Italy was in the throes of losing her independence, Ariosto could think only of obtaining a cozy sinecure and living a tranquil life in the company of the Muses. Of course, Ariosto, in his earnest mood, was totally unaware that there might be anything laughable about his position. In fact, he wrote his best tercets just when he was least consciously striving for an effect and most thoroughly absorbed in venting his spleen over the prosaic disappointments of his everyday life. While we may agree with De Sanctis that there is a certain dark comedy in the *Satires*, perhaps we should be reluctant to believe that it was unconscious on Ariosto's part. Why suddenly, when he comes to talking about himself, should Ariosto lose completely that acute sense of irony, that wry comic aloofness, which is a major source of interest and delight in the *Orlando Furioso*? In any case, Ariosto could not possibly have missed the striking incongruities between his own biography and Horace's and between the Augustan Age of Rome and Italy during the French invasions.

Although De Sanctis credited Ariosto with having revitalized poetic composition in *terza rima*, and although he obviously found the *Satires* charming, his reading of them fostered several unproductive but very persistent lines of critical thought in the twentieth century. Benedetto Croce expresses two of them. In the first place, he adopts unquestioningly De Sanctis's view that the *Satires* are pure autobiography. According to Croce, we have an Ariosto "in his dressing-gown, who experiences great delight in revealing, without the slightest reserve, his genuine character." Secondly, Croce refuses to consider the *Satires* poetry. They are merely a "*graziosissimo epistolario versificato.*" The letters are letters, prosaic in content, and the rime is only an embellishment.[8]

Giuseppe Fatini, with De Sanctis as his authority, pursues a third line of adverse criticism. According to Fatini, Ariosto never sees beyond an "*angusto orrizonte.*" The scope of the *Satires* is restricted to the interior life of a discontented man forced into servitude. There are too many monotonous laments, and there is too much declamation in a moral vein. A spacious and profound vision of reality is totally lacking. Fatini concludes that Ariosto did not bother to publish the *Satires* during his lifetime because he was aware of their artistic inferiority.[9] Aside from the consolation of viewpoints such as that of Bertani, who holds that there is an entire world of people and events in the *Satires*,[10] one wonders off-hand what there is about the inner life of a discontented man that may prevent it from being spacious and profound.

Clearly Croce's objection to the *Satires* is more serious than Fatini's and requires an answer. There have been several modern students of Ariosto who have seen in the *Satires* an artistic purpose beyond ingenious verse-making. Giuseppe Toffanin was the first to see that Ariosto might be creating an ideal picture of himself. He says that we are presented with "the flawless self-portrait of a consummate artist, who idealizes himself according to his own aesthetic model, that is, according to the demands of his own poetry."[11] Regrettably, Toffanin does not enlarge on this statement, suggestive as it is; but the requirements of his literary historical format prevent him from taking space adequate for the task. In any case, it is a statement of faith that Ariosto created a persona in the *Satires*—very close to life, but still a work of the imagination. If this is so, then Ariosto is inviting his readers to respond to a poetic fiction, born of a conceit, as the Renaissance used that term, and meaningful only if it is understood that the author kept a certain intellectual distance while in the act of creating.

Much later Santorre Debenedetti, in arguing that the *Satires* were not necessarily intended to be arranged in a strict chronological sequence, maintained that Ariosto organized the seven pieces with a view toward designing a complete and aesthetically pleasing work. His ideas are based largely on a close analysis of the text itself and are extremely convincing.[12]

However, we owe the most rewarding recent study of the *Satires* as poetry to Carlo Grabher, who uses Toffanin's observation as a point of departure for his own critical judgment. He claims that in the *Satires* Ariosto

> regards the affairs of life—including those of his own life—with an almost imperceptible detachment, with an almost inadvertent, but nearly constant, impetus to idealize. Events and feelings . . . live in abundance in an atmosphere which appears concretely real and has nevertheless its own contemplative remoteness. Ariosto succeeds often, especially in certain sketches and fables, in blending reality and fantasy in a style which powerfully exemplifies that kind of poetry which hides by design beneath the ingenuous and good-natured aspect of a confidence, or of a representation delivered in the manner of conversation.

According to Grabher, Ariosto created with the *Satires* a new poetic style, subdued, contemplative, expressive of emotion recollected in tranquillity—a style graced with an exquisite simplicity suited to show the poet's inner world reflected in the events of everyday life.[13]

Although Grabher does not make the connection, one cannot help but think of the major work of a French poet who was a member of the generation succeeding Ariosto's. The list of Joachim Du Bellay's models for *Les Regrets* includes Ovid's *Tristia*, Ronsard's sonnets for Marie, and the satirical sonnets of Berni and Burchiello. However, we know that Du Bellay had also read Ariosto's *Satires*, and that he used line 12 of Satire I in Sonnet 150 of *Les Regrets*. Beyond the simple translation of one line, there are enough affinities of tone and style between *Les Regrets* and the *Satires* to make one suspect that the *Satires* ought to be added to the list of Du Bellay's models. In the same restrained, apparently prosaic verse, embracing rhythms, phrases, and images possible in sophisticated speech, both poets voice their melancholy and their nostalgia over lost freedom, their exasperation with menial tasks which prevent them from writing poetry, and their bitterness at having learned through personal experience that disappointment, not wealth or preferment, is the reward of faithful service and reasonable hopes. In both poets, the traditional butts of satire—courtiers, prelates, and pedants—lose their abstract quality because they become parts of the mental life of a particular individual. Both poets have a mild, sardonic sense of humor, and they include themselves as targets of their own satire. Du Bellay, the fervent imitator of Ariosto in his *Olive*, could not have failed to see the similarities between Ariosto's servitude under "the yoke of the Cardinal of Este" and his own position in Rome in the service of his cousin, also a powerful cardinal more involved in diplomacy than in matters of religion.

Grabher's just attribution to Ariosto of the authorship of the plain style in the vernacular, generally held to be Du Bellay's contribution, only echoes the opinions of his sixteenth-century colleagues, Dolce and Sansovino; however, it should cause us to be more receptive to judgments like Vittorio Cian's, that the *Satires* are among the most original products of sixteenth-century poetry.[14] In any case, whatever originality the *Satires* exhibit is owing, paradoxically, to Ariosto's imitation of Horace, and can be appreciated only after a comparison has been made between the two. There have been scholars who have considered Ariosto's *Satires* a cold, unimaginative *pasticcio* of quotations and sentiments lifted out of Horace's *Satires* and *Epistles*.[15] However, they failed to recognize that there are strong similarities of temperament between Horace and Ariosto, and that Ariosto might easily have felt free to adapt as much of Horace as possible to his own purposes without fear of compromising his individuality. By the year 1517, Ariosto was aware of his "naturel"—to use Du Bellay's term—and would not have chosen a model unless he were certain that through imitation of it he would discover qualities which were distinctly his own.[16]

NOTES

[1] See Satire VI, preface.
[2] He did not complete his fifth comedy, entitled *I Studenti*. For more on

Ariosto as a dramatist, see Satires III and VII, prefaces.

[3] *I Dilettevoli Sermoni* . . . (Venice: Giolito, 1559), p. 12.

[4] Satire I.

[5] Venice: Giolito, 1570, p. 216.

[6] Venice: Geremia, 1731, pp. 112–113.

[7] *Saggi di critica*, I (Florence: 1859), pp. 24–25.

[8] *Ariosto* (Bari: Laterza, 1927), p. 63.

[9] "Umanità e poesia dell'Ariosto nelle Satire," *Archivium Romanicum*, XVII (October–December, 1933), 171.

[10] "Identificazioni di personaggi delle Satire di Ludovico Ariosto," *Giornale storico della letteratura italiana*, CII, 1933, 44.

[11] *Storia Letteraria d'Italia; Il Cinquecento* (Milan: Vallardi, 1954), p. 45. This history was first published in 1929.

[12] "Intorno alle *Satire* dell'Ariosto," *Giornale storico della letteratura italiana*, CXXII, 1945, 109–130. See also pp. 49–51 below.

[13] *La poesia minore dell'Ariosto* (Rome: Edizioni Italiane, 1947), pp. 83–98. The passage quoted is in my translation from p. 92.

[14] *Storia dei generi letterari italiani; La Satira*, II (Milan: Vallardi, 1939), 40.

[15] For instance, G. Marpillero, "I motivi tradizionali e le *Satire* di Ludovico Ariosto," *Fanfulla della Domenica*, XIX, 1897, 43–44.

[16] For supplementary histories of critical responses to the *Satires*, see Grabher, and Cian, II, 36–40.

ARIOSTO'S USE OF SOURCES

The classical *corpus satirarum* in Italy at the close of the fifteenth century consisted of the works of Horace, Persius, Juvenal, Martial, and Lucian. Satire was a very popular genre. By 1482 the *Satires* and *Epistles* of Horace had been honored by a commentary from Cristoforo Landino. During the academic year 1484–85, Angelo Poliziano gave a series of lectures on them, and during the following year he lectured on Juvenal. By this time the satires of Persius and Juvenal had also received their modern commentaries, and Juvenal had even been translated into Italian, albeit ineptly, by Giorgio Sommariva. The popular *Florilegia*, of the day were full of Martial's epigrams, and most of Lucian's satirical dialogues had found their way into Latin during the course of the century.

Horace had long been respected in Italy, though his popularity was never as great as Juvenal's. Dante refers to the *Ars poetica* in section XXV of the *Vita Nova*, and also in the second book, section XIV, of the *Convivio*. In limbo, among the poets he grants "Horace the satirical" a place next to Homer and Vergil. As early as November, 1347, Petrarch had received a copy of Horace's complete works, and the codex, filled with his marginal notes, remains a treasure of the

Laurentian Library. In Horace's love of solitude, art, and glory, Petrarch must have detected a kindred spirit. There are numerous echoes of the Latin poet throughout his works, and he may also have perceived in Horace a classical model for the creation of his own ideal autobiography. In this respect, he anticipated Ariosto's interest in the *Satires* and *Epistles,* and decisively assisted Dante in establishing a tradition in Italian literature. The concealment of art in Horace's plain style must also have influenced the style in some of Petrarch's Italian lyrics—though not, of course, as directly as the *trobar clar* of the troubadours.

In spite of Petrarch's interest in Horace, the *Satires* and *Epistles* did not find an enthusiastic reception among the learned until the end of the fifteenth century. In 1470 they were published in the first edition of Horace's complete works. Then Landino's commentary gave them the boost they needed in order to reach forty-four editions by 1500. They began to be imitated in the Latin writings of humanist scholars and poets, among whom the most important for Ariosto was the Ferrarese Tito Vespasiano Strozzi, father of Ercole, one the Ariosto's closest friends. In the *Sermonum liber,* published in the Aldine edition of his *Carmina* in 1513, the elder Strozzi became the first poet to imitate Horace by combining satire with the epistle form. This was no startling innovation, because the relationship between the *Satires* and the *Epistles* was considered complementary. The *Satires* rooted out vices in order for the *Epistles* to plant virtues in their place. To combine the forms merely increased moral efficacy and artistic harmony. In any case, the epistle had already been used for purposes of satire by Petrarch in his *Epistolae sine nomine* in prose, and also, though the satirical passages are less frequent and less virulent, in his *Epistolae metricae.* Tito Strozzi's accomplishment was to provide Ariosto with a worthy precedent in contemporary literature.

Ariosto's enthusiasm for Horace had become legendary well before the close of the sixteenth century. In his life of Ariosto prefacing the 1584 edition of the *Orlando Furioso* published in Venice, Pigna tells how the poet acquired great honor and reputation at the court of Pope Leo X as the result of a discourse he delivered explaining certain passages in Horace which were held in his day to be especially obscure. Pigna's story has a certain amount of verisimilitude. In Virginio's notes toward a biography of his father, we find the statement that Ariosto was not very studious, but that he greatly esteemed Horace and Catullus. However, notes of this sort are relatively unimportant. Echoes of Horace are to be found in almost all of Ariosto's works, from his earliest Latin lyrics to the final version of the *Orlando Furioso*. His *Satires* did more for Horace's reputation in Italy than all the work of his successors and predecessors put together.

Surprisingly, a reader of the *Satires* will not find himself bombarded every time he turns a page with ostentatious borrowings from Horace. When Ariosto does choose to take whole phrases and passages from his model, they fit so naturally within his context as to seem his own. In lines 94–96 of his sixth satire, he adapts lines 120–121 of Horaces's first satire in Book I. Just as Horace does not want to be thought of as having "rifled the rolls of blear-eyed Crispinus,"[1] Ariosto does not want Bembo to say that he is "robbing the wardrobes of Il Pistoia and Pietro Aretino." The Horatian echo fits smoothly within its context, and it has significance. The context was not manipulated to make room for the allusion. Ariosto is afraid that, if he turns his attack away from humanists to members of other professions, he will be identified with certain of his predecessors in vernacular satire. By placing them on a level with "blear-eyed Crispinus" and himself on a level with Horace, he makes a value judgment as to the merits of his own as opposed to their work. As the first poet to write classical satire in the vernacular, he does not wish to be placed in the same category with scribblers of lampoons and slanderous diatribes.

Apart from certain of his phrases, Horace's ideas also find themselves transmuted to serve the particular aims of the Italian poet. In his fifth satire, on the subject of women and marriage, Ariosto applies the concept of *aurea mediocritas* to the problem of choosing a proper wife.[2] He tells his cousin Annibale Maleguzzi, soon to become a husband, that a wise man always looks for a wife who is neither beautiful nor ugly. If she is beautiful everyone will wish to seduce her; but if she is ugly she will be unable to seduce her husband. This advice sounds very sensible, but, as Ariosto would have been the first to admit, it is difficult to follow. Annibale could not have failed to detect a touch of irony in it. Ariosto seems to have chosen the one situation to which it is most difficult to apply the golden mean, and then proceeded to apply it for the very sake of creating a humorous effect. Apart from this particular passage, the conclusion to all of Ariosto's fine advice in Satire V is that no amount of wisdom avails in keeping a wife shamefast and steadfast. The devil's ring works far better.

Throughout the *Satires* Ariosto's adaptations from Horace fit smoothly and often ingeniously into the contexts in which they appear, for the very reason that they contribute vitally to Ariosto's meaning. Horace's sense of humor, his thoughts and values, his style of life, and the studied ease of his conversational tone appear reincarnated in the work of a man who was Horace's equal, to say the least, as a poet, and who must have felt a great sympathy with him. However, every reference Ariosto makes to Horace's *Satires* and *Epistles* serves a satirical purpose of its own. Lines 95–128 of Horace's sixth satire in Book I influence greatly the sequence of thought throughout Ariosto's second satire. When Ariosto requests of his brother a small room with simple fittings, when he renounces the harried life of preferment-seeking within the clergy, and when he contrasts a prelate's life unfavorably with a page's, he does so in words reverberating with Horace's description of his own quiet life, free from ambition, unlike the life led by certain Roman statesmen, victims constantly of envy and slander. However, Ariosto focuses so sharply upon contemporary matters of particular concern to himself that the adaptation is scarcely apparent. A similarity of temperament seems to have produced a similarity of expression. Never do we fear that Ariosto has smothered his own personality beneath a heap of broken fragments chipped off a revered monument.

On the contrary, Ariosto distinguishes himself by his espousal of the Horatian outlook. Horace's love of the ethical life, his faith in the golden mean, his admonishment to men to recognize their limitations, his effort to bring consistency to his entire being, and his delight only in attainable pleasures all combine, along with certain facts about his life, to form the standard in Ariosto's *Satires* by which contemporary society is judged and found to be degenerate. In the *Satires* Ariosto portrays himself as poet and humanist, a quixotic individual, who has adopted as the fondest dream of his intellectual life the possibility, not only of attaining values implicit in the Horatian outlook, but also of receiving from his own society some of the rewards and recognition Horace received from his. In the course of the *Satires,* he describes some of the windmills with which he has ineluctably clashed. To the extent that we as readers identify with him, and feel the pathos of his alienation, and grow fond of his genial idealism, we also grow to dislike the society that not only cannot comprehend him, but also casually, inadvertently, does much to destroy him.

In the Satires a persona swiftly emerges of a man dedicated to the ideals of an age other than his own. He conducts himself as a stranger in contemporary society. He is able to perform the duties laid upon him by his superiors, but never with a full sense of commitment. His allegiance is to a golden world, of which day to day existence too often turns out to be the opposite. However, his ideal not only provides him with a standard for evaluating actual society, but also infuses irony into his words. Beneath his every description of current reality there lies a reference to analogous circumstances in an ideal world. A subtle, ironical comedy results. The events and the great men of contemporary society take on a mock heroic aspect, while the narrator of the *Satires* becomes a fool as Erasmus would have understood that term when he included the wise man in his list of fools. The persona Ariosto creates in the *Satires* is that of an individual who lives, thinks, and expresses himself within a polarity between the ideal and the real. His outlook lends itself to satire, of himself, as well as others.

Horace's seventh epistle in Book I provides Ariosto with a perfect instrument for satire. Evidently Maecenas had reproached Horace for staying too long in the country away from him. He had probably reminded the poet of his obligations toward his patron. Horace used his seventh epistle to quit himself of those obligations by providing Maecenas with another example of his poetry, and to issue at the same time a warning that he would be glad to give up all of Maecenas's gifts if they entailed the loss of his personal freedom. He offered his health as his excuse for avoiding the city. The striking differences between Ariosto's model and his imitation give rise to a virtuoso performance in satirical irony.

In the first place, Ariosto is unable even to address his Maecenas directly. The Cardinal is so enraged with him over his refusal to go to Hungary that he must request at second hand the information he desires as to his standing at the court. Far from caring about his health, the Cardinal would have him commit suicide by moving to just the cold climate that expert medical advice has warned him against. As for being quit of his obligations by writing a mere epistle, that can never be. The Cardinal has told him already that he cares no more for the entire *Orlando Furioso* than if it were toilet paper. The poet should have been busying himself around the court instead of writing nonsense. The Cardinal is no Maecenas; in fact, he is no patron in anything but name. Maecenas was discerning and scrupulous in his search for the worth in a man before he made him his friend and a recipient of his generosity. The Cardinal rewards anyone who caters to his petty desires. Meanwhile he cannot see that he has in his daily service, in the person of one man, the Vergil and the Horace of his age.

The fable of the fox and the weasel has a very different effect, coming at the end of Ariosto's satire, than it has inserted in the middle of Horace's epistle. Horace could be sure that Maecenas, who understood and valued him, would respect his love of freedom, considering any violation of it a threat to their friendship. On the other hand, Ariosto, who never had the Cardinal's friendship or appreciation, finds himself in the embarassing and somewhat foolish position of threatening to withdraw his allegiance from a man who never understood the value of it to begin with. To the Cardinal, Ariosto was never free. He was a servant. In Horace's refusal to return to Rome there is the affirmation of a principle, as well as the proof of a friendship. In Ariosto's refusal to go to Hungary there is merely the exasperation of a man who has reached the end of his endurance. The fox of the fable has become a donkey. The irony in Ariosto's comparing his own relationship with Cardinal Ippolito d'Este to that between Horace and Maecenas results in a withering condemnation of the Cardinal and a wry but gentle mockery of himself.

Not only Ippolito d'Este suffers the results of invidious comparison; his brother, Duke Alfonso, also suffers, though not as severely. From his second lord, Ariosto receives not a Sabine farm but a fortress in Garfagnana where he must govern a violent and seditious people. His second lord has no more intention than did his first of granting him leisure to write poetry. Furthermore, the Roman pontiff Leo X conveniently put aside the obligations of their former friendship as soon as he felt the tiara on his head. Through Ariosto's imitation of Horace, gradually all of contemporary Italian society comes in for a scathing comparison with a former golden age. Cynicism in the ethical sphere, expediency in the political, and opportunism in the intellectual combine to rule out the appreciation of beauty, truth, and goodness in a society on its way to enslavement under invading armies. If one individual, Ariosto seems to be saying, asserts amid the ruins his freedom and his values, he may seem a fool, and suffer disappointment and disillusionment, but his eccentricity will also serve to let men know how very debased they have permitted their lives to become.

Although parts of Satire V remind one vaguely of Juvenal's notorious satire against women, Ariosto's artistic discretion happily prevented him from being seduced into imitation of an all too popular model for satire in his day. Some of the situations he describes in the *Satires* might easily have provided occasion for the *saeva indignatio* of Juvenalian diatribe; however, by the exercise of exquisite restraint, Ariosto never dissipates the force of his satire in a rush of verbal acrobatics inspired by raging bitterness. We are outraged far more when we see a good man suffer injustice than we are when we hear a bitter man complain about his misfortunes. Ariosto as the Horatian father of Satire VI captures our compassion, and we think, without his having to tell us, that there must be something very wrong with a world in which a man of his quality must encounter continual failure. When, however, Ariosto does desire a model for invective, he turns to Dante as an author more in sympathy with the nobility of his conception than is Juvenal. In fact, he proves in the *Satires* that he is capable of rising to the Dantesque tone in all its moral seriousness.[3] In the *Orlando Furioso*, he had merely parodied Dante.[4]

With his *Satires* Ariosto succeeded so thoroughly in reviving the beauty and the effectiveness of Horatian satire, and expressed such a variety of ideas and moods so brilliantly in *terza rima,* that he ruled out the likelihood of having any successors who might equal him. In fact, Ariosto's only immediate successor in the Horatian mode who is worth a reader's time is Ercole Bentivoglio, and only because he wisely makes no effort to match the grandeur of Ariosto's accomplishment. He was a soldier and a nobleman of the Bolognese house who had lived in Ferrara since 1513. He was also a very good friend of Ariosto, as the following lines from his fifth satire attest:

> E men vado al cortil, dove una buona
> Ora passeggio con gl'amici meco
> Bramosi di poggiar spesso Elicona:
>   Se 'l Ariosto v'é, ragiono seco;
> Spesso insieme ridiam di Marco Guazzo
> E d'un altro romanzo cosí cieco,
>   Che si pensó con le sue rime il pazzo
> Di vincere il *Furioso* e d'altri molti
> Che di guerre cantâr, prendiam sollazzo.

And I betake myself to the courtyard, where I pass a pleasant hour with those friends of mine who desire frequently to scale Mt. Helicon. If Ariosto is there, I converse with him. Often

do we laugh together about Marco Guazzo,[5] and a certain other
writer of romances,[6] so blind he thought with his rimes, the
madman, to surpass the *Furioso;* and we take amusement at the
expense of many others who sang about wars.

Throughout his fifth satire, Bentivoglio informs his addressee of his
activities on an average day. When the beautiful dawn issuing from
her golden hostel sprinkles the heavens with fresh flowers and morning
roses, Bentivoglio leaps out of bed to comb the lice out of his hair.
He refuses to use a scent because he wishes to be as Nature made
him. In his first satire, on the subject of women, he declares himself
to be satisfied when his plain servant girl is beneath him, for he is
perfectly happy only to imagine her a Julia or a Lucretia. Thus does
he sweetly deceive himself. On the subject of war, he shows himself
to be a well-informed and powerful critic. He was present among the
Ferrarese troops at the siege of Florence in 1530 where he witnessed
the castration and incineration of a poor peasant by Spanish soldiers.
In his sixth satire, he gives an equally vivid description of a famine.
Every tercet of Bentivoglio's satires bears the impress of an engaging
personality involved in important events of the time, and also exhibits
a fluency in the adaptation of a difficult verse form to the rhythms
of ordinary speech. In these respects, he shows himself to be worthy
of his great predecessor, who had enriched the poetry of his age with
a new style.[7]

NOTES

[1] The Loeb Library translation.

[2] Ll. 151-165.

[3] See, for instance, Satires II, 11. 196-228, and VII, 11. 94-108. Dante, however,
did not provide Ariosto with his only inspiration to use *terza rima* in the *Satires*.
The *capitolo* in *terza rima* had long been in use for serious and satrical subjects.
Petrarch, Boccaccio, Lorenzo de' Medici, and Machiavelli offer notable examples.

[4] See *Orlando Furioso*, XXXIV, 7-11, and VI, 26-53.

[5] A soldier who took up the pen in hope of rivaling Ariosto with two clumsy
chivalric poems, the *Belisardo* and *Astolfo il Borioso*.

[6] According to Catalano, this would be Cassio Brecorelli, author of the *Morte
del Danese*.

[7] To the best of this writer's knowledge, Bentivoglio's satires can be found
only in the extant copies of Sansovino's *Sette libri di Satire*.

THE *SATIRES* AND THE *ORLANDO FURIOSO*

As interesting as the *Satires* are in their own right, their value will increase for us if they offer a significant aid in interpreting one of the classics of western literature. It would be peculiar indeed if the *Satires,* first in quality among Ariosto's minor works and the product of his maturity, did not shed some light on our understanding of the *Orlando Furioso.* A mere list, however, of parallel passages will not establish an enlightening relationship between the two works. Nor can a comparison be of much value if it confines itself to enumerating particular instances of satire in the *Furioso.* All that would be learned thereby is what everyone who has ever read the *Orlando Furioso* knows already—the work is full of satire, in all forms from invective to parody. We must try to determine whether a more meaningful connection exists between Ariosto's major work and his chief minor work.

We have already seen that the *Satires,* in accord with their Horatian model, offer us a persona adopted by their own creator. The *Satires* comprise essentially the careful rendering of an ideal self-portrait, complete and polished. It so happens that the genre to which the *Orlando Furioso* belongs also required the author to assume a persona and to step forward onto the stage of his own fiction. Even after the romantic epic, the *romanzo,* had moved up from the street corners and the market-place, and had entered the hands of such conscious literary craftsmen as Pulci and Boiardo, it managed to retain one of its most charming folk elements—the address of the *cantastorie,* or story singer, to his audience at the opening of each installment of his narrative. This brief address contained anything from a reference to weather conditions to an invocation of a local patron saint. It usually contained an outline of the story to follow and could also include homiletic sayings out of folk wisdom, a series of pleasantries, or, as far as we can tell, whatever the individual *cantastorie* was inspired to improvise. Its purpose was to ingratiate the *cantastorie* with his audience and to attract their attention to the story he was about to sing. Evidently the audience took an interest in the personality of the man about to entertain them, and indeed expected him to make casual remarks of a self-revelatory nature.

Both Pulci and Boiardo made clever use of the *cantastorie's* opening address in their own *romanzi.* Pulci creates with it the delightful portrait of a pious simpleton conscientiously narrating a story in complete unawareness of its frequently scurrilous and blasphemous passages. Boiardo steps forth at the opening of each canto of the *Innamorato* as very much the nobleman he was in real life, the Count of Scandiano, and he succeeds, after his hail-fellow manner, in adorning the values of the aristocracy to which he belonged with the beauty and enchantment of a remote golden world of chivalry. Ariosto, however, outdoes both his distinguished predecessors in the use he makes of the opening address.

In the *Orlando Furioso* the *cantastorie's* address becomes a miniature discourse. Ariosto uses it as a platform from which to hold forth on such diverse topics, among others, as the necessity of using deception in an imperfect world, the injustice of unrequited love, the battle of Ravenna as a Pyrrhic victory, and the inability of the uneducated to understand allegory. He deplores the fact that women spend more time in applying make-up to their faces than in educating themselves. He is certain that the French invasions are a scourge of God on Italy for her infinite sins. One distinction between the human race and the animals is that the males of our species use violence against the females. The discourse goes on and on. Nor is it confined only to the opening addresses. At the close of Canto IX there is Orlando's invective against firearms, and in the middle of Canto XVII the leaders of Christendom, specifically Charles V and Leo X, are admonished to stop making life miserable for their fellow Christians and to set out on a crusade to recover the Holy Sepulchre. Ariosto's penchant for discourse led one authority on the *Orlando Furioso* to suggest that the poet might well have had an even greater inclination towards satire than towards romance.[1] In fact, Ariosto's use of the *cantastorie's* opening address reminds one of Aristophanes use of the *parabasis* in Old Comedy. Interestingly, it was from the parabasis of Old Comedy that the Roman genre of satire probably derived.

Claiming for Ariosto's discourses a kinship with the earliest source of formal satire does not, however, solve the problem they create; namely, that of confusion. They bear a thematic relationship to the cantos they introduce; but, unlike the proems of Pulci and Boiardo, they do not seem to define a persona. We gather that the *cantastorie* of the *Orlando Furioso* is an intelligent, well-educated, well-informed gentleman with an interest in political, ethical, and literary matters, and that he has a bitter-sweet, ironical sense of humor. He also has a sharp eye fixed on the actual world outside his poem. We can only suspect that the persona Ariosto adopts for the *cantastorie* of the *Orlando*

Furioso is a reflection of himself, and find our suspicion confirmed in the proem of Canto XLVI when he launches into a paean of gratitude to all those friends who encouraged him in his long labor on the great poem.

At this pass, it might be good sense to declare the problem of the persona of the *Furioso's cantastorie* insoluble, or at least a mystery for biographical criticism. But the *Satires* were written during the period just after the *Furioso's* first publication, and were devoted almost exclusively to the creation of a persona which is, in fact, Ariosto's ideal self-portrait. If this is significant, the *Satires* should offer us not only a fuller account of the *Furioso's cantastorie*, but also a way in general to understand the work itself. The figure who emerges in the *Satires* has a talent for holding up to devastating contrast an acute vision of the actual world with a cherished illusion of his own intellectual life. The result is irony, at times bitterly condemnatory of the world, and at others gently self-mocking. Perhaps the *cantastorie* of the *Orlando Furioso* discourses so continually because he also wishes to create a contrast between illusion and reality. Perhaps he wishes to remind us with his discourses that the actual world is the background of the fantastical stories in his repertoire. The atmosphere of fantasy and enchantment in the *Furioso* may correspond psychologically to a world of illusions according to which we try in vain to live—illusions which meet the real with as much security as enchantments withstand Astolfo's terrible horn. The step may be not only easy, but obvious, from the image of the disillusioned poet of the *Satires* to an understanding of the image of Orlando, mad and naked, hauling his wounded horse on his shoulders.

The disillusionment we find in the *Satires*, the disillusionment of the humanist poet who has discovered himself to be out of tune with his age, and whose disappointed existence serves as a reproach to his unappreciative contemporaries, may explain the distinctly skeptical quality of much of the humor in the *Orlando Furioso*. The brilliant allegory begun and developed in Cantos VI, VII, and VIII, and concluded in Canto X, has been much commented upon. Briefly, it tells how Ruggiero, swept away by his winged horse, falls captive to the beautiful enchantress Alcina; how the good fairy Melissa, acting on behalf of the forlorn Bradamante, uses the magic ring to free Ruggiero from Alcina's garden of delights; and, at last, how Ruggiero, having conquered a host sent out against him by Alcina, joins forces with the lady Logistilla, who then instructs him in the bridling and management of his unruly hippogryph. In broad outline, the *significatio* is clear enough. A young man with promise allows his vagrant passions to carry him away into a life devoted exclusively to the enjoyment of sensual pleasures. Meanwhile he so forgets his responsibility to the better part of himself that only through the good will of someone concerned about him can reason enter in a flash to make him see the ugliness of his condition. But once aware, he submits to the instructions of wisdom and learns how to control his desires. This is an edifying story, but it is not over.

Ruggiero soars off from Logistilla's palace on his newly bridled hippogryph only to find the peerless Angelica tied naked to a rock where she is waiting to be devoured by the ravenous Orc. Ruggiero adroitly rescues her, then whisks her away to the nearest lonely spot. There he fails in an attempt to rape her only because he cannot free himself from his armor before she outwits him and disappears. With a magnificent gesture Ariosto bursts the bubble of his allegory. A young man's wisdom is no match for a pretty girl in the nude. In a world more closely resembling that of the *Decameron* than of Plato's *Republic*, wisdom, far from controlling the passions, is likely to serve them. In any case, Bradamante will have cause to weep.

If we remember that the literal translation of Logistilla is "a drop of wisdom," and not Wisdom, we shall not feel very shocked at Ruggiero's delinquency. What Ariosto has done is to use allegory for the purpose of dazzling us with one of our dearest illusions. Since the time of Socrates we have liked to think that in wisdom there is some salvation for us from our slavery to desire. A grinning Ariosto strokes up our illusions until we are purring comfortably, and then undeceives us. We find ourselves laughing at the breakdown of illusion before the real. We are forced to admit that we have been tricked. But it should not surprise us to find Ariosto, the disappointed humanist of the *Satires*, ironically mocking the excessive faith of his fellow humanists in reason and knowledge, and parodying their favorite technique for serious poetry, the allegory.

The source of comedy and satire in the *Orlando Furioso* lies in the confrontation of illusion with reality. The urbane, sophisticated conversationalist, who assumes the role of *cantastorie*, treats his subject matter with the greatest irony, unfurling a tapestry into which we find woven the pattern in detail of our most cherished illusions. There they appear dressed up as wizards and fairies, enchanted knights, bloodcurdling monsters, and beautiful ladies. However, the background of the pattern, at times receding, and at others brought up in sharp contrast, is the real world. The satirist who saw so clearly the futility of the humanist effort to lodge Augustan Age values in an Italy lacerated by the French invasions turns his attention in the *Orlando Furioso* mainly to the subject of love and the cherished illusions of his age concerning love.

The Innkeeper's Tale of Canto XXVIII has been notorious since the time of Elizabeth I, who ordered Sir John Harington to translate the other forty-five cantos as punishment for his bawdiness in having translated only that one in order to amuse her ladies-in-waiting. The main characters, Jocondo and King Astolfo, pride themselves on their surpassing beauty. Now Plato tells us, and so does Castiglione, that love is the desire to unite ourselves with the beautiful. Therefore Astolfo and Jocondo should be loved, and loved faithfully, at least by their wives, or so they think. But no sooner has Jocondo departed from his wife than she finds her way into the arms of a boy; worse for King Astolfo, he has the displeasure of witnessing his queen in the act of uniting herself with a hunchback dwarf. Worse yet, she spends most of her time grieving because the dwarf loves her so little that he will neglect her for a game of dice. The result for the two men is a disillusionment so thorough that they become ridiculous. The degree to which they deluded themselves in their overestimation of the importance of beauty is reflected in the absurd extreme they adopt when once they are confronted with reality.

After a year studiously devoted to the seduction of as many wives as they can find, the two weary men conclude that no woman is faithful to one man, no matter what fine qualities he may possess. The answer, they decide illogically, is to provide one woman with two men. Where beauty fails, let sexual satiety provide the cure. However, the girl they share has a chance to correct their reasoning. She contrives to enjoy a lover while nestled comfortably in bed between the two of them. They learn that love in this world admits of everything but absolutes. The will is subject to captivity by both reason and the senses, and may as a result develop preferences of the most contradictory and unpredictable sort. Confronted with the endless game of imperfect adjustment to each other which the senses and the spirit play, the individual must laugh or else become laughable. So Ariosto leaves Astolfo and Jocondo rolling in uncontrollable laughter on the floor of their bedroom. Let Plato and his Renaissance disciples confine their theory of love to the academy and the palace of Urbino, and let men accomodate themselves as best they can to a condition of love which infallibly proves all theories to be illusory.

Orlando must learn his lesson too, but in a different way. In Boiardo's romance Orlando's infatuation with Angelica was a delightful novelty, because it brought together two divergent traditions, the Arthurian and the Carolingian. The conflict in Orlando's character between *courtoisie* and *prouesse* made amusing entertainment, especially for the cultured Italian audience of the quattrocento, since Orlando, the brawny, hirsute paladin of France, expressed his love in Petrarchan terms. Boiardo delighted in this image of Orlando as the hulking, clumsy lover whose bushy eyebrows and habit of snoring clashed ridiculously with his protestations of eternal, worshipful love, and it was Boiardo's accomplishment to bring to life in the character of Angelica the lady of the Petrarchan *canzoniere*. However it was Ariosto's genius to see that certain difficulties of a psychological nature, beyond the obvious dilemma of having to choose between vassalage to a king or to a lady, might arise from Orlando's conflict of ideals and from the presence of a flesh and blood lady with a will of her own. It was Ariosto's special accomplishment to carry those difficulties out to their logical conclusion in the *Orlando Furioso*.

Orlando, as the knight of the *chanson de geste*, is a fighter who may expect to receive from his suzerain honor commensurate with his valor and loyalty. He may also expect as his due the total devotion of his lady. In *The Song of Roland*, the paladin, upon dying, says his last farewell to his sword and never bothers to mention Aude la belle; however, she, upon being told of his death, drops dead. Orlando, the soldier, we are supposed to believe, has earned a right to such devotion. On the other hand, Orlando, as the Petrarchan lover, is entitled to nothing. For his service to his lady to have any merit, it must be gratuitous, and the more obdurate she remains, the more ennobling that service becomes for him as a human being. The two traditions contradict each other. Of course Ariosto's Orlando, sunk beneath the burden of his dual identity, does not see this. He makes the mistake of thinking that his service as a lover entitles him to rewards as tangible as those accorded his service as a paladin. What increases the difficulty for him is that while Angelica in his concept of her remains the Laura of the *Canzoniere*, she is in reality more like the Lesbia of Catullus's

elegies. Ariosto lays stress on the complete metamorphosis the ideal
lady of the courtly tradition undergoes in assuming flesh and blood.
She becomes very much like the passionate, capricious, self-seeking
courtesan of Latin elegaic poetry. It would be far better for Orlando
if Angelica, like Laura, departed conveniently to another world, for
on this earth she will confer not glory, but madness, upon him. As
it is, he can think of no more fitting reward for his faithful services
than her maidenhead.[2]

Orlando is in for a double disenchantment. Angelica, being very much
in possession of her will, teaches him that no amount of worthiness
entitles one person to another's fancy. She jilts him, a hero of France
and of the Christian cause, for a foot soldier in the Saracen army.
His worth as a paladin, he learns, has nothing to do with his desirability
as a lover. Furthermore, his having honored and served her as a lover
in the Petrarchan mode entitles him to nothing when it comes time
for her to choose a mate. Orlando, in his confusion, fails to understand
that the sort of love he practiced towards her has its reward in seeing
one's lady take her place beside the angels, and that Angelica, despite
her name, never had any intention of taking her place anywhere but
beside an attractive man. She is an angel in an Ovidian pantheon,
not in the heaven of those who practiced the "dolce stil nuovo."
Orlando's identity, based as it is, not only upon two illusions, but
upon a confusion between them, must give way when it comes up
against reality. In learning of the deflowering of Angelica, Orlando
meets his Roncesvalles. He reads the elegant Horatian epigram inscribed
by Medoro on the wall of the Vergilian cave in which Angelica lost
her virginity and goes insane, tearing off his armor to run amuck and
to provide the master image—like the image of Don Quixote charging
the windmill—that gathers into itself the meaning of the narrative in
which he is the central figure.

Orlando's disillusionment finds its portrait in the image of the naked
paladin running mad with the weight of his wounded horse upon his
shoulders—not *his* horse actually, for he has taken it from Angelica.
False hopes and utopian dreams of personal gratification, ordered
theories and cherished illusions, may bear a man up, but sooner or
later, no matter how noble they appear, they must become a painful
and ludicrous burden. When once they are exposed to the truth, they
occasion madness if one persists in them. Ariosto was to have the
disconcerting experience of acting out in his life an incident in a work

he had already created. When in 1513, upon the election of Giovanni de' Medici to the papacy, Ariosto received no reward or recognition for his poetry, and when later, in the summer of 1517, he was forced to break with his ungrateful employer Cardinal Ippolito d'Este, he may well have seen in his own deluded condition and in his own bitter disappointment a reflection of Orlando's madness. His response was to write the *Satires* in which he delineates himself as the slightly preposterous, pathetic figure of the learned poet-humanist—an eccentric—resigned to being misunderstood and unappreciated by his contemporaries, forced thereby to use irony in his communications with them, and patient in the knowledge that he must confine his dreams only to a modest realization within the solitude of his private life. Orlando had thought to see the smile of a Laura on the lips of a coquette. Ariosto had dreamed of finding a Maecenas among the political ruins of early sixteenth-century Italy. The parallel is not close; but it is close enough.

The madness of Atalante's palace of illusions, in which all the residents chase in vain elusive images of their fondest desires, represents the prevalent condition of the world, Ariosto implies, and we are trapped there until an Astolfo comes to free us with his horn of horrible sound—horrible because it is the sound of truth. But where in the meantime have our wits departed? The answer to this question comes in one of the most ingenious and original passages in all satirical literature. Our wits, along with Orlando's, have flown up to the moon, where all collects that is lost on earth:

>   Le lacrime e i sospiri degli amanti,
> l'inutil tempo che si perde a giuoco,
> e l'ozio lungo d'uomini ignoranti,
>   vani disegni che non han mai loco,
> i vani desidèri sono tanti,
> che la più parte ingombran di quel loco:
>   ciò che in somma qua giu perdesti mai,
> là su salendo ritrovar potrai.[3]   (XXXIV, 75)

The tears and sighs of lovers, the unused time that one loses at play, the prolonged idleness of ignorant men, futile schemes that never take effect, and vain desires, all these are so many that they encumber the greatest part of that region: everything you have ever lost down here, you will be able to find if you ascend there.

Astolfo finds that the greatest single commodity on the moon, piled up in a high mountain of flasks, is human wits. Common sense, the sublunar world thinks it can do without. Of lunacy, however, there is not a trace on the moon. Madness dwells below and never leaves the company of men.

In this valley of the moon, through which Astolfo travels guided by St John the Evangelist, Ariosto may have placed some earthly jetsam of particular interest to himself:

> Ami d'oro e d'argento appresso vede
> in una massa, ch'erano quei doni
> che si fan con speranza di mercede
>   ai re, agli avari principi, ai patroni.
> Vede in ghirlande ascosi lacci; e chiede,
> et ode che son tutte adulazioni.
>   Di cicale scoppiate imagine hanno
> versi ch'in laude dei signor si fanno.   (77)

Next he sees hooks of gold and silver heaped in a mass, which were once those offerings that are made in hope of reward to kings, to greedy princes, and to patrons. He beholds in garlands hidden snares, and inquires, and hears that they are all flattering phrases. Verses composed in praise of lords have the image of cicadas who have burst themselves with droning.

The *Orlando Furioso* itself was written in celebration of the House of Este. In moments of disgust, perhaps Ariosto felt he had wearied himself for nothing in his long and thankless task. Certainly those great lords who should have granted him patronage never did—not during the time he was writing the *Orlando Furioso*, nor at any time after its publication. On the moon, services rendered in courts appear as a heap of broken bottles (79). In the pessimism of this episode on the moon, the disappointed poet of the *Satires* emerges at an earlier stage in his career. Indeed the *cantastorie* of the *Orlando Furioso* deserves to be considered a satirist of the first rank.

Another famous satirical passage also exhibits the pessimism that pervades much of the epic and finds its fullest expression in Astolfo's trip to the moon. However this passage is obviously comical. In Canto XIV, God hears Charlemagne's prayer for help and sends the Archangel Michael to find Silence and Discord, the one to cloak Rinaldo's return with reinforcements from England, and the other to stir up strife within the Saracen ranks. The angel in all his grandeur swoops down to the nearest monastery, where he expects to find Silence, where in fact silence is written over every door. But things on earth are not, he learns, as they are in the kingdom of heaven. Instead of Silence, he finds bedlam, and in the midst of it Discord keeping company with Fraud. In the angel's disillusionment at the reversal of his expectations, Ariosto has invented a superbly ingenious and novel means of reinvigorating a rather stale theme of satire, the corruption of the clergy. However, the master-stroke is yet to come. In Canto XXVII, the archangel proves that he has learned the ways of the world. Having discovered that Discord has deserted the Saracen camp, Michael becomes enraged and flies straight to the same monastery, where he knows this time he will find him. There he seizes a crucifix from the wall and proceeds to beat Discord over the head with it. No one is safe from corruption—not even angels.

Throughout the *Orlando Furioso* a false illusion of one sort or another provides the motive for satire. Sometimes an individual needs to be disabused of a misconception concerning himself and others, but often an entire society has to learn that at least one of the customs by which it lives engenders madness. The story of Ginevra and Ariodante, in Cantos IV, V, and VI, perhaps the best known of all the stories in the *Orlando Furioso*, presents an example. In the kingdom of Scotland, where the story takes place, the law is that a woman who takes a man into her bed, except her husband, shall die for the offence, unless a champion can be found to defend her in mortal combat against her accuser. What is at issue is the double standard between the sexes—one of Ariosto's favorite subjects. The long series of tales and sub-plots in the *Orlando Furioso* not only begins with this question, but also ends on it with the Mariner's Tale of Canto XLIII.

The special charm, as well as the significance, of the story lies in the way Ariodante responds to what he is certain is Ginevra's unfaithfulness and to the sentence her society passes upon her. He becomes a foil to Orlando. Although he goes mad and tries to drown himself, he changes his mind at the last minute. He retains his wits and uses them when he hears of Ginevra's approaching execution. He decides to act in a manner he knows to be consistent with his feelings and in a manner which is at the same time selfless. He will not let Ginevra die. He becomes her champion in spite of what he believes to be her betrayal of him. Ariodante sets out to meet his own brother Lurcanio in a fight to the death. His selflesssness results in revolutionary consequences. By the nobility of his behavior he reveals the law to be unjust and proves that it should be abolished.

However, a pall hangs over the story. What, we ask, would have happened if Rinaldo had not arrived in time to stop the battle between the brothers? Would Ariodante have behaved as he did if he had not been influenced by fear of death, first his own death and then Ginevra's? Besides, Ginevra is really innocent. What would have happened had she been guilty? Would the law have been abolished in that case? And even though the law is wiped off the books, the characters of Lurcanio and Polinesso give evidence of an ingrained woman-hatred which might bring into existence again an even worse law. In eloquent words, Rinaldo deplores the injustice of discriminating against women (IV, 63–7.). However, his thinking leaves much to be desired. Since men are promiscuous with impunity, says he, why should women be denied the same right? The law of Scotland is a delusion, and a destructive one, and must therefore go the way of all enchantments; but what, we ask ourselves, is left? If we are to be satisfied with Rinaldo's fine words, we must resign ourselves to a cynical existence under a condition of human nature which provides us merely with the intelligence to see and to laugh at our inconstancy. We must resign ourselves to the laughter of Astolfo and Jocondo. The human race is a complicated joke which takes its force from the incongruity of the ideal with the real.

A. Barlett Giamatti, in his introduction to the recent edition of Rose's translation, claims to see Ariosto's point of view in Rinaldo's pessimism. In the episode of the enchanted cup (XLII, 97–104 and XLIII, 1–9), Giamatti considers Ariosto to have given Rinaldo the only solution to existence in a self-seeking, self-deluding world where the truth too often turns out to be abhorrent. Rinaldo's grief-stricken host bids him drink some wine from a magical goblet. If his wife is faithful to him, he will succeed in bringing the wine to his lips; if not, it will spill out on his breast. Rinaldo refuses to drink. Why, he reasons, if he is happy with his wife, should he seek to become unhappy by learning the truth? So much the better if she is faithful to him; but if she is not, he had might as well avoid misery by continuing to think that she is. In Rinaldo's philosophy, it is best not to place too great a demand upon life, and in crucial matters better to let oneself be deceived than to know the truth. Although Ariosto's ingenuity in storytelling is as striking here as elsewhere, this reasoning must impress the reader as facile and out of correspondence with the impression that the *Orlando Furioso* as a whole creates. Perhaps it would be more profitable not to rely too heavily, in determining the author's point of view, on a minor episode. We should also remember that Rinaldo is not in love when he faces the trial of the enchanted cup. Disdain has already conquered Jealousy in his breast, and he has drunk eternal hatred at the fountain of Merlin (XLII, 45-65).

Paradoxically, the *Satires,* just as they help us to see the ironical and the caustic in the *Orlando Furioso,* help us also to see our way out of the pessimism of the work and into the world it offers beyond satire. They remind us of Ariosto's nostalgia for the Rome of Augustus, and remind us also that Ariosto's innovation in the romance genre was to add the *matiere de Rome la grande* to Boiardo's amalgamation of the Arthurian and Carolingian subject matters. They counsel us not to consider complete any determination of the author's point of view that leaves unmentioned the Vergilian element in the *Orlando Furioso,* and they prevent us from considering the marriage of Ruggiero and Bradamante as nothing more than an elaborate compliment to the Estensi. Just as in the *Satires* Ariosto introduces a classical theme, the golden life of measured, harmonious unaffectedness, in contrast to the greed-rotten, self-deceiving existence led by prelates, courtiers, and certain humanists of his own time, in the *Orlando Furioso* he contrasts the story of Aeneas and Lavinia with the deluded passion of Orlando for Angelica. Like Aeneas and Lavinia, Ruggiero and Bradamante share in a destiny to accomplish a work beyond personal desire. They suffer delays and separations, and they exhibit shortcomings toward each other, but their conviction that their union is in the service of humanity carries them through. Appropriately, it is Ruggiero, and not Orlando, who plunges his sword into Rodomonte, the spirit who always denies.

Furthermore, it is no accident that Angelica finally gives herself to Medoro, for he is the reincarnation of Vergil's Euryalus. Medoro, like Euryalus, displays selfless devotion to his lord. However, he is luckier than his Trojan counterpart. Instead of ending with his head on the point of an enemy spear, he is rewarded by a beautiful woman. Touched by his selflessness, Angelica gives herself to him, and simultaneously to the ideal which he embodies. In the union of Angelica and Medoro beauty comes to rest in the arms of magnanimity. We can forgive Angelica her former caprices, because Medoro is the opposite of Orlando, who neglected all of Christendom to pursue a personal desire. Orlando needs to be disillusioned before he can regain his wits and see how far he has departed from the ideal.

The once ambitious poet of the *Satires* had also to learn through disappointment to find his salvation in espousing the ideal. However, his difficulty was not as severe as Orlando's, for he did not permit his desire for glory to bring him to the point of madness. He did not mistake for the ideal a delusion fostered by personal desire. Orlando does, and it is the genius of the *cantastorie* of the *Orlando Furioso* to see this. Just as the poet of the *Satires* sees reality in the light of a cherished ideal, the *cantastorie* of the *Orlando Furioso* opposes Orlando's madness to the ideal loves of Angelica for Medoro and of Ruggiero and Bradamante for each other. As a classicist and an admirer of Vergil, he deserves to be considered one person with the modern Horace to whom we are introduced in the *Satires*.

NOTES

[1] Pio Rajna, *Le Fonti dell'Orlando Furioso* (Florence: Sansoni, 1900), pp. 103-4.

[2] It is difficult to understand why Angelica's maidenhead has not become a subject of scholarly debate, since early in the *Orlando Furioso* we are left in doubt as to its very existence. See Canto I, 54-6.

[3] *Orlando Furioso*, ed. Lanfranco Caretti (Milan: Ricciardi, 1954).

THE TEXT

With the loss of the Malaguzzi MS., known to Giannandrea Barotti,[1] who refers us to two variant readings from it, the text of the *Satires* derives chiefly from MS. Cl. I, B of the Biblioteca Comunale Ariostea di Ferrara, which we shall call F. It was considered an autograph from the time of its rediscovery in the middle of the eighteenth century by Barotti and by Girolamo Baruffaldi until the early years of the present century. It is actually an apograph with only the corrections in Ariosto's hand. MS. I, vi, 41 of the Biblioteca Comunale di Siena, containing only Satires I and III, provides additional material, and there is also the *editio princeps* of June, 1534, (*LE SATIRE // DI. M. LVDOVICO ARIOSTO, / VOLGARI, IN TERZA RIMA, / DI NVOVO STAMPATE, / DEL MESE DI / GIUGNO. // M. D. XXXIIII.*).

Not only is all of Ariosto's preparatory work on the *Satires* missing—rough drafts and rejected copies—but also the copies he sent to the addressees. According to Santorre Debenedetti's reconstruction of the early history of the work,[2] we know the *Satires* only from a period commencing about seven years after the writing of the first satire, when Ariosto decided to regather whatever scattered copies were available into a single volume, which is now lost. But three copies issued from this lost volume: the first is the Malaguzzi MS., known to us only through Barotti's variants; the second is the Sienese MS.; the third, retouched with some attention given to corrections made by Ariosto at an earlier date in F, is the copy that was reproduced in the *editio princeps*.

After these three copies had derived from the lost volume, Ariosto retouched it once more and had a clean copy made. On this copy, all in the hand of an unknown copyist except for the last four verses, which are in Ariosto's own hand, he did further work, especially on the grammar. He may have intended to publish the final product of his work, but he was distracted by other cares—possibly by the labor he had to expend upon the third edition of the *Orlando Furioso*. In any event, he put the copy aside without giving it its final polish, and it (F) remains to this day in Ferrara in the municipal library named after Ariosto. Its authority is unquestionable because it contains the last corrections the author was able to make before his death. We know from Virginio Ariosto that his father began, beyond the seven satires in F, two or three more, one of which was addressed to Castiglione. But they remained unfinished, and the fragments are lost.

The *editio princeps* is a clandestine edition, the work of Francesco Rosso da Valenza, a Ferrarese printer. It was probably intended to celebrate the first anniversary of the poet's death, but it came out a month too early. In this edition, the *Satires* are reproduced in a text similar to F before Ariosto made his final corrections, and in the same order as in the manuscript except that the fifth satire is arbitrarily placed before the others, perhaps because the printer saw profit in associating his little volume with the popular *querelle des femmes* literature of the period. The *editio princeps* underwent fifteen reprints by the year 1550.

Giolito's edition of 1550, *LE SATIRE DI / M. LODOVICO / ARIOSTO. / TRATTATE DALL'ORIGI / NALE DI MANO DELL'AV- / tore con due Satire non / piu uedute; e con molta /*

diligenza ristam- / *pate.* // *IN VINEGIA APPRESSO* / *GABRIEL GIOLITO* / *DE FERRARI.* / *MDL.*, edited by Doni, is the first to reproduce the order and the text, with Ariosto's final corrections, of F. It is thought that Virginio Ariosto himself provided the editor with the copy. The two satires never before seen were not seen in Giolito's edition and have remained unseen to the present day.

From the *editio princeps* (A) and from Giolito's edition (B), two types of texts originated, the first of which (A) was not entirely superseded, as would have been logical, by the second (B), by far the better and the more popular of the two. Giolito's edition underwent numerous reprints—from 1557 on in union with the *Rime*—and became the basis of most subsequent editions. According to Cesare Segre, the modern editor of Ariosto's *opere minori*, "it is upon the alternating fortunes of these two types of text that the history of the text of the *Satires* is woven."[3] The first return of type A resulted from a rivalry between editors. Ruscelli, after having severely criticized Giolito's edition, could find nothing better to do than to republish, with corrections not always of much use, a text in the tradition of A: *LE SATIRE* / *DI M. LODOVICO* / *ARIOSTO,* / *ET DEL S. LVIGI* / *ALAMANNI.* / *Nuouamente ristampate, con le correcttioni, et annotatic-* / *ni di GIROLAMO RUSCELLI.* // *IN VENETIA, PER PLINIO* / *PIETRASANTA MDLIIII.*)

Placed on the Index published at Parma in 1580, the *Satires* suffered clerical and moralistic alterations from 1583 through the seventeenth century, which saw only expurgated editions. The first edition worthy of notice is that of Rolli published in the early eighteenth century (*Delle SATIRE E RIME di M. Ludovico Ariosto, Libri Due. LONDRA, Per Giovanni Pickard, MDCCXVI.*), based upon a text of type A. This is the first edition with a commentary. Barotti, on the other hand, in his 1766 edition of the complete works, returned to type B, preferring Giolito's edition of the *Satires* to F itself, with which he was very well acquainted since he owned it.

During the nineteenth century, studies towards Ariosto's biography, of which the *Satires* constitute an important, though misunderstood, part, inspired Baruffaldi in his *Vita Dell'Ariosto* (Ferrara: 1807) with the idea that the *Satires* should be ordered chronologically. Hence Baruffaldi proposed a sequence (II, I, III, IV, V, VII, VI), and every subsequent editor felt obliged to order the *Satires* in his own way according to his own interpretation of the historical and biographical data. Molini (*Poesie varie di Ludovico Ariosto, con annotazioni, Firenze, presso G. Molini, 1824*) kept the order of type A, but gave the text according to the reading of F. Tortoli (*Commedie e Satire di Ludovico Ariosto, annotate da G. Tortoli, Firenze 1856*) gave the order as V, I, II, III, IV, VII, VI, and Polidori (*Opere minori in verso e in prosa di Ludovico Ariosto, ordinate e annotate per cura di Filippo-Luigi Polidori, Firenze 1857*) as II, I, V, III, IV, VII, VI. The process continued into the twentieth century with the added reinforcement of the decisive biographical contributions of Bertani and Catalano. This is, of course, the editorial equivalent of the critical train of thought described in section I of this introduction. For a period of almost one hundred and fifty years, editors and critics were for the most part unable to see that the *Satires* might be autobiographical in content, and might also comprise a work of conscious literary art.

Catalano's chronology[4] is considered definitive by modern students of Ariosto. He arranges the *Satires* in the following order: I (September–October, 1517), II (November–December, 1517), III (April–June, 1518), V (the latter part of 1521), IV (February, 1523), VII (March–April, 1524), VI (the latter part of 1524 or the beginning of 1525). But Catalano goes on to conclude from Ariosto's two notes in F, calling for a rearrangement of the first two satires into chronological order, that Ariosto intended all of the satires to follow a strict chronological sequence. Ariosto, he conjectures, simply forgot to make further notes calling for rearrangement of the rest of the satires, or perhaps illness and death overtook him before he could bring his revision to completion. This train of thought, however, must strike any reader as being more than a trifle arbitrary. Could illness and death have overtaken Ariosto so swiftly that he had no time to scribble down a few brief, but crucially important, notes? After all, F contains more than two hundred corrections in Ariosto's hand, the majority of which could not be said, by any stretch of the imagination, to deal with matters more important than the sequence of the entire work.

Debenedetti[5] argues, and this translator wholeheartedly concurs, that Ariosto intended Satire I, second in F, but accompanied by the author's note calling for its replacement in the first position, to be an introduction to the entire sequence. Debenedetti points out that Ariosto covers numerous general headings in Satire I to which he returns in the later satires—his responsibility to his family; his life with and his disappointment at the hands of his patron; his services and his meagre recompenses;

the poor condition of his health and his finances; his refusal to be tempted into fruitless, menial labors by offers of wealth and prestige; his love of learning, literature, and freedom. The appropriateness of Ariosto's choice of an introductory piece only serves to underline the arbitrariness of the choice of the printer of the *editio princeps*. A humorous *trattatello* on the ups and downs of married life is far from typical of the content or even of the form of the other satires. Although Satire I, second in F, was written first, we have no right to conclude that chronological accuracy was the author's sole or even his most important reason for indicating that it should be placed first in the sequence—much less to beg the question by assuming that he intended all of the satires to be placed in chronological order. It is easy to see how Satire VII, sixth in Catalano's chronology, serves as a perfect conclusion to the group, containing, as it does, Ariosto's final renunciation of the quest for official recognition in the form of a lucrative sinecure and his most emphatic endorsement of the life of private contentment in the company of his friends and loved ones. We can conclude that Ariosto gave heed to chronology when, and only when, it served his poetic purpose. While no one disputes Catalano's dates, and while the *Satires* do provide tantalizing material for the author's biography, a student of literature cannot be satisfied with the suggestion that Ariosto's major consideration in the ordering of his work could be mere chronological accuracy.

As for how the order of the first two satires ever became reversed to begin with, Debenedetti speculates, with superb common sense, that Ariosto finished correcting the satire addressed to Galasso and gave it to the copyist before he finished the satire addressed to Alessandro. He merely reserved that they should be restored to their proper order when they came to the printer. Hence the two notes. In general, Debenedetti's approach is refreshing, and well worth a student's time, because it insists upon treating the *Satires* as a unified work.

Toward the close of the nineteenth century, Wenk's lithographic reproduction (*Le Satire Autografe di Ludovico Ariosto*, with a preface by Viani, Bologna 1875) made F widely available to scholars. Upon this reproduction Tambara based a critical edition (*Le Satire di Ludovico Ariosto, testo critico con intr. e note a cura di G. Tambara, Livorno 1903*). Since many modern editions have reproduced his text, it might be worthwhile here to mention a new error which Tambara authored, and which amounted in its way to a final misguided effort to restore type A. Tambara declared, on the basis of ink densities, that the corrections in F were written by two different hands. To Ariosto's would belong only those relatively unimportant corrections entered in the *editio princeps*. Consequently, in Tambara's edition, Ariosto's notes calling for the reversal of the first two satires in F are ignored, and we have a II-I order. This division of inks was discussed immediately by Bertana in a review,[6] but he arrived at no clear conclusion and therefore had no influence. Meanwhile Fatini, reviewing[7] Berardi's edition (*Le Satire di Ludovico Ariosto, con introduzione e commento per gli scolari e per le persone colte di Cirillo Berardi, Campobasso 1918*), which follows Tambara's text, proposed a method of editing which is of interest only because it represents one of those rare instances when a scholar has seen that there might be some merit in comparing the *Satires* with the *Orlando Furioso* in a systematic way. Fatini would have established as a foundation the Ferrarese apograph (F), and supplemented it with readings from the earliest editions of the *Satires*, using for verification of these readings the diction and the grammar of the *Orlando Furioso*. Finally Bertani[8] and Catalano,[9] working independently, disposed of Tambara's distinction between inks, demonstrating that all the corrections in F are in the hand of Ariosto, except for a very few. Consequently, Fatini accepted in his edition (*Le Satire di Ludovico Ariosto, a cura di G. Fatini, Firenze 1933*) all the corrections in F.

Debenedetti, in preparation for a critical edition of the *Satires*, examined anew the corrections in F and confirmed the findings of Catalano. Cesare Segre, to whose critical notes to the texts of the minor works this history of the *Satires* is heavily indebted, used Debenedetti's text in his edition of the *Opere minori* (Milan: 1954), and I have translated that text, keeping close at hand Wenk's lithographic reproduction of F. Debenedetti's text follows F both in the order of the satires and in the readings desired by Ariosto in what, for lack of other materials, we must consider his final revision.

For the annotations to my translation, I am indebted to the editions of Segre and Fatini for the many leads they provided me, but more useful for my purposes were Catalano's *Vita di Ludovico Ariosto* and Angelo Stella's recent edition of the letters. My endeavor has been, with prefaces as well as annotations, to place the text of the *Satires* within its various *specific* historical and biographical contexts. In the *Satires*, Ariosto recorded his judgments of specific events in his life, which he carefully selected for the insights they might provide, not only into his own beliefs as a man, but into the character of his age as well. Hence we must begin with those particulars and work outward from them toward a comprehension of the poet and his view of life.

NOTES

[1]The compiler of *Memorie istoriche dei letterati ferraresi*, Ferrara 1777, and the editor of an esteemed edition of the *Opere* of Ludovico Ariosto published in Venice in 1766.

[2]"Intorno alle *Satire*. . . ."

[3]*Opere minori* (Milan: Ricciardi, 1954), p. 1179.

[4]Outlined in his *Vita di Ludovico Ariosto*, in *Biblioteca dell'Archivium Romanicum*, XV, 1931.

[5]"Intorno alle *Satire*. . . ."

[6]*Giornale storico* . . ., XLII, 1903, 418–22.

[7]*Giornale storico* . . ., LXXIV, 1919, 292–302.

[8]"Sul testo e sulla cronologia delle *Satire* di Ludovico Ariosto," *Giornale storico* . . ., LXXXVIII, 1926, 256–281; LXXXIX, 1927, 1–36.

[9]"Autografi e pretesi autografi," *Biblioteca dell'Archivium Romanicum*, IX, 58–64.

THE TRANSLATION

We have no record of any sixteenth-century translation of the *Satires* into any language. Furthermore, there is no Spanish translation at all. Due either to the popularity of Harington's *Orlando Furioso* or to a vogue for satire at the close of the sixteenth century, credit goes to the English for the first translation:

Ariosto's Satyres, in seven famous discourses, showing the state, 1 Of the court and courtiers. 2 Of libertie, and the clergie in generall. 3 Of the Romane clergie. 4 Of marriage. 5 Of soldiers, musitians, and lovers. 6 Of schoolemasters, and scholars. 7 Of honour, and the happiest life. In English, by Garvis Markham. London, Printed by N. Okes, for R. Iackson, 1608.

In 1611, the same translation was published as *Ariosto's seven planets governing Italie*. It is uncertain whether Markham or Robert Tofte is the translator. The work is in couplets, its meter striving too conscientiously to be iambic pentameter. It is a clumsy performance, very free,

bordering at times on incoherence and forced frequently by the rime
into infidelity. In addition, the translator seems often to have been
baffled by the syntactical difficulties of the original, and to have thought
nothing at such times of compensating by interpolating lines entirely
of his own device. His translation is entertaining nevertheless. At the
slightest hint of lubricity, his Muse takes heart, breaking out, for instance,
into a series of jaunty sixains when it comes time to tell the story
of the painter Galasso at the close of Satire V. This is perhaps the
high point of the entire translation. The translator accompanies his
work with notes to the text, often droll, with introductions to each
satire, and with a general introduction to the whole, in which he concocts
a lurid tale of love and violence involving Cardinal Ippolito and a
kinswoman of the poet. The order of the satires is that of F, except
that the positions of IV and V are reversed. But this first translation
never gained popularity, since the mode for English satire at the time
was Juvenalian, not Horatian.

There is an eighteenth-century English translation on record (*The
Satires of Ludovico Ariosto*. London, 1759.), attributed to Rev. H—rt—n
and Rev. T. H. Croker, an example of which resides in the British
Museum of London. This translator has not had the opportunity to
see it. There is also a nineteenth-century English translation (*The seventh
SATIRES of Ariosto*. Translated into English by Lord Holland. LON-
DON, 1827.), also in the British Museum of London. In France the
Satires were translated only once in their entirety:

> *Satires de l'Arioste,* traduites en francois, avec le texte en regard,
> précedées d'un apercu sur l'auteur et accompagnées de notes
> explicatives (par J. J. Trelis). Lyon, Laurent, 1826.

However, a *Traduction libre de la Cinquième Satire de l'Arioste* by
Méchin-Desquins appeared in 1846. It should also be mentioned that
Vauquelin de la Fresnaye performed an uninspired adaptation of Ariosto's Satires III-VII in his *Satyres Françoises*. Vauquelin probably wrote
his satires at intervals between 1574 and 1595.

The *Satires* fared best of all in Germany, where there was a translation
as early as 1794 by Christian Wilhelm Ahlwardt, *Lodovico Ariosto's
SATYREN*. The twentieth century has seen two translations, that of
Otto Gildemeister, *Lodovico Ariosto's SATIREN*, published in 1904,
and considered the better, and that of Alfons Kissner, published in

1909 in *Kleinere Werke, KOMODIEN LYRISCHE GEDICHTE, SA-TYREN.* This latter was reprinted in 1922 as part of Kissner's *Sämtliche poetischen Werke* of Ariosto. In fact, we have owed to Germany the only twentieth-century translations of the complete *Satires* we have had up to now. It should also be noted that in 1774 Jagemann, the continuator of Meinhard, in a third volume attached to the second edition of Meinhard's *Versuche über den Charakter und die Werke der besten italienischen Dichter,* included a prose translation of the *Satires.* And finally, J. G. Fucilla[1] cites Ettore Lo Gatto's *Studi di letterature slave* (III, Rome, 1931, 212) for a Czechoslovakian translation of some of the satires by Jaroslav Vrchlicky, translator of the *Orlando Furioso* at the close of the nineteenth century.

With the present translation I hope to fill an obvious and long-standing gap in English and American Renaissance studies by supplying a readable version of Ariosto's second masterpiece. Although the original is in *terza rima,* I have chosen not to rime the translation for reasons of accuracy and humility, considering myself fortunate if I have been able to achieve fidelity to some of the many intellectual and emotional subtleties of the original, and if I have succeeded in preserving some of the dignity and the urbanity of Ariosto's style. The bilingual format of this edition should gratify experts in the Italian language, and be of service as well to those whose knowledge of Italian is modest and to beginners who must still struggle along with dictionary and grammar book in hand. For the many believers that poetry can never be translated successfully into prose, Joseph Tusiani's *Italian Poets of the Renaissance* (New York: 1971) is to be recommended very highly for its skillful and graceful renditions of extended passages from the *Satires.*

NOTES

[1] "European Translations and Imitations of Ariosto," *The Romanic Review,* XXV (January–March, 1934), 50.

SATIRE I

To Messer Alessandro Ariosto
and Messer Ludovico da Bagno

PREFACE

In the year 1517 a permanent break with his employer, Cardinal Ippolito d'Este, seems to have provided Ariosto with the occasion of his first satire. From the beginning of his service in the early months of 1503, the poet had occupied the position of factotum to the Cardinal. He was charged with missions, often futile and hazardous, to chiefs of state and high ranking prelates, including two popes; he was employed as a courier, as a gatherer of intelligence, as a political and military aide, and as a companion on journeys; he was also assigned the responsibility of entertaining the Ferrarese court as official playwright and as director of numerous theatrical productions. No one knows precisely where his duties ended, mainly because they went on to include such menial tasks as the procurement of clothes for the Cardinal's back and delicacies for his table. But, during those years of constant labor, Ariosto managed somehow to find the time he needed to bring the *Orlando Furioso* through all the stages of its development from its initial conception up to its first publication in 1516 in forty cantos. The Cardinal, however, to whom the work was dedicated and in praise of whose family it had been written, condescended to reward his poet with no more than a flippant remark,[1] so little was he inclined to approve of time spent on literature by a servant who should have been occupying his every waking moment with official business.

Ariosto was now loaded with even heavier extra-literary duties. No sooner was the *Orlando Furioso* off the press than Ippolito was off to Rome. Evidence points to the poet's having accompanied him from 23 June to 7 July 1516.[2] By 30 August, Ariosto was in the saddle once again on a mission to Florence. Then in October he went on a journey to Milan for the purpose of renting out the proceeds of his share, a gift from the Cardinal, of that episcopal chancery to which he refers in the present satire and also in Satires II and IV[3] as more of a nuisance to him than a benefit. Although Ariosto made this trip on private business, the Cardinal contrived to profit from the occasion by burdening the poet with the task of purchasing for him certain barrels of wine which he had to accompany through snow, past customs agents, and across swollen rivers back to Ferrara. From 17 February to 28 March 1517, the Cardinal progressed to Mantua, Milan, and Pavia, and the poet trotted along as leader of part of the entourage. Once back in Ferrara, Ippolito made frequent forays into the countryside to hunt water fowl, with the faithful poet reluctantly at his master's side. One can imagine Ariosto's disappointment after having hoped that the *Orlando Furioso* would win him a respite from the drudgery of his life as a courtier.

One should reserve, however, a certain amount of sympathy for the Cardinal. During much of the time Ariosto served him, Ippolito had dire need of resourceful followers. The times were critical from the League of Cambrai and the Holy League through Francis I's conquest of Lombardy, and Ippolito would have been wasting the human resources of his court had he given sinecures to men of Ariosto's capabilities. While he observed all around him the collapse of states many times larger and far wealthier than his own, he had to defend his family's right to govern Ferrara against two successive popes, Julius II and Leo X, the former a fierce warrior and the latter a superb diplomat. The Estensi had need of couriers, diplomats, and soldiers; they did not need poets.

When on 25 August 1517 news came that the Cardinal had decided, perhaps at the request of King Louis II of Hungary, to take up a lengthy residence at his Bishopric of Eger near Budapest, the entire court began to grumble. Postumo, one of the court physicians whom Ariosto mentions in the present satire,[4] wrote to Isabella d'Este that if God permitted him to return home safely from that accursed Hungary, reserved in ancient times by the Romans as a place of exile for their criminals, he would henceforth be certain of entering Paradise in full dress, not to mention body and soul, since no sin of his was so grievous that a single month in that land would not serve as sufficient penance.[5] Ariosto flatly refused to accompany the Cardinal. He gave sound reasons. Ippolito took his refusal as a mark of ingratitude. No doubt, Ippolito believed a courtier should consider himself honored in the knowledge that he was needed. But Ariosto remained obstinate, and the break between them became final.

It must have been during the days just following the Cardinal's departure on 25 October 1517 that Ariosto drafted his first satire and addressed it to two men upon whose friendship he could depend. Alessandro Ariosto (1492-1569), the poet's youngest brother, was in the Cardinal's service from 1507 until 1520. He made the journey, his second to Hungary, survived his master and his four brothers, and spent the rest of his years in the priesthood. Although he was the more successful courtier, he owed his introduction into the Cardinal's service to his eldest brother and often had need of Ludovico's help when it came to obtaining benefices. Ludovico da Bagno, who had acted as godfather to the poet's son Virginio, also followed the court to Hungary as Ippolito's secretary. He too was a member of the clergy. Ariosto had already remembered his friendship in the first edition of the *Orlando Furioso* (XL, 4).

In this satire, an apparently personal letter, Ariosto seeks information as to the Cardinal's present opinion of him, wonders whether or not he will be deprived of former gifts, and hints that he would accept a reconciliation, on his own terms. Ariosto did not, in fact, lose any of the benefices he had acquired during his former service. He lost what was probably more precious to him—the promised grant of secular lands of considerable value. There was never to be a reconciliation. By spring of the following year, Ariosto was officially in the service of Duke Alfonso d'Este, the Cardinal's brother.

After almost three years in Eger, Ippolito returned to Ferrara in the spring of 1520. He died on 2 September of that year of a severe attack of indigestion. Food was his only weakness. In his will he remembered many of his servants, including those of the lowest rank; but he made no mention of the one servant to whom he owes, more than to anyone, the immortality of his name.

NOTES

[1] See ll. 94–96 of the present satire and the accompanying note.
[2] Michele Catalano, *Vita di Ludovico Ariosto* (Geneva: Olschki, 1931), I, 439.
[3] I, ll. 109–114; II, ll. 99–102; IV, ll. 181–183.
[4] See ll. 28–30 and the accompanying note.
[5] Catalano, I, 443.

Io desidero intendere da voi,
Alessandro fratel, compar mio Bagno,
s'in corte è ricordanza più di noi;

    se più il signor me accusa; se compagno
per me si lieva e dice la cagione   5
per che, partendo gli altri, io qui rimagno;

    o, tutti dotti ne la adulazione
(l'arte che più tra noi si studia e cole),
l'aiutate a biasmarme oltra ragione.

    Pazzo chi al suo signor contradir vole,   10
se ben dicesse c'ha veduto il giorno
pieno di stelle e a mezzanotte il sole.

    O ch'egli lodi, o voglia altrui far scorno,
di varie voci subito un concento
s'ode accordar di quanti n'ha dintorno;   15

    e chi non ha per umiltà ardimento
la bocca aprir, con tutto il viso applaude
e par che voglia dir: — anch'io consento. —

    Ma se in altro biasmarme, almen dar laude
dovete che, volendo io rimanere,   20
lo dissi a viso aperto e non con fraude.

    Dissi molte ragioni, e tutte vere,
de le quali per sé sola ciascuna
esser mi dovea degna di tenere.

    Prima la vita, a cui poche o nessuna   25
cosa ho da preferir, che far più breve
non voglio che 'l ciel voglia o la Fortuna.

    Ogni alterazione, ancor che leve,
ch'avesse il mal ch'io sento, o ne morei,
o il Valentino e il Postumo errar deve.   30

    Oltra che 'l dicano essi, io meglio i miei
casi de ogni altro intendo; e quai compensi
mi siano utili so, so quai son rei.

    So mia natura come mal conviensi
co' freddi verni; e costà sotto il polo   35
gli avete voi più che in Italia intensi.

I wish to hear from you, Alessandro, my brother, and Bagno, my dear friend, whether at the court there lingers any recollection of me; whether my lord continues to revile me; whether a comrade rises to defend me and explains why I am staying here while everyone else is leaving; or whether you are all schooled in sycophancy (the art among us most studied and revered) and help him to blame me beyond reason.

Mad is the man who would contradict his lord, even if he were to say he had seen the day full of stars and at midnight the sun. Whether he praise a man or disgrace him, suddenly one hears a concert of as many voices as he has around him in accord; and he who has not for meekness the courage to open his mouth applauds with all his face and seems to yearn to say, "I too agree." But blame me though you must in other respects, you should at least praise me, because I declared openly, without deception, that I wanted to stay. I gave him many reasons, and all of them true, and each one by itself alone should have been sufficient to keep me here.

First of all, I possess little or nothing that I prefer to the one life I do not want Fortune or the heavens to abbreviate. With every change for the worse, though slight, of this illness[1] I suffer, either I shall die or Valentino and Postumo[2] must be mistaken. Aside from their opinion, I know my own affairs better than anyone; I know which conditions may help me, just as I know which are bad. I know how ill-adapted my constitution is to cold winters, and there beneath the pole[3] you have them more intense than here in

E non mi nocerebbe il freddo solo;
ma il caldo de le stuffe, c'ho sì infesto,
che più che da la peste me gli involo.
   Né il verno altrove s'abita in cotesto   40
paese: vi si mangia, giuoca e bee,
e vi si dorme e vi si fa anco il resto.
   Che quindi vien, come sorbir si dee
l'aria che tien sempre in travaglio il fiato
de le montagne prossime Rifee?   45
   Dal vapor che, dal stomaco elevato,
fa catarro a la testa e cala al petto,
mi rimarei una notte soffocato.
   E il vin fumoso, a me vie più interdetto
che 'l tòsco, costì a inviti si tracanna,   50
e sacrilegio è non ber molto e schietto.
   Tutti li cibi son con pepe e canna
di amomo e d'altri aròmati, che tutti
come nocivi il medico mi danna.
   Qui mi potreste dir ch'io avrei ridutti,   55
dove sotto il camin sedria al foco,
né piei, né ascelle odorerei, né rutti;
   e le vivande condiriemi il cuoco
come io volessi, et inacquarmi il vino
potre' a mia posta, e nulla berne o poco.   60
   Dunque voi altri insieme, io dal mattino
a la sera starei solo a la cella,
solo a la mensa come un certosino?
   Bisognerieno pentole e vasella
da cucina e da camera, e dotarme   65
di masserizie qual sposa novella.
   Se separatamente cucinarme
vorà mastro Pasino una o due volte,
quattro e sei mi farà il viso da l'arme.
   S'io vorò de le cose ch'avrà tolte   70
Francesco di Siver per la famiglia,
potrò mattina e sera averne molte.

Italy. And not only would the cold do me harm, but
also the heat of the stoves, which I find so noxious
that I avoid them more than the plague. Nor in winter
does one live far from them in that land; one eats,
drinks, and games near them, and near them one sleeps
and performs all the rest as well. How should one
who comes away from them imbibe the air of the
nearby Riphaeian mountains,[4] which continually bela-
bors one's breathing? By the vapor which, rising from
the stomach, gives the head a catarrh and settles in
the chest, I would be suffocated one night. And the
heavy wine, far worse for me than poison, is gulped
down in toasting there, and it is a sacrilege not to
drink it straight and in abundance. All of their foods
are prepared with pepper and ginger and other aromat-
ics, all of which the doctor considers harmful to me.

There, you may say, I should find retreats, where
beneath the chimney I might sit beside the fire; nor
feet, nor armpits would I smell, nor belches; and the
cook would dress me my viands as I wished them,
and I could dilute as I wish my wine with water and
drink none of it or just as little as I choose. How
now! While all you others are together, should I from
morning to evening stay in my cell alone and dine
alone like a Carthusian monk? I should need pots
and crockery for the kitchen and the bedroom; it would
be necessary to dower me with furnishings like a new
bride. If Master Pasino[5] were content to cook specially
for me once or twice, the next few times he would
glower at me menacingly. If I desired some of the
stuff Francesco di Siver[6] scrapes up for the servants,
morning and evening I could have my fill. If I were

S'io dirò: — Spenditor, questo mi piglia,
che l'umido cervel poco notrisce;
questo no, che 'l catar troppo assottiglia —   75
per una volta o due che me ubidisce,
quattro e sei mi si scorda, o perché teme
che non gli sia accettato, non ardisce.
Io mi riduco al pane; e quindi freme
la colera; cagion che a li dui motti   80
gli amici et io siamo a contesa insieme.
Mi potreste anco dir: — De li tuoi scotti
fa che 'l tuo fante comprator ti sia;
mangia i tuoi polli alli tua alari cotti. —
Io, per la mala servitude mia,   85
non ho dal Cardinale ancora tanto
ch'io possa fare in corte l'osteria.
   Apollo, tua mercé, tua mercé, santo
collegio de le Muse, io non possiedo
tanto per voi, ch'io possa farmi un manto.   90
   — Oh! il signor t'ha dato... — io ve 'l conciedo,
tanto che fatto m'ho più d'un mantello;
ma che m'abbia per voi dato non credo.
   Egli l'ha detto: io dirlo a questo e a quello
voglio anco, e i versi miei posso a mia posta   95
mandare al Culiseo per lo sugello.
   Non vuol che laude sua da me composta
per opra degna di mercé si pona;
di mercé degno è l'ir correndo in posta.
   A chi nel Barco e in villa il segue, dona,   100
a chi lo veste e spoglia, o pona i fiaschi
nel pozzo per la sera in fresco a nona;
   vegghi la notte, in sin che i Bergamaschi
se levino a far chiodi, sì che spesso
col torchio in mano addormentato caschi.   105
   S'io l'ho con laude ne' miei versi messo,
dice ch'io l'ho fatto a piacere e in ocio;
più grato fòra essergli stato appresso.

to say, "Steward, get this for me, because it does
not feed my rheumy head, and not this, because it
loosens my catarrh too much," for every once or
twice that he would obey me, he would forget me
four or six times, or, fearing that his provision might
not be approved, he would not try to please me. So
I reduce my diet to bread, and anger rumbles forth,
and quarrels ensue between myself and my friends
over every two words.

You might also tell me, "Make your servant the
purchaser of your share out of your own pocket; eat
your chickens cooked over your own grill." I, in return
for my wretched servitude, have not as yet, from
the Cardinal, acquired enough to equip a hostelry at
the court. Apollo, thanks to you, and thanks to you,
sacred college of the Muses, I do not earn enough
to make myself a cloak. "Oh, but your lord has
given you . . ." -yes, I grant you that, enough to
make more than one cape, but I doubt that he has
remunerated me because of you. He himself has said
so. And I wish to repeat it to all. I can send my
verses to the Cloacasseum for its seal whenever I
please.[7]

He does not consider his praises, composed by me,
as work worthy of any thanks, but to be a galloping
postman is worth a reward. He rewards those who
follow him into the Barco,[8] and to his villa; the servant
who dresses and undresses him is rewarded, and the
man who lowers bottles into the well at noon to keep
them cool till evening; and the servant who keeps
watch all night, until the Bergamasks wake up to make
nails, so that he often buckles, torch in hand, numb
with sleep. If I have praised him in my verses, he
says I have done so to please myself and at my leisure;
better if I had been at hand to wait upon him. And

E se in cancellaria m'ha fatto socio
a Melan del Constabil, sì c'ho il terzo   110
di quel ch'al notaio vien d'ogni negocio,
   gli è perché alcuna volta io sprono e sferzo
mutando bestie e guide, e corro in fretta
per monti e balze, e con la morte scherzo.
   Fa a mio senno, Maron: tuoi versi getta   115
con la lira in un cesso, e una arte impara,
se beneficii vuoi, che sia più accetta.
   Ma tosto che n'hai, pensa che la cara
tua libertà non meno abbi perduta
che se giocata te l'avessi a zara;   120
   e che mai più, se ben alla canuta
età vivi e viva egli di Nestorre,
questa condizïon non ti si muta.
   E se disegni mai tal nodo sciorre,
buon patto avrai, se con amore e pace   125
quel che t'ha dato si vorà ritorre.
   A me, per esser stato contumace
di non voler Agria veder né Buda,
che si ritoglia il suo sì non mi spiace
   (se ben le miglior penne che avea in muda   130
rimesse, e tutte, mi tarpasse), come
che da l'amor e grazia sua mi escluda,
   che senza fede e senza amor mi nome,
e che dimostri con parole e cenni
che in odio e che in dispetto abbia il mio nome.   135
   E questo fu cagion ch'io me ritenni
di non gli comparire inanzi mai,
dal dì che indarno ad escusar mi vienni.
   Ruggier, se a la progenie tua mi fai
sì poco grato, e nulla mi prevaglio   140
che li alti gesti e tuo valor cantai,
   che debbo far io qui? poi ch'io non vaglio
smembrar su la forcina in aria starne,
né so a sparvier, né a can metter guinzaglio?

if he has made me Constabili's partner in the chancery
in Milan, so I get a third of all that goes to the notary
from each transaction,[9] it is because I sometimes spur
and whip, changing horses and guides, and dash in
haste over cliffs and mountains, and toy with death.

Take my advice, Marone.[10] Toss your verses into
a privy and your lyre after them, and learn a more
acceptable skill if you desire to earn benefices. But
as soon as you have received them, remember you
have lost your precious liberty no less than if you
had gambled it away with dice, and even if you and
he live to the grey old age of Nestor, this condition
of yours will never change. And if you ever plan
to untie this knot, you will strike a good bargain if,
with peace and good will, he repossesses himself of
his former gifts.

That he may take back his gifts in reprisal for my
obstinacy in refusing to see either Eger or Buda does
not so profoundly disturb me (even if he were to
put my best plumes back into the mew and altogether
clip my wings) as the thought that he may bar me
from his affection and good graces, and speak of me
as loveless and faithless, and demonstrate with words
and signs that he holds my name in hatred and
contempt. And that is why, from the day I came to
excuse myself in vain, I contrived never to show him
my face again.

Ruggiero,[11] if you make me so little welcome among
your progeny, and I achieve no distinction by singing
of your noble deeds and valor, what should I do at
your court? For I am no good at dismembering
partridges suspended on a fork; I do not know how
to manage the jesses of a hawk or how to hold a

Non feci mai tai cose e non so farne:
alli usatti, alli spron, perch'io son grande,
non mi posso adattar per porne o trarne.

Io non ho molto gusto di vivande,
che scalco io sia; fui degno essere al mondo
quando viveano gli uomini di giande.   150

Non vo' il conto di man tòrre a Gismondo;
andar più a Roma in posta non accade
a placar la grande ira di Secondo;

    e quando accadesse anco, in questa etade,
col mal ch'ebbe principio allora forse,   155
non si convien più correr per le strade.

Se far cotai servigi e raro tòrse
di sua presenza de' chi d'oro ha sete,
e stargli come Artofilace a l'Orse;

    più tosto che arricchir, voglio quïete: 160
più tosto che occuparmi in altra cura,
sì che inondar lasci il mio studio a Lete.

Il qual, se al corpo non può dar pastura,
lo dà a la mente con sì nobil ésca
che merta di non star senza cultura.   165

Fa che la povertà meno m'incresca,
e fa che la ricchezza sì non ami
che di mia libertà per suo amor esca;

    quel ch'io non spiero aver, fa ch'io non brami,
che né sdegno né invidia me consumi   170
perché Marone o Celio il signor chiami;

    ch'io non aspetto a mezza estade i lumi
per esser col signor veduto a cena,
ch'io non lascio accecarmi in questi fumi;

    ch'io vado solo e a piedi ove mi mena   175
il mio bisogno, e quando io vo a cavallo,
le bisacce gli attacco su la schiena.

E credo che sia questo minor fallo
che di farmi pagar, s'io raccomando
al principe la causa d'un vasallo;   180

dog in leash. I have never done such things. They are not my trade. Since I am large in stature, I cannot bend myself to pull on and slip off my lord's boots and his spurs. I have not the taste for meats that makes a carver. I would have been well qualified to enter life in the days when men lived on acorns.[12] I do not want to take the accounts out of Gismondo's hands,[13] and there is no longer occasion for me to go posting to Rome in order to sooth the rage of Secondo.[14] And even if there were, at my age and with my illness, which perhaps had its inception then, it no longer befits me to go racing over the roads.

If he who thirsts for gold here must perform such menial tasks, and rarely remove himself from my lord's presence, and play the Hunter to his Little Bear, then let me have peace instead of wealth, and let me not occupy myself with such distractions as will cause my studies to drown in Lethe. Although my studies serve not to nourish my body, they serve my mind with such a noble food that they should not go uncultivated. Through them my poverty grieves me less, and they prevent me from loving wealth so much as to forego my liberty in pursuit of it. They cause me not to long for what I cannot hope to have; they prevent envy and resentment from consuming me, because my lord summons Marone and Celio[15] to his presence. In midsummer, because of them, I do not await the torches in order to be seen at supper with my lord. I do not let myself be blinded in this smoke of vanity. They persuade me to go alone on foot wherever necessity leads me, and when astride to carry my belongings in saddlebags on my horse's back. And I esteem them to be a lesser failing in my duty than to extort a payment from a vassal whose cause I plead before my prince, or to commence

o mover liti in benefici, quando
ragion non v'abbia, e facciami i pievani
ad offerir pension venir pregando.

Anco fa che al ciel levo ambe le mani,
ch'abito in casa mia commodamente,   185
voglia tra cittadini o tra villani;

e che nei ben paterni il rimanente
del viver mio, senza imparar nova arte,
posso, e senza rossor, far, di mia gente.

Ma perché cinque soldi da pagarte,   190
tu che noti, non ho, rimetter voglio
la mia favola al loco onde si parte.

Aver cagion di non venir mi doglio:
detto ho la prima, e s'io vuo' l'altre dire,
né questo basterà né un altro foglio.   195

Pur ne dirò anco un'altra: che patire
non debbo che, levato ogni sostegno,
casa nostra in ruina abbia a venire.

De cinque che noi siàn, Carlo è nel regno
onde cacciaro i Turchi il mio Cleandro,   200
e di starvi alcun tempo fa disegno;

Galasso vuol ne la città di Evandro
por la camicia sopra la guarnaccia;
e tu sei col signore ito, Alessandro.

Ecci Gabriel; ma che vuoi tu ch'ei faccia?   205
che da fanciullo la sua mala sorte
lo impedì de li piedi e de le braccia.

Egli non fu né in piazza mai, né in corte,
et a chi vuol ben reggere una casa
questo si può comprendere che importe.   210

A la quinta sorella che rimasa
n'era, bisogna apparecchiar la dote,
che le siàn debitori, or che se accasa.

L'età di nostra matre mi percuote
di pietà il core; che da tutti un tratto   215
senza infamia lasciata esser non puote.

litigations over benefices to which I have no right
and to force the parish priests to come to me praying
to pay me tribute money.[16] My studies also cause
me to raise both hands in thanks to heaven that I
live in my house comfortably, whether in the city
or among peasants, and that I am able to support
the remainder of my life with my patrimony, without
having to learn a new craft and without making my
household blush for shame.

But because I do not have five *soldi*[17] to pay you,
who take note, I wish to bring my story back to the
place where I began it. It grieves me to have reasons
not to come. You have heard the first, and if I desired
to enumerate the others, neither this nor another sheet
of paper would suffice.–Still I shall give you one more.
I must not suffer that, every support removed, our
House fall into ruin. Of the five that we are, Carlo[18]
is in the kingdom whence the Turks chased my
Cleandro,[19] and he plans to linger there awhile. Galasso[20] desires to put a shirt over his bathrobe[21] in the
city of Evander,[22] and you, Alessandro, have gone
away with my lord. Gabriele[23] is here, but what do
you expect of him? From boyhood his ill-fortune has
left him crippled in his arms and legs. He was never
in the market-place nor at the court, and what this
means can be understood by anyone who desires to
manage a household well. For our fifth sister,[24] who
remained with us, we must provide a dowry, for we
are her debtors now that she is entering another's
house. Our aged mother[25] touches my heart with
compassion. She cannot be deserted by all of us at
once without disgrace.

Io son de dieci il primo, e vecchio fatto
di quarantaquattro anni, e il capo calvo
da un tempo in qua sotto il cuffiotto appiatto.

La vita che mi avanza me la salvo   220
meglio ch'io so: ma tu che diciotto anni
dopo me t'indugiasti a uscir de l'alvo,

gli Ongari a veder torna e gli Alemanni,
per freddo e caldo segui il signor nostro,
servi per amendua, rifa i miei danni.   225

Il qual se vuol di calamo et inchiostro
di me servirsi, e non mi tòr da bomba,
digli: — Signore, il mio fratello è vostro. —

Io, stando qui, farò con chiara tromba
il suo nome sonar forse tanto alto   230
che tanto mai non si levò colomba.

A Filo, a Cento, in Arïano, a Calto
arriverei, ma non sin al Danubbio,
ch'io non ho piei gagliardi a sì gran salto.

Ma se a voglier di novo avessi al subbio   235
li quindici anni che in servirlo ho spesi,
passar la Tana ancor non starei in dubbio.

Se avermi dato onde ogni quattro mesi
ho venticinque scudi, né sì fermi
che molte volte non mi sien contesi,   240

mi debbe incatenar, schiavo tenermi,
ubligarmi ch'io sudi e tremi senza
rispetto alcun, ch'io moia o ch'io me 'nfermi,

non gli lasciate aver questa credenza;
ditegli che più tosto ch'esser servo   245
torrò la povertade in pazïenza.

Uno asino fu già, ch'ogni osso e nervo
mostrava di magrezza, e entrò, pel rotto
del muro, ove di grano era uno acervo;

e tanto ne mangiò, che l'epa sotto   250
si fece più d'una gran botte grossa,
fin che fu sazio, e non però di botto.

I am the first of ten, and aged forty-four years, with my bald head concealed for some time now beneath a skull-cap. I preserve what life remains to me as best I can. But you, who delayed to leave the womb until eighteen years after me, return to see the Hungarians and the Germans, follow our lord through heat and cold, serve for both of us, and make good my errors. If he wishes to make use of me with ink and quill, and not budge me from my firm resolve, tell him, "My lord, my brother is yours." Dwelling here, I will with a shining clarion make his name ring out higher perhaps than ever flew a dove. I would go for him as far as Filo, Cento, Ariano, or Caltro,[26] but not as far as the Danube, for my feet are not valiant enough to take so long a leap. But if I had the fifteen years I spent in serving him all over now to weave upon the warp, I would not hesitate to cross even the Don in his service.

If he thinks that having granted me the means to collect every four months twenty-five uncertain *scudi*, frequently contested, gives him the right to bind me with chains and make a slave of me, or to obligate me to sweat and shiver without any consideration whatsoever, whether I am ill or dying, then let him remain no longer in this error. Tell him that sooner than to be a lackey I would choose to live my life in patient poverty.

Once there was a donkey,[27] so thin that he displayed his every bone and sinew, and he entered, through a hole in the wall, a place where there was a mighty heap of grain. And he ate so much that his belly grew bigger than a tun, and he guzzled until he was full, and that was not all in a moment. Fearing

Temendo poi che gli sien péste l'ossa
si sforza di tornar dove entrato era,
ma par che 'l buco più capir nol possa.   255

Mentre s'affanna, e uscire indarno spera,
gli disse un topolino: — Se vuoi quinci
uscir, tràtti, compar, quella panciera:

a vomitar bisogna che cominci
ciò c'hai nel corpo, e che ritorni macro,   260
altrimenti quel buco mai non vinci. —

Or, conchiudendo, dico che, se 'l sacro
Cardinal comperato avermi stima
con li suoi doni, non mi è acerbo et acro

renderli, e tòr la libertà mia prima.   265 afterwards that he might be beaten for his temerity, he strained to get out where he had entered, but he could no longer fit through the hole. While he puffed and panted and tried in vain to squeeze through, a tiny mouse said to him "If you wish to get through that hole, cousin, remove your belly-armor first. You must begin by vomiting up all you have taken into your carcass, and get thin again, otherwise you will never manage to get out of the hole you are in.

Now, in conclusion, I declare that, if the reverend Cardinal thinks he has purchased me with his gifts, I find it neither bitter nor harsh to return them and to resume my former freedom.

NOTES

[1] Ariosto was troubled most of his adult life by a stomach condition. He himself says later (l. 155) that it might have resulted from the harrowing experiences he underwent during his missions to Julius II.

[2] Giovanni Andrea Valentino, a Modenese physician, went with Ippolito to Hungary. The Pesarese Guido Silvestri, called Postumo because he was born after the death of his father, was also a physician in the Cardinal's service. However, at the last minute, he managed to avoid the trip to Hungary. He was a close friend of Ariosto, who remembered him in the *Orlando Furioso* (XLII, 89) as an excellent poet in Latin and as an accomplished physician. He in turn warmly praised Ariosto in his Latin verses. He died in 1521.

[3] Ariosto exaggerates merely to indicate what would have been his discomfort, as an Italian, had he been forced to go north for the winter.

[4] Another exaggeration, and perhaps also a reminiscence of Vergil's "*talis Hyberboreo septem subiecta trioni/gens effrena virum Riphaeo tunditur Euro . . .*" (*Georgics*, III, 381). The Romans called a certain range in Scythia Riphaeian.

[5] The Cardinal's cook, whose name appears frequently in the registers of expenses for the years 1513 and 1514. The title *mastro* indicates that he was a commoner.

[6] A member of the nobility, as the title *messere* before his name in the official registers indicates, who was charged with the day to day provision of foodstuffs for the court.

[7] "Cloacasseum" is a translation of *culiseo*, a pun in Italian on the word for colosseum, *colosseo*, the popular version of which is *coliseo*. A reference to the Flavian Amphitheatre in Rome is intended. It may have been this passage and the lines directly following that gave rise to the notorious account of the Cardinal's words when in 1516 he received the dedication copy of the *Orlando Furioso* from the poet in person: "*Messer Ludovico, dove mai avete trovato tante corbellerie?*" In English: "Ludovico, where in the world did you find so many silly stories?" Since our earliest sources for this utterance date from the late seventeenth century and are not Italian, perhaps we should lend less credence to its historical veracity than its popularity seems to call for. But regardless of whether or not the Cardinal actually spoke the words attributed to him, they do serve apothegmatically to acquaint us with the tone of Ariosto's relationship with his lord.

[8] A spacious forest and meadow land to the north between the Po and the walls of Ferrara. It was set aside by the House of Este as a private game preserve and as pasturage for their horses. The Cardinal was a passionate hunter.

[9] On 1 October 1516 the Cardinal gave Ariosto a one-third share in the revenues of the archepiscopal chancery of Milan. The other shareholders were Antonio Costabili and Benedetto Fantino. On 9 August 1517, after having renounced a Ferrarese benefice in favor of the cleric Vincenzo Silvestri, Ariosto received in exchange Fantino's one-sixth share. Later in this same satire (1.239) he states that his annual income from the Milanese benefice amounted to twenty-five *scudi*.

[10] Andrea Marone of Brescia competed against his fellow poet Celio Calcagnini for the privilege of accompanying the Cardinal to Hungary and lost. Both had been in the Cardinal's service since 1510 and both were friends of Ariosto, who remembered them in the *Orlando Furioso* (III, 56; XLII, 90; XLVI, 13-14). Marone, like Ariosto, was employed as a courier, but Celio Calcagnini, a member

of the clergy, had better luck. He received many benefices in Ferrara and Modena and ended his career as an apostolical protonotary. Apart from his fame as a Latin poet and orator, he was a numismatist, a philosopher, and the owner of a rich library. One of his writings, on the movement of the earth, entitles him to be numbered among the precursors of Copernicus; another, as a source useful to Rabelais.

[11] A major character in the *Orlando Furioso*, in which he and the warrior maiden Bradamante, after many vicissitudes, finally become united as the progenitors of the House of Este.

[12] During the Golden Age, we are told, men lived on acorns and enjoyed the simple life (Ovid, *Metamorphoses*, I, 106).

[13] Sigismondo Cestarelli held the position of accountant for Duke Alfonso and later for the Cardinal.

[14] Ariosto's first important missions for the Cardinal were to the court of Julius II. Although Ariosto's embassies were consistently unwelcome to the Pope, he never held a personal grudge against the poet. In fact, at critical moments Julius was more disposed to listen to him than to any of the Cardinal's other ambassadors. Only once did the Pope's uncontrollable temper ever jeopardize Ariosto's life. During the height of hostilities between the Papacy and the House of Este over the latter's refusal to break its alliance with France and join the Holy League, the Pope commanded Cardinal Ippolito to appear before him in Rome within fifteen days. Ippolito sent Ariosto to the papal court three times in rapid succession in order to defend him before the Pope, to get extensions of time, and to obtain for him, if possible, a safe conduct. On his second trip Ariosto learned from certain cardinals friendly to his lord that it would be extremely hazardous for Ippolito to enter Rome without a safe conduct. Therefore, on his third trip, the poet was instructed to tell the Pope that his master would flatly disobey the order to appear unless he were granted the safe conduct. Luckily he was not given an audience this time. When Julius heard at second hand the contents of his mission, he flew into such a rage that he ordered Ariosto to be fed to the fish. Fortunately, some friends helped him to escape. While this was the Pope's only direct attack, Ariosto's life was in danger during the entire period of hostility, which lasted until Julius II's death in 1513.

[15] See note 5.

[16] Parish priests, against whose benefices lawsuits were advanced by false claimants, often found it easier to buy off their persecutors with annual payments out of their revenues than to undertake the expenses of the ecclesiastical courts.

[17] A speaker who had digressed from his argument and could not remember where to take it up again had to pay his listener a token fine.

[18] Carlo (1485–1527), the third eldest, is the least known to us of Ariosto's brothers. In 1514, after Ludovico had contracted a loan of 200 *lire marchesane* to pay his expenses, Carlo departed for the kingdom of Naples in order to enter the grain and cattle businesses.

[19] Cleandro, the aged lover in Ariosto's comedy *I Suppositi*, took refuge in Ferrara after having been expelled by the Turks from his native city of Otranto.

[20] Galasso (1490–1546), the penultimate brother, entered upon an ecclesiastical career. He was in the service of Cardinal Riario and later in that of Cardinal Cibò. Although he gained secure posts, he was always in need of help from his eldest brother, especially in the administration of the benefices which were granted him. Duke Ercole II used him on political missions to Venice and to the Emperor. He died in Ingolstadt, Bavaria.

²¹ A jocular reference to Gallasso's desire to put a rochet about his soutane. Evidently he aspired to become a bishop or an abbot.

²² Rome. According to Roman legend, Evander, the son of Carmentis, founded a colony of his fellow Arcadians on the banks of the Tiber where Rome was afterwards to stand. Ariosto borrows the phrase from the *Aeneid* (XI, 26), in which Evander helps Aeneas defeat Turnus.

²³ Gabriele (1477-1549), Ludovico's eldest brother, had been rendered a semi-paralytic for life by a disease suffered during infancy. However, the poet grossly exaggerates his disability. Gabriele was in fact the real manager of the family's domestic affairs. His father bequeathed him the largest share of the patrimony, and through careful management he was able to support himself with it. Gabriele was also a competent poet in Latin and Italian. It was he who completed Ludovico's *I Studenti* and gave it the title *La Scolastica*. Among his Latin poems (*Carmina*, Ferrara 1582), one is noteworthy, "*In obitu L. Areosti.*" He remembers his brother as his tutor in poetry: "*Tu me, tu primum docuisti inflectere carmen,/Tu musarum umbram, suosque ostendis amictus.*"

²⁴ The poet refers to his youngest sister Taddea (1493-1520), who towards the end of 1517 or the beginning of 1518 married Antonio dal Leone, a citizen of Ferrara. Her brothers had to amass a dowry of 700 gold ducats for the occasion. As for Ariosto's other sisters, the eldest was Taddea Giovanna (1475-1492), who entered the convent of S. Caterina in Ferrara. No doubt the younger Taddea, born a year after her death, was named after her. Laura Margherita (1479-?), along with the younger Taddea. She was married in the spring of 1501 to Andrea Guirino, and the brothers were of course burdened with raising her dowry, which amounted to somewhat more than 1600 *lire marchesane* by the time it was fully paid in 1512. They paid 563 *lire* immediately and then were saddled with installments of approximately 100 *lire* for each of the next eleven years. Giulia Giovanna (1480-?), the third sister, was married also, but during her father's lifetime. Of Virginia, the fourth in line, we know only that she too entered the convent of S. Caterina in Ferrara.

²⁵ Daria, daughter of the scholar and poet Gabriele Malaguzzi, was born in April, 1453. She married Niccolò Ariosto in September of 1473 during his captaincy of the citadel of Reggio. She brought a dowry of 1000 gold ducats. She died sometime between September, 1519 and February, 1522.

²⁶ Small towns on the borders of Ferrarese territory.

²⁷ To emphasize his Horatian model, Ariosto turns in closing to the seventh epistle of the *Liber Primus* (ll. 29-33) in order to adapt to his own purpose the fable of the fox and the weasel. See pp. xxi-xxii above.

SATIRE II

To Messer Galasso Ariosto
His Brother

During the several months between his break with the Cardinal and his enrollment in the service of Duke Alfonso, Ariosto probably sought relief from all troublesome employments. But he was not completely successful. An obligation to an old friend of his family sent him galloping once more to Rome and also gave him the subject matter for his second satire.

Giovanni Fusari, priest of the parish church of Santa Agata sul Santerno in the diocese of Faenza, had probably first become acquainted with the Ariosto family in 1496 when Niccolò, the poet's father, was serving Ercole I of Ferrara as his commissioner at Lugo. By 1499 the relationship had progressed so far that the priest could entrust Niccolò with the purchase of some real estate for him, leaving the location and price largely up to his friend's discretion. After the death of the elder Ariosto, Fusari transferred his confidence to Ludovico.

By 1511 the "old priest," as Ariosto refers to him in the present satire, must have begun to lose some sleep over the possession of the rich benefice of Santa Agata, worth approximately three hundred gold ducats a year. It was by no means an unheard-of practice for someone who desired a rich benefice to assassinate its occupant in order to accelerate its availability. One means by which the occupant could insure his life against such an attempt was to sign over his title to a trustworthy friend with the reservation that he, the assignor, would continue to enjoy its revenues until his death when the friend would automatically succeed to them. Two lives and a much more precarious enterprise would then stand in the way of the would-be assassin. Fusari found, in Ludovico, the trustworthy friend he needed.

There exists, in fact, a letter dated 25 November 1511 from Ariosto to Cardinal Giovanni de' Medici, then serving as Legate in Bologna, in which the poet requests free of charge an exemption from sacerdotal duties along with a special dispensation to hold three benefices at once. Ariosto would have needed both the exemption and the dispensation in order to enter into an agreement with Fusari, since he already held one benefice in Ferrara and another in Milan, and he had never submitted to the tonsure. As bearer of the letter, Fusari, to whom Ariosto refers affectionately as a second father, was charged with dispatching all necessary details involved in the request. Although in the letter Ariosto does not mention Santa Agata specifically, there can be no doubt that he is asking the Florentine cardinal, endowed with the requisite legatine powers, to remove the ecclesiastical impediments which would prevent him from accepting that benefice. This letter, incidentally, is extremely interesting for the indication it gives that Ariosto had for some time prior to 1511 enjoyed a very friendly relationship with Giovanni de' Medici.

The request was granted. Fusari sent his resignation to the Curia. All that remained was for Ariosto to obtain the bull which would confirm his occupancy. But the year 1511 had seen an outbreak of hostilities between the House of Este and Pope Julius II over the former's refusal to support the Holy League. Consequently, the bull had to await a more auspicious moment. That moment came when Giovanni de' Medici assumed the tiara in the spring of 1513 as Leo X. Ariosto set out immediately for Rome with hopes that must have soared far beyond the parish church of Santa Agata. He could call himself the pope's friend, and this new pope had a reputation for favoring men of letters. Ariosto was granted an audience with Leo, and describes it in Satire III.[1] He came away sorely disappointed. But at least he took with him the bull confirming him in the benefice of Santa Agata, along with a forgiveness of the fee normally charged for the compilation of a bull. He still had to pay the annate and a registration fee. And since the annate came to a considerable sum, he decided to postpone paying it until he had outlived his elderly friend. Consequently, the bull, though signed by Leo on 8 June 1514, remained in the possession of the Curia until such time as the necessary payments would render it operative.

Several years passed. Suddenly, Fusari received alarming news from Rome that a conspiracy was under way to assassinate him. He begged the poet to pay the fees before it was too late. And so toward the middle of December, 1517, Ariosto left for Rome on the journey which gave him occasion to write the present satire. This vivid attack upon the greed, pride, and ambition of clerics is addressed appropriately to his brother Galasso,[2] an aspiring member of the priesthood, who happened to be residing at the time in Rome, probably in the service of Cardinal Cibò. Ludovico requests his brother to make the necessary preparations for his arrival.

Ariosto used this visit to Rome not only to put in force the bull regarding Santa Agata but also to acquire another bull assuring him of the revenues from his other two benefices, the episcopal chanceries of Ferrara and Milan. It was a profitable trip. But he did not have the opportunity to enjoy the proceeds from his new benefice for quite some time. Fusari, with his fears removed, encamped himself firmly among the living. Only in 1527 did Ariosto begin to collect revenues from Santa Agata. But he did not collect them in his own name. Three years earlier he had arranged for the benefice to provide his fifteen-year-old son Virginio with a yearly pension for life.

NOTES

[1] See ll. 175–186.
[2] See Satire I, ll. 202–203, and note 20.

Perc'ho molto bisogno, più che voglia,
d'esser in Roma, or che li cardinali
a guisa de le serpi mutan spoglia;
    or che son men pericolosi i mali
a' corpi, ancor che maggior peste affliga   5
le travagliate menti de' mortali:
    quando la ruota, che non pur castiga
Issïon rio, si volge in mezzo Roma
l'anime a crucïar con lunga briga;
    Galasso, appresso il tempio che si noma   10
da quel prete valente che l'orecchia
a Malco allontanar fe' da la chioma,
    stanza per quattro bestie mi apparecchia,
contando me per due con Gianni mio,
poi metti un mulo, e un'altra rózza vecchia.   15
    Camera o buca, ove a stanzar abbia io,
che luminosa sia, che poco saglia,
e da far fuoco commoda, desio.
    Né de' cavalli ancor meno ti caglia;
che poco gioveria ch'avesser pòste,   20
dovendo lor mancar poi fieno o paglia.
    Sia per me un mattarazzo, che alle coste
faccia vezzi, o di lana o di cottone,
sì che la notte io non abbia ire a l'oste.
    Provedimi di legna secche e buone;   25
di chi cucini, pur così a la grossa,
un poco di vaccina o di montone.
    Non curo d'un che con sapori possa
de vari cibi suscitar la fame,
se fosse morta e chiusa ne la fossa.   30
    Unga il suo schidon pur o il suo tegame
sin a l'orecchio a ser Vorano il muso,
venuto al mondo sol per far lettame;
    che più cerca la fame, perché giuso
mandi i cibi nel ventre, che, per trarre   35
la fame, cerchi aver de li cibi uso.

Since I have great need, greater than any wish,
to visit Rome now in the season when the cardinals,
like snakes, are changing skins,[1] when diseases are
not so dangerous to the body,[2] but a surpassing plague
afflicts the tormented minds of mortals, in the season
when the Wheel[3] that punishes others besides the
evil Ixion turns in the center of Rome, torturing souls
with long vexation, Galasso, nearby the temple named
after that competent priest who made Malchus' ear
depart from his head,[4] prepare a lodging for four beasts
of burden, counting me and my Gianni[5] as two,
together with a mule and a tired old jade.

I desire a room or a hole where I can live, and
the light can penetrate and there are few steps to
climb and a place to make a fire. Do not devote less
care to the horses, for it would be useless for them
to have a stall if they had to go without hay or straw.
Make sure there is a woolen or a cotton mattress
to caress my aching back, so I will not be forced
to do my sleeping at an inn. Provide me with firewood,
good and dry, and with someone to cook simply for
me a small amount of beef or mutton.

I would not know what to do with the kind of cook
who with flavors of different dishes can resuscitate
hunger, even though it lies dead and buried in the
grave. Let him lard his spit and oil his frying pan
right up to the muzzle and the ears of Master Vorano,[6]
who came into the world for the sole purpose of
producing dung. For he craves hunger in order to
send food into his stomach, more often than he craves
food to relieve his hunger. The new gentleman in

Il novo camerier tal cuoco inarre,
di pane et aglio uso a sfamarsi, poi
che riposte i fratelli avean le marre,
    et egli a casa avea tornati i boi;   40
ch'or vòl fagiani, or tortorelle, or starne,
che sempre un cibo usar par che l'annoi.
    Or sa che differenzia è da la carne
di capro e di cingial che pasca al monte,
da quel che l'Elisea soglia mandarne.   45
    Fa ch'io truovi de l'acqua, non di fonte,
di fiume sì, che già sei dì veduto
non abbia Sisto, né alcun altro ponte.
    Non curo sì del vin, non già il rifuto;
ma a temprar l'acqua me ne basta poco,   50
che la taverna mi darà a minuto.
    Senza molta acqua i nostri, nati in loco
palustre, non assaggio, perché, puri,
dal corpo tranno in giù che mi fa roco.
    Cotesti che farian, che son ne' duri   55
scogli de Corsi ladri o d'infedeli
Greci o d'instabil Liguri maturi?
    Chiuso nel studio frate Ciurla se li
bea, mentre fuori il populo digiuno
lo aspetta che gli esponga gli Evangeli;   60
    e poi monti sul pergamo, più di uno
gambaro cotto rosso, e rumor faccia,
e un minacciar, che ne spaventi ogniuno;
    et a messer Moschin pur dia la caccia,
al fra Gualengo et a' compagni loro,   65
che metton carestia ne la vernaccia;
    che fuor di casa, o in Gorgadello o al Moro,
mangian grossi piccioni e capon grassi,
come egli in cella, fuor del refettoro.
    Fa che vi sian de' libri, con che io passi   70
quelle ore che commandano i prelati
al loro uscier che alcuno entrar non lassi;

waiting procures himself such a cook, even though
he was recently accustomed to appease his hunger
with bread and garlic after his brothers had laid down
their hoes and he had herded the oxen to their stalls.
Now he desires pheasant, or young doves, or sometimes partridge, for he would tire of the same dish
day after day. Now he can taste the difference between
the meat of a buck or a boar that ranged the mountain
and the meat of those which Elisea[7] is wont to send
us.

Arrange for me to find, not from a fountain, but
from a river, water which has not seen the Sistine
nor any other bridge for six days.[8] I am no connoisseur
of wine, though I do not abstain. But I need only
a small amount to flavor my water, and a tavern will
sell it to me at retail. If I dare not without much
water drink our wines, born in marshy soil, because
undiluted they would draw down to my chest the
catarrh that makes me hoarse, what then would those
wines do to me which are matured on the rocky slopes
of Corsican thieves or treacherous Greeks or fickle
Ligurians? Let Brother Ciurla,[9] hidden in his cell,
drink them, while outside the ignorant populace fasts
and waits for him to expound the Gospels. Let him
mount the pulpit redder than a boiled lobster and
rumble and threaten so as to frighten everyone. And
let him even upon Messer Moschino and Brother
Gualengo[10] and all their companions hurl down his
curses, because they create a scarcity of *vernaccia*,
and because, out in the open, at Gorgadello or the
Moro,[11] they eat big squabs and fat capons; just as
he does in his cell, if not in the refectory.

See to it that there are some books in my room,
which I can use to pass those hours when the prelates
command their porters to admit no one, just as certain

come ancor fanno in su la terza i frati,
che non li muove il suon del campanello,
poi che si sono a tavola assettati.   75
    — Signor, — dirò (non s'usa più fratello,
poi che la vile adulazion spagnola
messe la signoria fin in bordello)
    — signor, — (se fosse ben mozzo da spuola)
dirò — fate, per Dio, che monsignore   80
reverendissimo oda una parola. —
    — *Agora non si puede, et es meiore*
che vos torneis a la magnana. — Almeno,
fate ch'ei sappia ch'io son qui di fuore. —
    Risponde che 'l patron non vuol gli siéno   85
fatte imbasciate, se venisse Pietro,
Pavol, Giovanni e il Mastro Nazereno.
    Ma se fin dove col pensier penètro,
avessi, a penetrarvi, occhi lincei,
o' muri trasparesser come vetro,   90
    forse occupati in cosa li vedrei
che iustissima causa di celarsi
avrian dal sol, non che da gli occhi miei.
    Ma sia a un tempo lor agio di ritrarsi,
e a noi di contemplar sotto il camino   95
pei dotti libri i saggi detti sparsi.
    Che mi mova a veder Monte Aventino
so che voresti intendere, e dirolti:
è per legar tra carta, piombo e lino,
    sì che tener, che non mi sieno tolti,   100
possa, pel viver mio, certi baiocchi
che a Melan piglio, ancor che non sian molti;
    e proveder ch'io sia il primo che mocchi
Santa Agata, se avien ch'al vecchio prete,
supervivendogli io, di morir tocchi.   105
    Dunque io darò del capo ne la rete
ch'io soglio dir che 'l diavol tende a questi
che del sangue di Cristo han tanta sete?

monks make sure their bell does not disturb them
three hours after sunrise while they are all still seated
round the table. "Sir," I will say ("brother" is no
longer used among us since that vile Spanish
pompousness managed to find a place for aristocracy
even in the bordello), "Sir," I will say, even though
he is a sniveling footman, "for the love of God,
persuade the most reverend monsignor to hear one
word." "Is no possible now, and is better you come
back mañana."[12] "At least let him know that I am
waiting outside." And he answers that his master
would not care to receive an embassy, even if Peter,
Paul, John, and Master Nazerene in person were to
pay a visit. But if I had Lynceus' eyes to see as
far as my thought penetrates, or if the walls were
made of glass, perhaps I would see those prelates
occupied in matters which give them ample cause to
hide, not only from my eyes, but from the sun itself.
While it is their pleasure to withdraw themselves, at
the same time let it be ours to contemplate beside
the hearth wise words set down in learned books.

I know that you would like to hear what moves
me to visit the Aventine, and I will tell you. It is
to bind with paper, lead, and linen[13] my right to live
on certain episcopal farthings which I collect in
Milan,[14] for, though they be few, they might otherwise
be taken from me. And I must also arrange to be
the first to get Santa Agata if her old priest should
die before I do. Will I then jump head first into the
net that I myself have said the devil spreads for those
who thirst so mightily for the blood of Christ? If

Ma tu vedrai, se Dio vorrà che resti
questa chiesa in man mia, darla a persona   110
saggia e scïente e de costumi onesti,
   che con periglio suo poi ne dispona:
io né pianeta mai né tonicella
né chierca vuo' che in capo mi si pona.
   Come né stole, io non vuo' ch'anco annella   115
mi leghin mai, che in mio poter non tenga
di elegger sempre o questa cosa o quella.
   Indarno è, s'io son prete, che mi venga
disir di moglie; e quando moglie io tolga,
convien che d'esser prete il desir spenga.   120
   Or, perché so come io mi muti e volga
di voler tosto, schivo di legarmi
d'onde, se poi mi pento, io non mi sciolga.
   Qui la cagion potresti dimandarmi
per che mi levo in collo sì gran peso,   125
per dover poi s'un altro scarricarmi.
   Perché tu e gli altri frati miei ripreso
m'avreste, e odiato forse, se offerendo
tal don Fortuna, io non l'avessi preso.
   Sai ben che 'l vecchio, la riserva avendo,   130
inteso di un costì che la sua morte
bramava, e di velen perciò temendo,
   mi pregò ch'a pigliar venissi in corte
la sua rinuncia, che potria sol tòrre
quella speranza onde temea sì forte.   135
   Opra feci io che si volesse porre
ne le tue mani o d'Alessandro, il cui
ingegno da la chierca non aborre;
   ma né di voi, né di più giunti a lui,
d'amicizia fidar unqua si volle: 140
io fuor de tutti scelto unico fui.
   Questa opinïon mia so ben che folle
diranno molti, che a salir non tenti
la via ch'uom spesso a grandi onori estolle.

God wills that this church should rest in my hands, you will see me give it in charge to a person wise and learned and of honest behavior, and then let him minister to it at his own peril. For my part I never wish the chasuble, the alb, or tonsure to come near my head. I desire neither the stole nor the ring to bind me, so I no longer hold it in my power to choose the one or the other. In vain, if I were a priest, would the desire for a wife befall me; and if I were to take a wife, I would have to renounce the wish to become a priest. Because I know how mutable my intentions are, I avoid binding myself in such a way that I cannot loose myself if later I repent.

And here you may ask me why I wish to hoist so heavy a load upon my neck only to have to unload it later upon someone else. It is because you and my other brothers would have reproached, and perhaps hated me, if I had not accepted this gift when Fortune offered it. Full well you know that the old priest, mindful of his right to choose a successor, having heard that a certain one desired his death, and fearing poison, begged me to go to Rome to possess myself of his benefice, knowing that in that way alone he might forestall the murderous intent he feared so much.[15] I contrived that he might be content to place himself in your hands or in Alessandro's since your genius is not averse to the tonsure, but neither did he wish to entrust himself in any way to your friendship nor to that of others much closer to him: he chose me alone over everyone else.

Well do I know that the world calls foolish my firm resolve not to climb the path that frequently exalts men to great prestige. This path has indeed

Questa povere, sciocche, inutil genti,   145
sordide, infami, ha già levato tanto,
che fatti gli ha adorar dai re potenti.

Ma chi fu mai sì saggio o mai sì santo
che di esser senza macchia di pazzia,
o poca o molta, dar si possa vanto?   150

Ogniun tenga la sua, questa è la mia:
se a perder s'ha la libertà, non stimo
il più ricco capel che in Roma sia.

Che giova a me seder a mensa il primo,
se per questo più sazio non mi levo   155
di quel ch'è stato assiso a mezzo o ad imo?

Come né cibo, così non ricevo
più quïete, più pace o più contento,
se ben de cinque mitre il capo aggrevo.

Felicitade istima alcun, che cento   160
persone te accompagnino a palazzo
e che stia il volgo a riguardarte intento;

io lo stimo miseria, e son sì pazzo
ch'io penso e dico che in Roma fumosa
il signore è più servo che 'l ragazzo.   165

Non ha da servir questi in maggior cosa
che di esser col signor quando cavalchi;
l'altro tempo a suo senno o va o si posa.

La maggior cura che sul cor gli calchi
è che Fiammetta stia lontana, e spesso   170
causi che l'ora del tinel gli valchi.

A questo ove gli piace è andar concesso,
accompagnato e solo, a piè, a cavallo;
fermarsi in Ponte, in Banchi e in chiasso appresso:

piglia un mantello o rosso o nero o giallo,   175
e se non l'ha, va in gonnelin liggiero;
né questo mai gli è attribuito a fallo.

Quello altro, per fodrar di verde il nero
capel, lasciati ha i ricchi uffici e tolto
minor util, più spesa e più pensiero.   180

raised beggars, nitwits, and good-for-nothings, both
the sordid and the infamous, so high that powerful
monarchs revere them. But who was ever so wise
or so holy that he could boast of being unstained
by insanity, in some degree.[16] To each man his own
madness. This is mine. I value not the richest hat[17]
in Rome if freedom must be lost to gain it.

What good is it to sit at the head of the table if
I therefore rise not more satisfied than the man who
sits at the middle or at the foot? Just as with food,
I would not win more peace, more tranquillity or more
contentment, even if I buried my head under five
mitres. Some esteem it felicity to have a hundred
retainers accompany you to the Palace[18] and to have
the common people crowd around to gaze at you.
I esteem it misery, and I am mad enough to think,
and say, that in this Rome befogged by vanity the
master is more the servant than his page.

The page has to serve in no greater business than
to accompany his lord when he goes riding. The rest
of the time he may do as he pleases. The greatest
care that oppresses his heart is that the Fiammetta[19]
is far away, and often causes the hour to slip by
without him when the servants gather to dine. To
him it is granted to go where he pleases, alone or
in company, on foot or on horseback, and to stop
at the Piazza di Ponte, the Banchi, or an alley nearby.[20]
He can wear a cloak, red, black, or yellow, and if
he has no cloak, he can go in a thin gown, and no
one will find fault with him for it.

But the master, in order to line his black hat with
green,[21] has sacrified rich prebends and settled for
less profit, more expense, and more worry. He has

Ha molta gente a pascere e non molto
da spender, che alle bolle è già ubligato
del primo e del secondo anno il ricolto;
    e del debito antico uno è passato,
et uno, e al terzo termine si aspetta   185
esser sul muro in publico attaccato.
    Gli bisogna a San Pietro andare in fretta;
ma perché il cuoco o il spenditor ci manca,
che gli sien dietro, gli è la via interdetta.
    Fuori è la mula, o che si duol d'una anca,   190
o che le cingie o che la sella ha rotta,
o che da Ripa vien sferrata e stanca.
    Se con lui fin il guattaro non trotta,
non può il misero uscir, che stima incarco
il gire e non aver dietro la frotta.   195
    Non è il suo studio né in Matteo né in Marco,
ma specula e contempla a far la spesa
sì, che il troppo tirar non spezzi l'arco.
    — D'uffici, di badie, di ricca chiesa
forse adagiato, alcun vive giocondo,   200
che né la stalla, né il tinel gli pesa. —
    Ah! che 'l disio d'alzarsi il tiene al fondo!
Già il suo grado gli spiace, e a quello aspira
che dal sommo Pontefice è il secondo.
    Giugne a quel anco, e la voglia anco il tira   205
a l'alta sedia, che d'aver bramata
tanto, indarno San Georgio si martira.
    Che fia s'avrà la catedra beata?
Tosto vorrà gli figli o li nepoti
levar da la civil vita privata.   210
    Non penserà d'Achivi o d'Epiroti
dar lor dominio; non avrà disegno
de la Morea o de l'Arta far despòti;
    non cacciarne Ottoman per dar lor regno,
ove da tutta Europa avria soccorso   215
e faria del suo ufficio ufficio degno;

a large household to feed and not much money to
spend, because from the start he owes, in return for
the bulls, the revenues of the first and second years.[22]
And for an older debt one deadline is past, and still
another, and at the third he expects to see his name
tacked up in public.[23] He must go to St Peter's in
haste on business, but because his cook and his steward
are missing, who should be in his entourage, the way
is barred. The mule stands outside, one of his haunches
sore, his harness broken or his saddle, or perhaps
he has just come back from the Ripagrande[24] weary
and unshod. If even the kitchen boy fails to trot along,
the wretch cannot issue forth, because he considers
it a hardship to travel without a crowd behind him.
His study is not in Matthew and Mark; he puzzles
and meditates how to moderate his expenditures, so
that too hard a pull will not break his bow.

"With prebends, with abbeys, with a rich parish,
perhaps someone lives joyfully and profitably, burdened neither by his stables nor his servants' hall."
But, ah, how his desire to rise will hold him down!
His present rank displeases him already, so he aspires
to that which is second only to the Supreme Pontiff.
And he attains it, but his desire drags him up to the
lofty throne for which St George hungered so mightily
that he martyred himself in vain.[25] And what if he
gets the blessed cathedral? Soon he will desire to
raise his sons or his nephews up from civil private
life, but he will not think of giving them the dominions
of the Achaeans or the Epirots. He will not plan to
make them despots of Arta or Morea.[26] He will not
ponder how to expel the Ottoman Turks in order to
bestow crowns upon his sons, so that all Europe may
benefit and he make worthy use of his office. To

ma spezzar la Colonna e spegner l'Orso
per tòrgli Palestina e Tagliacozzo,
e darli a' suoi, sarà il primo discorso.

E qual strozzato e qual col capo mozzo 220
ne la Marca lasciando et in Romagna,
trionferà, del crestian sangue sozzo.

Darà l'Italia in preda a Francia o Spagna,
che sozzopra voltandola, una parte
al suo bastardo sangue ne rimagna. 225

L'escomuniche empir quinci le carte,
e quindi ministrar si vederanno
l'indulgenzie plenarie al fiero Marte.

Se 'l Svizzero condurre o l'Alemanno
si dee, bisogna ritrovare i nummi, 230
e tutto al servitor ne viene il danno.

Ho sempre inteso e sempre chiaro fummi
ch'argento che lor basti non han mai,
o veschi o cardinali o Pastor summi.

Sia stolto, indòtto, vil, sia peggio assai, 235
farà quel ch'egli vuol, se posto insieme
avrà tesoro; e chi baiar vuol, bai.

Perciò li avanzi e le miserie estreme
fansi, di che la misera famiglia
vive affamata, e grida indarno e freme. 240

Quanto è più ricco, tanto più assottiglia
la spesa; che i tre quarti si delibra
por da canto di ciò che l'anno piglia.

Da le otto oncie per bocca a mezza libra
si vien di carne, e al pan di cui la veccia 245
nata con lui, né il loglio fuor si cribra.

Come la carne e il pan, così la feccia
del vin si dà, c'ha seco una puntura
che più mortal non l'ha spiedo né freccia;

o ch'egli fila e mostra la paura 250
ch'ebbe, a dar volta, di fiaccarsi il collo,
sì che men mal saria ber l'acqua pura.

smash the Column and kill the Bear will be his first design, in order to seize Palestrina and Tagliacozzo and give them to his own.[27] Leaving one man strangled in the Marches and another beheaded in the Romagna, he will triumph, drenched in Christian blood. He will give Italy in prey to France or Spain, so that, after she is turned upside down, one part will remain for his bastard blood.[28] In one place excommunications will fill pages, while in another plenary indulgences will be administered to savage Mars himself.[29] If he needs to hire the Germans or the Swiss, he must find money, and all his loss devolves upon his servants.

I have always clearly understood that prelates never have money enough to satisfy themselves, whether they be bishops, cardinals, or popes. Whether they be stupid, ignorant, disgraceful, or worse, they will do as they please, provided they have heaped up a treasure, and whoever desires to bark, let him bark! To get treasure, they institute niggardly savings and extreme miseries, which make the wretched household starve and cry out in vain and tremble. The richer he becomes, the more he thins out his expenses, for he is determined to put aside three quarters of all the year brings in. From eight ounces a mouth to six the meat diminishes, and the bread fares no better, when the darnel and the vetches are no longer sifted out. And not only do the bread and the meat suffer, but also the wine-dregs that are served have a sharpness more deadly than swords and arrows. Or else the wine trickles and shows the fear it has, in spilling, of breaking its neck, so that one would be better off to drink plain water. But if the gong only

Se la bacchetta pur levar satollo
lasciasse il capellan, mi starei cheto,
se ben non gusta mai vitel né pollo.   255
    — Questo — dirai — può un servitor discreto
patir; che quando monsignor suo accresce,
accresce anco egli, e n'ha da viver lieto. —
Ma tal speranza a molti non riesce;
che, per dar loco a la famiglia nuova,   260
più d'un vecchio d'ufficio e d'onor esce.
Camarer, scalco e secretario truova
il signor degni al grado, e n'hai buon patto
che dal servizio suo non ti rimova.
Quanto ben disse il mulatier quel tratto,   265
che, tornando dal bosco, ebbe la sera
nuova che 'l suo padron papa era fatto:
    — Che per me stesse cardinal meglio era;
ho fin qui auto da cacciar dui muli,
or n'avrò tre; che più di me ne spiera,   270
    comperi quanto io n'ho d'aver dui iuli.

let the chaplain[30] get up from the table satisfied, I
would keep silent, even if I never tasted veal or
chicken.

"This," you will say, "a prudent servitor can
endure, for if his master prospers, he will prosper
also and have enough to live happily." But that hope
goes unfulfilled for many. More than one old man
has left his office and his honors to make room for
a new retainer. The newly exalted lord finds a gentleman in waiting, a carver, a secretary, more suitable
to his rank, and you have made a good bargain if
he does not quite remove you from his service. How
well the mule-driver spoke when, having returned from
the woods, he heard the news one evening that his
master had been made pope: "Better for me had he
stayed a cardinal. So far I have had two mules to
drive, but soon I shall have three. Whoever expects
to get more out of this, let him buy my share for
a fig."

NOTES

[1] At Advent, cardinals change their red vestments for violet. In the year 1517, Advent began on 29 November.

[2] The winter months in Rome provided a respite from malaria.

[3] An allusion to the reopening in mid-November of the *Tribunale della Rota* ("wheel"), before which causes were pleaded regarding benefices. It was well known for dragging out its proceedings interminably. Ariosto compares it with the wheel upon which Ixion was bound and condemned forever to turn in Hades.

[4] A periphrasis for St. Peter's Cathedral. Peter the apostle with a blow of his sword lopped off the ear of Malchus, a servant of Caiaphas, when the Romans and the officers of the Pharisees came to apprehend Jesus in the garden of Gethesemane. John 18:10.

[5] Gianni da Pescia succeeded the aged Carlo da Prato as Ariosto's manservant. Carlo had also served the poet's father.

[6] A nickname meaning voracious. It is not known whether there was actually a particular individual at the Estensi court who merited such a nickname. Alfonso I was very fond of nicknaming his courtiers.

[7] This new gourmet claims to be able to tell the difference in taste between game caught in mountainous territory and game caught in lowlands near the sea. The Lisea, or the Elisea, in the lowlands of Comacchio near the sea, was a forest where the Estensi liked to hunt.

[8] Water from rivers was considered more hygienic than water from fountains, providing that it was left to stand for several days so the impurities could settle. Ariosto specifies that he wants water from the Tiber that has been left to stand for six days.

[9] The proverbial hypocrite, the monk who preaches abstinence and temperance and gorges and swills in private. "Ciurlo" in various Italian dialects means "tipsy."

[10] Messer Moschino was actually a certain Antonio Magnanino, a courtier in the service of Ercole I and one of the most celebrated drunkards and revelers in the Ferrara of his day. He probably gained his nickname, which means roughly "Little Fly," as the result of an easily excitable, testy disposition. Ariosto became friendly with Messer Moschino during his years in the university, for this solemn tippler made it his special duty to uphold the rights of the student class. Ariosto remembered him in the *Orlando Furioso* (XIV, 124) and in the revision in verse of his comedy *La Cassaria* (Act V, scene iv). In the *Orlando*, Moschino, who actually died in 1497, meets his end during the assault on Paris after Rodomonte tosses him into the moat where he drowns in that very same element he had always fled so assiduously during his life—water. Brother Gualengo was Messer Moschino's favorite companion in drunkeness. He met his end in 1496, stabbed in broad daylight by a man whom he had grossly insulted.

[11] Two famous inns of Ferrara.

[12] The Spanish porter is making a clumsy attempt to speak Italian.

[13] Ariosto describes a bull, written on paper or parchment and bearing a lead seal hanging on a strip of linen or hemp.

[14] That share in the episcopal chancery of Milan granted him by the Cardinal. See Satire I, ll. 109-111, and the accompanying note.

[15] The meaning of ll. 130-135 is not clear. Catalano sees in the text a precise

reference to the purpose for which Ariosto made the journey to Rome in mid-December, 1517, the journey which occasioned the present satire. According to this reading, the lines should be translated, "Full well you know that the old priest, though he reserved his right to collect revenues from the benefice, begged me, once he heard that a certain man wished to poison him, to go to Rome in order to put in force the bull securing my succession and to destroy thereby any hope an assassin might have of succeeding him." Catalano bases his reading upon a comparison of the vocabulary used in these lines with the technical terms used in the documents relevant to the transaction between Fusari and the poet. With all due respect to Ariosto's very scrupulous biographer, the present translator prefers to concur with the majority of modern editors of the *Satires* in seeing a general reference in ll. 130-135 to the entire Fusari affair, which by 1517 embraced a period of roughly six years. This second reading is easier to arrive at from the Italian of the passage. And Galasso, who held an influential post in Rome, almost certainly did not have to be apprized of the details. No doubt he had already been employed in the affair.

[16] "*Nullum magnum igenium sine mistura dementiae fuit,*" Seneca, *De Tranquillitate Animi,* XVII, 10.

[17] A cardinal's hat.

[18] The Vatican Palace.

[19] During Ariosto's time, one of the most famous courtesans in Rome was named Fiammetta. She lent her name to a piazza which was probably in a red light district.

[20] The Piazza di Ponte is a Roman square connecting with the bridge of Sant'Angelo. It was a meeting place of gamesters and vagabonds. The neighborhood nearby was called the Banchi after the Bank of the Hospital of the Holy Spirit. The area was much frequented by businessmen because the offices of the magistrates and the Curia were located there.

[21] See Satire III, l. 105, and the accompanying note.

[22] In order to obtain a bull guaranteeing the possession of a benefice or an ecclesiastical office, one had to pay, apart from fees and registration expenses, tips to the solicitors and the clerks. The heaviest fee was that called the annate, which usually amounted to a year's income from the benefice payable in two annual installments.

[23] The prelate in question is in debt not only for the fees due on his new benefice but also for those which he has delayed to pay on a benefice received in the past. If he fails to meet his payments on this older benefice, his name will be posted on a list of delinquents. Ariosto knew something of the worry attached to this situation. As fee for the bull granted him on 8 June 1514 guaranteeing him the succession to Santa Agata, he was supposed to pay 150 ducats. He did not begin his payments until 1517 and did not complete them until 1525. He was forced, in fact, to obtain a postponement of his debt in order to keep his name from being posted.

[24] The Ripagrande, on the banks of the Tiber, was a place of commerce.

[25] Raffaele Riario, the Cardinal of St George, had been a contender for the tiara in the conclave of 1513. In the spring of 1517 he was found to be implicated in the Conspiracy of Cardinals. Leo fined him an enormous sum of money, and he was forced consequently to retire from Rome. He died in 1521.

[26] Ariosto first gives the ancient names of these peoples and then the names of their modern states. The Achaeans were, of course, the Greeks, and the Epirots were the inhabitants of Epirus, the nation which extended in ancient

times over the area occupied today by Albania. The town still named Arta is slightly to the south of Albania near the Ambracian Gulf. It was once the residence of Pyrrhus. The Morea, in Ariosto's day, was the name of the Peloponnesus. In the sixteenth century, both Greece and Albania were under the domination of the Ottoman Turks.

[27] Column and Bear are an allusion to the Colonna and the Orsini, the two most powerful Roman families. Since the Middle Ages, they had fought each other and the pope for supremacy in Rome and the Romagna. Pope Alexander VI (1492–1503) turned against them with exceptional vigor. From the Colonna he seized the fief of Palestrina, and from the Orsini that of Tagliacozzo.

[28] These two tercets seem also to allude to Alexander VI. "Bastard blood" describes Alexander's descendants, probably Cesare Borgia in particular. Alexander sanctioned the Italian enterprises of Louis XII of France in the hope that Cesare might, through alliance with the French, carve out a kingdom for himself in central Italy. But the part about giving Italy in prey to France and Spain fits Pope Julius II (1503–1513) very well. He brought France into the League of Cambrai for the purpose of crushing the Venetians. Then he turned to Spain and formed the Holy League for the purpose of expelling the French, with the result that the Spanish remained in possession of Italy. He did not, however, practice excessive nepotism.

[29] Both Leo X (1513–1521) and Julius II were well known for launching excommunications, issuing indulgences, and selling benefices according to the changing requirements of their military and political policies. Duke Alfonso I of Ferrara had been excommunicated by both of them.

[30] "*Capellano*" (chaplain) was slang for "stomach."

SATIRE III

To Messer Annibale Malaguzzi

On 23 April 1518 Ariosto was officially enrolled in the service of
Duke Alfonso I of Ferrara at a salary of 21 *lire marchesane* per month
plus his board and the cost of maintaining two horses. No sooner
was he established than his cousin Annibale Malaguzzi sent to inquire
about the state of his affairs. Was he any better off with the Duke
than he had been with the Cardinal? Why did he not share the opinion
of those who thought that he should have gone to Rome to seek his
fortune at the court of his old friend Pope Leo X? Ariosto took the
opportunity to reply with a satire, his third, in which he deals briefly
with the first question and at length with the second. In Satire III,
as well as in Satire VII, the poet settles his accounts with the Medici.

By May, 1518, the probable date of composition for this epistle to
his friend and cousin, Ariosto had not had enough experience in his
new position to be able to compare it with his previous one. His salary
was slightly higher. And the Duke, of course, would reside in Ferrara
for longer periods than had his brother the Cardinal; consequently,
his servants would enjoy more time at home with their families and
friends. Ariosto would have more time to spend with his beloved
Alessandra Benucci. And perhaps the Duke would entrust him with
missions more honorable than those he had executed for the Cardinal.
As early as December, 1509, when the Venetians were practically at
the gates of Ferrara, Alfonso had sent him on a mission to Pope Julius
II to seek assistance, a mission upon which the security of Ferrara
might have depended if the Cardinal had not gone out in haste to
destroy the Venetian fleet at the battle of Polesella. Above all, the
Duke might even appreciate his poetic gift. Alfonso had condescended
in July, 1509, to read a rough draft of the *Orlando Furioso*. A poet's
life, Ariosto might have thought, would have its rewards at the court

of a sophisticated, pleasure-loving master with a taste for elegance
and adventure.

But Ariosto, on the verge of this new departure in his life, could
not have foreseen that within only one year he would become entangled
in a bitter and endless litigation with both Duke and Cardinal over
his cousin Rinaldo Ariosto's inheritance, and that his profits from the
second edition in 1521 of the *Orlando Furioso* would be consumed
by the payment of legal expenses. He could not have foreseen that
the Duke, short of money due to his constant need to defend himself
against the schemes of Leo X, would by 1521 be forced to cancel
his salary. Ariosto would never have dreamed that by February, 1522,
a mere four years off, he would have to accept, in order to support
himself, the grueling and dangerous job of governing a province torn
by lawlessness and civil strife. At the outset of his service, the poet
must have expected, if not to prosper, at least to improve his lot,
at the court of Alfonso d'Este.

On the other hand, in the spring of 1518, Ariosto did not need
exceptional insight to realize that he could hope for nothing from the
Medici. His acquaintance with the leading family of Florence had been
long and disillusioning. From his letter of 28 February 1516 to Ottaviano
Fregoso, Doge of Genoa, we know that Ariosto was at the court of
Urbino in 1507 when Fregoso, along with Bibbiena and the Magnifico
Giuliano de' Medici, presumably took part in those conversations which
Castiglione claimed to have recorded in *The Courtier*. It must have
been then that, with verses from his newly conceived *Orlando Furioso*,
Ariosto helped to make the Medici exile "less harsh and desolate."[1]
From his letter of 25 November 1511 to Cardinal Giovanni de' Medici,
in which he requests the dispensation and exemption necessary for
his investiture in the benefice of Santa Agata, we know that the years
from the Urbino meeting until Giovanni's elevation to Papal Legate
in Bologna had seen a strengthening of the friendly relations between
Ariosto and the Medici. As an "affectionate servitor" delighted at
the success of "his patron" and as a "most devoted servant" assured
in time of need of finding his master favorably disposed toward him,
Ariosto congratulates Giovanni upon his appointment as Legate. The
"love and graciousness" that His Most Reverend Lordship the Cardinal
Legate had "always" displayed toward him gives him the courage to
have recourse directly to His Lordship "in the hope of obtaining any
favor whatsoever."[2] Such was the language of this request, which

Giovanni was able to grant with no difficulty. If Ariosto had remembered to keep his hopes regarding the Medici always in the realm of what could be granted with no difficulty, perhaps he would never have suffered the severe disillusionment which was awaiting him.

No sooner had Giovanni de' Medici become Leo X than Ariosto was on his way to Rome to visit his "old friend." The poet requested the audience, which he describes in the present satire,[3] for purely private reasons. He had not been commissioned by the Estensi to offer their official congratulations to the new pope. Ostensibly the audience was for the purpose of requesting the bull securing his succession to Santa Agata; however, Ariosto's real intention was to reap the fruit of those seeds of friendship he had sowed for so long in the Medici garden. At last he might achieve recognition, and obtain the sinecure he needed to work full time on his poem. Perhaps he thought he would leave the pope's presence with the promise of a bishopric or even a cardinal's hat. But he was painfully disappointed. He left with nothing but the bull he had requested and a forgiveness of the fee attached to its compilation. In a letter of apology, dated 7 April 1513, Ariosto, still in Rome, awaiting Leo's coronation, reports his disappointment to his friend Benedetto Fantino in Ferrara:

Concerning your business I have done nothing as yet, not because I have forgotten about it, but because I have been unable to find the ways and means. I arrived here in the costume of a courier and for lack of clothes to wear, I have avoided visiting any person of quality; because here, more than anywhere else, no people are held in esteem save the well-dressed. It is true that I kissed the pope's foot and that in appearance he listened willingly to me. But I doubt that he saw me, for, since he became pope, he no longer carries his spy-glass. Not a single offer has been made me. Not from His Holiness nor from my friends who have recently become great lords. It seems to me that they are all imitating the pope in near-sightedness. But I will force myself. I will begin today, so this affair does not drag out, to see whether I can get any assistance from Messer Paride.[4] To seek help from Messer Bernardo,[5] I think, would be too difficult, for he has become too grand a man. It is only with surpassing labor that one can get near him, both because he is always surrounded by so large a crowd of people that he can scarcely be reached and because it is necessary to besiege twenty doors before arriving

in his presence. Fighting with porters is so hateful to me that
I do not know if I shall ever get to see him.[6] And indeed I
do not try to see him, nor anyone else who lives in this palace.
Yet for the sake of our friendship I shall do violence to my
nature, but I shall be able to accomplish little, because, once
the coronation is over, which will be within four days, I intend
to return to Ferrara. I hear that in Ferrara they think I have
become a great man here. I beg you to remove them from this
error, at least those with whom you converse, and tell them that
I amount to much less here than ever I did in Ferrara. I do
not want them to accuse me of discourtesy if I find it impossible
to perform any services they may expect of me.[7]

During the remainder of his service under Cardinal Ippolito d'Este,
Ariosto resided for long periods of time in the Rome of Leo X. He
may even have been present in the autumn of 1517 for the pope's
colossal creation of thirty-one cardinals in one day.

By the time of his entrance into the service of Alfonso d'Este, Ariosto
had had his fill of the Medici. The disappointment, so vivid in his
letter of 1513 from Rome, reappears in the present satire, addressed
to his cousin Annibale, and reappears again, as late as 1524, in Satire
VII. There can be no doubt that he had expected to assume the leading
role in Roman society that his friends in Ferrara expected would be
his. His only recourse was, four years later, to exalt in poetry the
life of moderation, and to condemn the futility of ambitious striving.
Annibale Maleguzzi must have known how thoroughly the epistle that
lay before him in the spring of 1518 represented a sardonic self-con-
demnation on the part of his gifted, but unappreciated, cousin, and
how difficult that ideal life bounded by the golden mean must have
appeared to the poet whose imagination, borne on wings of desire,
had soared over the face of the earth in search of the peerless Angelica.

A year later, Ariosto's hopes may have got the better of him once
again. On 6 March 1519, his comedy *I Suppositi* was presented before
the pope in the Vatican Palace.[8] Leo enjoyed the entertainment and
even scandalized some Frenchmen in the audience by marking with
laughter an indecent pun in the prologue. But Leo probably enjoyed
the decor of the production more than the play itself. Raphael had
painted the backdrop, a representation of the city of Ferrara in perspec-
tive, which was illuminated by candles arranged in groups of five,

each group forming a letter of the rubric LEO X PONTIFEX MAXIMUS. Leo's dream of causing the Medici sun, the light and power of his House, to rise over the domain of the Estensi dazzled his eyes. Not without just cause were the rulers of Ferrara to break out in wild rejoicing two years later at the death of this pope, their mortal enemy.

Ariosto's reputation in Ferrara as a papal favorite, however misleading, must have been strengthened by the success of *I Suppositi*. But during this period of scarcely veiled hostility between the papacy and the Estensi, any Ferrarese who enjoyed the slightest esteem from the pope must have been considered a Medici favorite by his compatriots. In May, 1519, Alfonso chose Ariosto to present the official condolences of the House of Este to Lorenzo de' Medici, Duke of Urbino, on the occasion of the death of his wife Madeleine de la Tour d' Auvergne. She had died after giving birth to that Catherine de' Medici who would in turn give birth to three French kings and preside over the horrors of St. Bartholomew's Day. Ariosto arrived in Florence on the fourth of the month to find that Lorenzo himself had died that morning. He was thereupon commissioned to represent Alfonso at the funeral. It might be unfair to suppose that Ariosto rejoiced at the death of the nephew upon whom all of Leo's plans to carve out a Medici kingdom in central Italy depended. Nevertheless there is unmistakable satisfaction in those lines of Satire VII[9] in which the poet pictures the Medici at the height of their happiness as all doomed to die within a few turns of the sun through the zodiac.

Ariosto's last business with Leo was to send him a copy of his comedy *Il Negromante* in January, 1520. He had begun the play ten years earlier and finished it hastily at the express desire of the pope. But the play never had a production in Rome, and it had to wait another nine years before being produced in Ferrara. During his pontificate, Leo had granted Ariosto various petitions concerning benefices. He had granted him financial rights to the *Orlando Furioso*, and had legitimated his son Virginio. He had even recommended to Alfonso that he examine with benevolence the poet's claims to his deceased cousin Rinaldo's estate. But Leo was never to reward Ariosto for having honored Italy with the finest vernacular poetry in the world—and this in spite of Leo's lavishness toward every variety of poetaster in Latin and the vernacular. One reason, however, for Leo's lack of generosity may have been that he considered it unwise to elevate a Ferrarese courtier who might easily have become a deadly enemy with his pen.

NOTES

[1] See ll. 85-93 of the present satire.
[2] Cf. ll. 100-103 of the present satire.
[3] Ll. 175-186.
[4] Paris de Grassis, Leo's master of ceremonies, and afterwards Bishop of Pesaro. He is the author of an important diary.
[5] Bibbiena. See note 24 to the present satire.
[6] Cf. Satire II, ll. 70-96.
[7] I have used the text of Angelo Stella's *Lettere di Ludovico Ariosto* (Verona: 1965) for all of my translations from Ariosto's letters.
[8] See Catalano, II, 195, for Alfonso Paolucci's letter to the Duke, describing the performance.
[9] 94-108.

Poi che, Annibale, intendere vuoi come
la fo col duca Alfonso, e s'io mi sento
più grave o men de le mutate some;
    perché, s'anco di questo mi lamento,
tu mi dirai c'ho il guidalesco rotto,   5
o ch'io son di natura un rozzon lento:
    senza molto pensar, dirò di botto
che un peso e l'altro ugualmente mi spiace,
e fòra meglio a nessuno esser sotto.
    Dimmi or c'ho rotto il dosso e, se 'l ti piace,   10
dimmi ch'io sia una rózza, e dimmi peggio:
insomma esser non so se non verace.
    Che s'al mio genitor, tosto che a Reggio
Daria mi partorì, facevo il giuoco
che fe' Saturno al suo ne l'alto seggio,   15
    sì che di me sol fosse questo poco
ne lo qual dieci tra frati e serocchie
è bisognato che tutti abbian luoco,
    la pazzia non avrei de le ranocchie
fatta già mai, d'ir procacciando a cui   20
scoprirmi il capo e piegar le ginocchie.
    Ma poi che figliolo unico non fui,
né mai fu troppo a' miei Mercurio amico,
e viver son sforzato a spese altrui;
    meglio è s'appresso il Duca mi nutrico,   25
che andare a questo e a quel de l'umil volgo
accattandomi il pan come mendico.
    So ben che dal parer dei più mi tolgo
che 'l stare in corte stimano grandezza,
ch'io pel contrario a servitù rivolgo.   30
    Stiaci volentier dunque chi la apprezza;
fuor n'uscirò ben io, s'un dì il figliuolo
di Maia vorrà usarmi gentilezza.
    Non si adatta una sella o un basto solo
ad ogni dosso; ad un non par che l'abbia,   35
all'altro stringe e preme e gli dà duolo.

Annibale, since you wish to hear how I am succeeding with Duke Alfonso and whether or not I feel myself
heavier with my shifted burdens—because, if now
I continue to lament, you will tell me I have a ruptured
harness sore or that I am by nature a reluctant
jade—without much thought I will say swiftly that
this weight galls me as much as the other and it would
be better not to be under any.

Now tell me I have a broken back and, if it pleases
you, tell me I am a jade and tell me worse. In short,
I do not know what to be if not truthful. If, as soon
as Daria gave birth to me in Reggio,[1] I had played
the same trick on my father[2] that Saturn played on
his in the lofty throne, so that mine alone were this
pittance in which it is necessary that ten brothers
and sisters have a share, I would never have committed
the folly of the frogs, to have gone in search of someone
to whom I could bare my head and bend my knee.
But since I was not the only son and since Mercury[3]
was never friendly to my family and I am forced
to live at another's cost, better for me to nourish
myself at the Duke's table than to go to one after
the other among the rabble begging my bread like
a pauper.

Well do I know that I reject the opinion of the
world, which esteems it an honor to live at the court,
for I on the contrary consider it servitude. Let the
man who prizes that life gladly stay there. I will escape
indeed, if someday the son of Maia cares to treat
me with courtesy. Not every back can endure the
same saddle and the same load; one mule may feel
nothing, while the same load may pinch and crush
and pain another. The nightingale can scarce abide

Mal può durar il rosignuolo in gabbia,
più vi sta il gardelino, e più il fanello;
la rondine in un dì vi mor di rabbia.

Chi brama onor di sprone o di capello,   40
serva re, duca, cardinale o papa;
io no, che poco curo questo e quello.

In casa mia mi sa meglio una rapa
ch'io cuoca, e cotta s'un stecco me inforco,
e mondo, e spargo poi di acetto e sapa,   45

 che all'altrui mensa tordo, starna o porco
selvaggio; e così sotto una vil coltre,
come di seta o d'oro, ben mi corco.

E più mi piace di posar le poltre
membra, che di vantarle che alli Sciti   50
sien state, agli Indi, a li Etiopi, et oltre.

Degli uomini son varii li appetiti:
a chi piace la chierca, a chi la spada,
a chi la patria, a chi li strani liti.

Chi vuole andare a torno, a torno vada: 55
vegga Inghelterra, Ongheria, Francia e Spagna;
a me piace abitar la mia contrada.

Visto ho Toscana, Lombardia, Romagna,
quel monte che divide e quel che serra
Italia, e un mare e l'altro che la bagna.   60

Questo mi basta; il resto de la terra,
senza mai pagar l'oste, andrò cercando
con Ptolomeo, sia il mondo in pace o in guerra;

 e tutto il mar, senza far voti quando
lampeggi il ciel, sicuro in su le carte   65
verrò, più che sui legni, volteggiando.

Il servigio del Duca, da ogni parte
che ci sia buona, più mi piace in questa:
che dal nido natio raro si parte.

Per questo i studi miei poco molesta,   70
né mi toglie onde mai tutto partire
non posso, perché il cor sempre ci resta.

a cage, while the goldfinch and the linnet remain there longer; but there the swallow will go mad and die in a single day. Let the man who hungers for the honor of the spurs or of the hat[4] serve a king, a duke, a cardinal, a pope. I will not. Such trifles do not interest me.

In my house a turnip tastes better to me that I cook myself and, when it is done, fork on a stick and peel and season with vinegar and must, than at someone else's table thrush, partridge, or wild boar; and I go to bed at home beneath a humble covering, as if it were made of silk or of gold brocade. And I am more pleased to rest my idle limbs than to boast that they have been to Scythia, India, Ethiopia, and beyond. Men's appetites are various. The tonsure pleases one man, while the sword befits another. Some love their homeland, while others delight in foreign shores. Let him wander who desires to wander. Let him see England, Hungary, France, and Spain. I am content to live in my native land. I have seen Tuscany, Lombardy, and the Romagna, and the mountain range that divides Italy, and the one that locks her in, and both the seas that wash her. And that is quite enough for me. Without ever paying an innkeeper, I will go exploring the rest of the earth with Ptolemy,[5] whether the world be at peace or else at war. Without ever making vows when the heavens flash with lightning, I will go bounding over all the seas, more secure aboard my maps than aboard ships.

The service of the Duke pleases me more in this than in any other part of it, that one rarely departs from one's native nest. For this reason my studies are scarcely disturbed, and I am not torn from the place I can never leave completely, because my heart

Parmi vederti qui ridere e dire
che non amor di patria né de studi,
ma di donna è cagion che non voglio ire.   75
Liberamente te 'l confesso: or chiudi
la bocca, che a difender la bugia
non volli prender mai spada né scudi.
Del mio star qui qual la cagion si sia,
io ci sto volentier; ora nessuno   80
abbia a cor più di me la cura mia.
S'io fossi andato a Roma, dirà alcuno,
a farmi uccellator de benefici,
preso a la rete n'avrei già più d'uno;
tanto più ch'ero degli antiqui amici   85
del papa, inanzi che virtude o sorte
lo sublimasse al sommo degli uffici;
e prima che gli aprissero le porte
i Fiorentini, quando il suo Giuliano
si riparò ne la feltresca corte,   90
ove col formator del cortigiano,
col Bembo e gli altri sacri al divo Appollo,
facea l'essilio suo men duro e strano;
e dopo ancor, quando levaro il collo
Medici ne la patria, e il Gonfalone,   95
fuggendo del Palazzo, ebbe il gran crollo;
e fin che a Roma se andò a far Leone,
io gli fui grato sempre, e in apparenza
mostrò amar più di me poche persone;
e più volte, e Legato et in Fiorenza,   100
mi disse che al bisogno mai non era
per far da me al fratel suo differenza.
Per questo parrà altrui cosa leggiera
che, stando io a Roma, già m'avesse posta
la cresta dentro verde e di fuor nera.   105
A chi parrà così farò risposta
con uno essempio: leggilo, che meno
leggerlo a te, che a me scriverlo, costa.

is always there. I seem to see you laughing at me
now and saying that, not love of country or of study,
but of a lady,[6] is the reason I do not wish to leave.
Frankly do I confess it to you. Now shut your mouth.
I am not one to take up sword and shield to defend
a lie. Whatever the reason is for my staying here,
I stay willingly. Now, may no one have more at heart
the care of me than I.

But if I had gone to Rome, someone will say, to
make myself a snarer of benefices, I would have caught
more than one in my net by now; and so much the
more readily since I was among the pope's[7] old friends
before merit or chance exalted him to the highest
of offices, and before the Florentines opened their
gates to him,[8] in the days when his Giuliano repaired
to the court of Montefeltro,[9] where, with the one
who formed the courtier,[10] with Bembo,[11] and with
the others consecrated to the god Apollo, he made
his exile less harsh and desolate. And afterwards too,
when the Medici raised their heads in their homeland,
and the Gonfalon, fleeing the palace, had its great
defeat, and to the time he went to Rome to become
Leo, I was always welcome to him, and in appearance
he gave out to love few persons more than he did
me. Both as Legate and in Florence,[12] he told me
many times that he was never inclined to consider
my case as different from his own brother's in time
of need. And so it would seem to one a matter of
slight consequence, if I had remained in Rome, that
he should already have crested me with green inside
and outside black.[13] To whomever it would thus
appear, I will make answer with a parable. Read it,
for it costs you less to read than it costs me to write
it.

Una stagion fu già, che sì il terreno
arse, che 'l Sol di nuovo a Faetonte   110
de' suoi corsier parea aver dato il freno;
    secco ogni pozzo, secca era ogni fonte;
li rivi e i stagni e i fiumi più famosi
tutti passar si potean senza ponte.
    In quel tempo, d'armenti e de lanosi   115
greggi io non so s'i' dico ricco o grave,
era un pastor fra gli altri bisognosi,
    che poi che l'acqua per tutte le cave
cercò indarno, si volse a quel Signore
che mai non suol fraudar chi in lui fede have;   120
    et ebbe lume e inspirazion di core,
ch'indi lontano troveria, nel fondo
di certa valle, il desiato umore.
    Con moglie e figli e con ciò ch'avea al mondo
là si condusse, e con gli ordegni suoi   125
l'acqua trovò, né molto andò profondo.
    E non avendo con che attinger poi,
se non un vase picciolo et angusto,
disse: — Che mio sia il primo non ve annoi;
    di mógliema il secondo; e 'l terzo è giusto   130
che sia de' figli, e il quarto, e fin che cessi
l'ardente sete onde è ciascuno adusto:
    li altri vo' ad un ad un che sien concessi,
secondo le fatiche, alli famigli
che meco in opra a far il pozzo messi.   135
    Poi su ciascuna bestia si consigli,
che di quelle che a perderle è più danno
inanzi a l'altre la cura si pigli. —
    Con questa legge un dopo l'altro vanno
a bere; e per non essere i sezzai,   140
tutti più grandi i lor meriti fanno.
    Questo una gazza, che già amata assai
fu dal padrone et in delizie avuta,
vedendo et ascoltando, gridò: — Guai!

There was once a season when the earth was so badly scorched that the Sun seemed to have given anew the reins of his coursers to Phaethon. Every well was dry and so too every fountain. The brooks and ponds and most famous rivers could all be crossed without a bridge. In those days, there was one needy shepherd among others. I do not know if I should say he was rich, or burdened, with herds and woolly flocks. After he had searched in vain for water through all the hollows, he turned to that Lord who is not in the habit of deceiving those who have faith in Him. And he received enlightenment and in his heart felt certain that he would find far away at the bottom of a certain valley the liquid he desired. With his wife and sons and all his worldly goods he betook himself there, and with his tools found water, nor did he have to dig so deep. Then, having nothing with which to draw it forth except a small and narrow vase, he said, "Let it not displease you if the first draught be mine and the second be my wife's, and it is just that the third and fourth go to my sons, and as many more as it takes to quench the burning thirst with which they are parched. I desire that the succeeding draughts be conceded to those of my household, according to their labors, who worked with me to dig the well. Then concerning each animal let it be recommended that care be taken, before the others, of those which it is a greater harm to lose." In accord with this pronouncement they came to drink one after another, and each exaggerated his merits so as not to be the last. A magpie, once very much beloved and pampered by his master, after he had seen and heard all this, cried, "Woe is me! I am

Io non gli son parente, né venuta   145
a fare il pozzo, né di più guadagno
gli son per esser mai ch'io gli sia suta;
    veggio che dietro a li altri mi rimagno:
morò di sete, quando non procacci
di trovar per mio scampo altro rigagno. —   150
    Cugin, con questo essempio vuo' che spacci
quei che credon che 'l Papa porre inanti
mi debba a Neri, a Vanni, a Lotti e a Bacci.
    Li nepoti e i parenti, che son tanti,
prima hanno a ber; poi quei che lo aiutaro   155
a vestirsi il più bel de tutti i manti.
    Bevuto ch'abbian questi, gli fia caro
che beano quei che contra il Soderino
per tornarlo in Firenze si levaro.
    L'un dice: — Io fui con Pietro in Casentino,   160
e d'esser preso e morto a risco venni.
— Io gli prestai danar —, grida Brandino.
    Dice un altro: — A mie spese il frate tenni
uno anno, e lo rimessi in veste e in arme,
di cavallo e d'argento gli sovenni. —   165
    Se, fin che tutti beano, aspetto a trarme
la voluntà di bere, o me di sete,
o secco il pozzo d'acqua veder parme.
    Meglio è star ne la solita quïete,
che provar se gli è ver che qualunque erge   170
Fortuna in alto, il tuffa prima in Lete.
    Ma sia ver, se ben li altri vi sommerge,
che costui sol non accostasse al rivo
che del passato ogni memoria absterge.
    Testimonio sono io di quel ch'io scrivo: 175
ch'io non l'ho ritrovato, quando il piede
gli baciai prima, di memoria privo.
    Piegossi a me da la beata sede;
la mano e poi le gote ambe mi prese,
e il santo bacio in amendue mi diede.   180

not a relative, nor did I help to dig the well, nor will I ever be worth more to him than I have been up to now. I see I shall remain far behind the rest. I shall die of thirst, if I do not set out to find another stream for my relief.''

Cousin, with this parable I desire you to dismiss those who believe that the pope must rank me ahead of Neri, Vanni, Lotti, and Bacci.[14] The nephews and the relatives,[15] who are so many, must drink first, and then those[16] who helped to dress him in the most beautiful of all mantles. After these have drunk, he will take special pleasure in seeing those[17] drink who rose up against Soderini in order to bring him back to Florence. One says, ''I was with Piero in Casentino,[18] and I came at the risk of being captured and killed.'' ''I lent him money,'' cries Brandino.[19] Says a third,[20] ''I maintained your brother at my expense a year and restored him to the possession of arms and goods. With horses and silver I assisted him.'' If I wait until all have drunk before I free myself of the desire to drink, either I must see the well dry of water or myself dry with thirst.

Better to repose in one's accustomed tranquillity than to try by experience whether it be true that Fortune first plunges in Lethe whomever she desires to raise on high. But it may still be true that, though she submerges others, she failed to bring this one man to the stream that washes away all memory of the past. I am testimony to what I write, for I did not find him devoid of memory when I kissed his foot the first time. He leaned over to me from the blessed seat and took my hand and then took both my cheeks and graced me with the holy kiss on each

Di mezzo quella bolla anco cortese
mi fu, de la quale ora il mio Bibiena
espedito m'ha il resto alle mie spese.
     Indi col seno e con la falda piena
di speme, ma di pioggia molle e brutto,   185
la notte andai sin al Montone a cena.
     Or sia vero che 'l Papa attenga tutto
ciò che già offerse, e voglia di quel seme
che già tanti anni i' sparsi, or darmi il frutto;
     sie ver che tante mitre e dïademe   190
mi doni, quante Iona di Cappella
a la messa papal non vede insieme:
     sia ver che d'oro m'empia la scarsella,
e le maniche e il grembio, e, se non basta,
m'empia la gola, il ventre e le budella;   195
     serà per questo piena quella vasta
ingordigia d'aver? rimarrà sazia
per ciò la sitibonda mia cerasta?
     Dal Marocco al Catai, dal Nilo in Dazia,
non che a Roma, anderò, se di potervi   200
saziare i desiderii impetro grazia;
     ma quando cardinale, o de li servi
io sia il gran Servo, e non ritrovino anco
termine i desiderii miei protervi,
     in ch'util mi risulta essermi stanco   205
in salir tanti gradi? meglio fòra
starmi in riposo o affaticarmi manco.
     Nel tempo ch'era nuovo il mondo ancora
e che inesperta era la gente prima
e non eran l'astuzie che sono ora,   210
     a piè d'un alto monte, la cui cima
parea toccassi il cielo, un popul, quale
non so mostrar, vivea ne la val ima;
     che più volte osservando la inequale
luna, or con corna or senza, or piena or scema,   215
girar il cielo al corso naturale;

of them. He also graced me with a half-share of that bull, the rest of which my Bibbiena²¹ has expedited for me at my own expense. From his presence, with my breast and with the fold of my cloak filled with hope, I travelled, drenched with rain and spattered with mud, all the way to the Ram for supper.

But even though the pope may keep his word about all that he once promised me and give me now the fruit of those seeds which I sowed for so many years, even though he may bestow upon me as many mitres and diadems as Jonah of the Chapel²² ever sees assembled at a Papal Mass, even though he may stuff my purse with gold, and fill my sleeves and my lap, and if that does not suffice, my throat, my stomach, and my bowels, for all this will that gaping gluttony for wealth be filled? Will the thirsty horned viper within me thus be sated? From Morocco to Cathay, from the Nile to Dacia, to say nothing of Rome, would I journey if I could obtain from the haughty the grace to satisfy my desires. But if I were to become a cardinal, or if of all the servants I were to become the great Servant, and yet my impudent desires were to find no end, what profit would my weariness from having climbed so many steps result in for me? Better for me to relax or to tire myself less.

In the days when the world was young and the first people were still inexperienced and shrewdness did not exist as it does now, at the foot of a lofty mountain, whose peak seemed to touch the heavens, a certain people, such as I cannot describe, lived at the bottom of a valley. Frequently observing the unstable moon revolve through heaven on its natural course, sometimes with horns and sometimes not, sometimes diminished and sometimes full, and believ-

e credendo poter da la suprema
parte del monte giungervi, e vederla
come si accresca e come in sé si prema;
    chi con canestro e chi con sacco per la   220
montagna cominciar correr in su,
ingordi tutti a gara di volerla.
    Vedendo poi non esser giunti più
vicini a lei, cadeano a terra lassi,
bramando in van d'esser rimasi giù.   225
    Quei ch'alti li vedean dai poggi bassi,
credendo che toccassero la luna,
dietro venian con frettolosi passi.
    Questo monte è la ruota di Fortuna,
ne la cui cima il volgo ignaro pensa   230
ch'ogni quïete sia, né ve n'è alcuna.
    Se ne l'onor si trova o ne la immensa
ricchezza il contentarsi, i' loderei
non aver, se non qui, la voglia intensa;
    ma se vediamo i papi e i re, che dèi   235
stimiamo in terra, star sempre in travaglio,
che sia contento in lor dir non potrei.
    Se di ricchezze al Turco, e s'io me agguaglio
di dignitate al Papa, et ancor brami
salir più in alto, mal me ne prevaglio;   240
    convenevole è ben ch'i' ordisca e trami
di non patire alla vita disagio,
che più di quanto ho al mondo è ragion ch'io ami.
    Ma se l'uomo è sì ricco che sta ad agio
di quel che la natura contentarse   245
dovria, se fren pone al desir malvagio;
    che non digiuni quando vorria trarse
l'ingorda fame, e abbia fuoco e tetto
se dal freddo o dal sol vuol ripararse;
    né gli convenga andare a piè, se astretto   250
è di mutar paese; et abbia in casa
chi la mensa apparecchi e acconci il letto,

ing that they could reach it from the highest peak and see how it grew and how it shrank, they all began to scale the mountain, one with a basket and another with a sack, all rivaling each other in their greed to make off with the moon. When afterwards they found themselves no closer, the first few fell worn out to the ground and wished in vain that they were down below; but the others lower down, seeing their leaders so high and believing they had touched the moon, came scurrying after with hurried steps. This mountain is the wheel of Fortune, on whose top the ignorant herd thinks all serenity resides—but it is not there.

If contentment were to be found in prestige or in immense riches, I would praise a disposition directed nowhere save toward them; but when we see popes and kings, whom we consider gods on earth, remain forever in travail, how can I say that contentment resides in honors and in wealth? If I make myself equal to the Turk in opulence and to the pope in dignity, and still long to climb higher, I take small advantage of my gains; but it is proper that I lay the warp and weave the cloth so that I do not suffer discomfort during the one life I should love more than all I own on earth.

A man should be rich enough to live in comfort, content with what befits his nature, and he should bridle his villainous desire. He should not have to fast when he wants to quell his aching hunger, and he should have a hearth and a roof to shelter him from the cold and the sun, nor should he have to walk if he is forced to travel from land to land, and he should have someone to prepare his meals and

che mi può dare o mezza o tutta rasa
la testa più di questo? ci è misura
di quanto puon capir tutte le vasa.   255
 Convenevole è ancor che s'abbia cura
de l'onor suo; ma tal che non divenga
ambizïone e passi ogni misura.
 Il vero onore è ch'uom da ben te tenga
ciascuno, e che tu sia; che, non essendo,   260
forza è che la bugia tosto si spenga.
 Che cavalliero o conte o reverendo
il populo te chiami, io non te onoro,
se meglio in te che 'l titol non comprendo.   265
 Che gloria ti è vestir di seta e d'oro,
e, quando in piazza appari o ne la chiesa,
ti si lievi il capuccio il popul soro;
 poi dica dietro: — Ecco che diede presa
per danari a' Francesi Porta Giove   270
che il suo signor gli avea data in difesa —?
 Quante collane, quante cappe nuove
per dignità si comprano, che sono
publici vituperii in Roma e altrove!
 Vestir di romagnuolo et esser bono,   275
al vestir d'oro et aver nota o macchia
di baro o traditor sempre prepono.
 Diverso al mio parere il Bomba gracchia,
e dice: — Abb'io pur roba, e sia l'acquisto
o venuto pel dado o per la macchia: 280
 sempre ricchezze riverire ho visto
più che virtù; poco il mal dir mi nòce:
se riniega anco e si biastemia Cristo.
 — Pian piano, Bomba; non alzar la voce:
biastemian Cristo li uomini ribaldi,   285
peggior di quei che lo chiavaro in croce;
 ma li onesti e li buoni dicon mal di
te, e dicon ver; che carte false e dadi
ti dànno i beni c'hai, mobili e saldi.

make his bed. What better life than this can I have whether I shave my whole head or only half?[23] All vases have a limit as to how much they can hold.

It is also right that a man pay attention to his honor, but not so diligently that honor becomes ambition and passes all measure. The true honor is that everyone consider you a good man and that you be a good man, for if you are not, the facade soon vanishes. The populace may call you Knight or Count or Reverend, but I do not honor you unless I perceive something more in you than your title. What glory do you gain by wearing silk and gold and by having the simple people doff their bonnets to you when you appear in the market place or church, if they say behind your back, "There is the man who for money surrendered Porta Giove to the French after his lord had given it to him to defend?"[24] How many new chains[25] and how many new hats are bought for honor's sake, which are public disgraces in Rome and elsewhere! For my part, I prefer to wear sackcloth and be good than to wear gold and to have the mark and stain of cheat or traitor.

Bomba[26] croaks in opposition to my opinion, and says, "Give me property nonetheless, even if it come by dice or marked cards! I have always seen riches revered more than virtue. Malicious rumors disturb me little, when Christ is also cursed and denied." Softly, softly, Bomba. Do not raise your voice. Evil men blaspheme against Christ, worse men than those who nailed him to the cross. But honest and good men speak evil of you, and they speak the truth, because marked cards and dice do bring you your estates and furnishings. And you give people plenty

E tu dài lor da dirlo, perché radi
più di te in questa terra straccian tele   290
d'oro e broccati e veluti e zendadi.
    Quel che devresti ascondere, rivele:
a' furti tuoi, che star dovrian di piatto,
per mostrar meglio, allumi le candele:
    e dài materia ch'ogni savio e matto   295
intender vuol come ville e palazzi
dentro e di fuor in sì pochi anni hai fatto,
    e come così vesti e così sguazzi;
e rispondere è forza, e a te è avviso
esser grande uomo, e dentro ne gavazzi.   300
    Pur che non se lo veggia dire in viso,
non stima il Borna che sia biasmo, s'ode
mormorar dietro che abbia il frate ucciso.
    Se bene è stato in bando un pezzo, or gode
l'ereditate in pace, e chi gli agogna   305
mal, freme indarno e indarno se ne rode.
    Quello altro va se stesso a porre in gogna
facendosi veder con quella aguzza
mitra acquistata con tanta vergogna.
    Non avendo più pel d'una cuccuzza,   310
ha meritato con brutti servigi
la dignitate e 'l titolo che puzza
    a' spirti umani, a li celesti e a' stigi.

to talk about. Few men in this district consume more
cloth of gold, more silks, brocades and sendals, than
you. What you ought to hide, you reveal. In order
to show them off better, you light candles to your
robberies, when they ought to be done secretly. And
you provide every sage and every dimwit with cause
to wonder how you have built near and far so many
villas and palaces in so few years, and how you dress
as you do and how you wallow in so much wealth.
And it would do you violence to inform them, and
you think yourself a great man and revel inwardly.

Provided that he does not hear it said to his face,
Borna[27] does not consider it an insult if he hears
it whispered behind his back that he slew his brother.
Although he was in exile a short time, now he enjoys
his inheritance in peace. And whoever wishes him
ill trembles and consumes himself with rage in vain.
That other fellow there is going to put himself in
the pillory, letting himself be seen In public with that
pointed mitre he acquired with so much shame. Having
no more hair than a gourd, he has earned with filthy
services the dignity and the title that stink in the nostrils
of humans, and in those of celestial and Stygean spirits.

NOTES

[1] For Daria see Satire I, note 25. Most students of Ariosto agree that he must have been born in the palace of the Citadel of Reggio, his father's official residence at the time. Twenty years after Ludovico's birth, Matteo Maria Boiardo, Count of Scandiano, died within the walls of the same edifice, perhaps in the same room in which the great continuator of his poem first saw the light of day.

[2] Niccolò Ariosto led an active life as diplomat, soldier, and husband. For an account of his many children, see Satire I, preface, and notes 18, 20, 23, and 24. Perhaps he deserves the title of Count, since he bought it in 1472 when Emperor Frederick III made a fund-raising journey to Italy. The elder Ariosto, unlike his famous son, had an acute respect for protocol. From 1462 until 1471, he was in the service of the Gonzaga of Mantua. But the Estensi also made use of him. Depending on which court he happened to be residing at for the moment, his job was to keep the other minutely informed of all significant happenings. Although his post lent itself to gossip-mongering and to mixed loyalties, he was not an espionage agent playing a double game. The rulers of Ferrara and Mantua had close ties of friendship and wanted for practical reasons to be well-informed of each other's doings. In times of discord Niccolò's position could, however, have become dangerous. Eventually it did.

Borso d'Este took to his death bed in the spring of 1471, and immediately a power struggle ensued between Ercole, his brother almost twenty years his junior, and Niccolò his nephew. Ercole, resident in Ferrara, and a legitimate son of Niccolò I, held the legal succession to the Dukedom. But in fifteenth-century Italy technicalities of this sort were frequently overlooked. Borso himself was illegitimate. Niccolò d'Este, son of the illegitimate Leonello d'Este, Borso's brother, was under the protection of the Gonzaga at Mantua and was making a convincing attempt to take over the family leadership. Ercole soon realized that he would need, for a very special mission, someone with family ties in Ferrara and with freedom of movement at the Mantuan court. Consequently, he chose Niccolò Ariosto to play a leading role in an attempt to assassinate Niccolò d'Este. It made no difference to Ariosto that he had earned his livelihood from the Gonzaga for almost eleven years. He accepted the assignment. At the last minute, however, his accomplices lost heart and confessed their intentions to Ludovico Gonzaga. They met with horrible punishment, but Niccolò Ariosto, managed to escape to Ferrara.

Ercole won the Dukedom and, recognizing a servant who would hazard his life, his honor, and his immortal soul for the sake of a generous master, named Ariosto Captain of the Citadel of Reggio. Niccolò held this important post from 1472 until 1481 and prospered, acquiring many real estate holdings, and a richly dowered wife of an old and noble family. She presented him with five of their ten children during the stay in Reggio. Then in 1481 Ercole appointed Niccolò Captain of the Citadel of Rovigo. But no sooner had the captain installed himself there than the Venetians took the town from him without a fight, even though its defenses were supposed to be impregnable. One wonders whether or not Niccolò dabbled in a conspiracy which the Venetians were fostering within the walls of Ferrara. But Ercole I must never have been suspicious of his Captain, for in 1482 he named him Treasurer General of the Ferrarese Militia. And in 1485, after peace had been concluded, Niccolò accompanied his Duke on a splendid visit of state to Venice.

By 1486 Niccolò had attained to the office of Judge of the Twelve Sages, the highest civilian post in Ferrara. But certain accusations of barratry and embezzlement, which had been trailing him ever since his days as Captain of Reggio, suddenly burst into the open at this zenith of his career in the form of handbills and sonnets posted in all the public places of Ferrara. Twenty-three of these sonnets have survived, and have been attributed by some to that Antonio Cammelli, called II Pistoia, to whom Ludovico refers in Satire VI, 1.96. One can imagine what must have been the eldest son's shame and anger over his father's public disgrace. To avoid further scandal Ercole was forced to transfer Niccolò in 1489 to the Captaincy of Modena, where he stayed until 1492. But Ludovico was unable to escape his father's bad reputation. He had to remain in Ferrara as a student at the university.

From 1492 until 1496 the elder Ariosto seems to have had no steady employment. Perhaps it was during this time that he forced Ludovico to study law (see Satire VI, 11. 154-162). Finally, in 1496, Ercole appointed Niccolò Commissioner of the Romagna, one of the most honorable and well paid posts a Duke of Ferrara could offer. But Niccolò lost it within the year on account of his harshness and cruelty. At Lugo, where the commissioner resided, a certain married woman was about to receive her lover into her bedroom when her husband's servants took the pair by surprise. The lover managed to escape, but in such haste that he left his cloak behind. The husband guessed the lover's identity, but chose discreetly to pass over the entire affair in silence. Unfortunately, word leaked out to the Commissioner. Niccolò took the case in hand, and to make sure that justice would prevail, tortured the outraged husband into confessing the name of his wife's lover. The husband then appealed to the Duke against his legal tormentor, and Ercole, once again in the throes of a public scandal, was forced to discharge his commissioner and fine him 500 gold ducats, 100 of which were to serve as damages to the mistreated husband. This puritan zeal is amusing to observe in the man whose son was to delight the world with the Innkeeper's Tale, and the stories of Ginevra and Ariodante and of Anselmo and the Ethiopian. The ex-commissioner died in 1500, having never again held public office.

During his life, Niccolò was treacherous, cruel, dishonest, and greedy, a moderately competent official, and a good husband. Each of his successive testaments provides with exceptional care for his wife's rights and comforts after his death. His biography should be interesting to students of the Satires for reasons apart from the portrait it presents of a fifteenth-century Italian public official. Perhaps it explains why that especially memorable and endearing character in Horace's Satires and Epistles, the benevolent, sympathetic, and upstanding father, is conspicuously absent from Ludovico's imitation. And who knows whether that irony and that skepticism which pervade all of the poet's major works may not have been nourished in his father's house?

[3] Mercury was the god of luck and wealth, the patron of merchants, and also of thieves. He was the son of Maia, the earth-goddess.

[4] Spurs were the symbol of knighthood. "Hat" refers to the birretta, worn by priests, bishops, and cardinals in black, purple, and red respectively, or to the broad-brimmed red hat with tassels, the exclusive property of cardinals.

[5] During Ariosto's lifetime the name of Claudius Ptolemaeus, the celebrated Alexandrian mathematician, astronomer, and geographer of the second century A.D., was synonymous with astronomy and geography. Ariosto means that he confines his exploration to maps.

[6] Alessandra Benucci. See Satire V, preface.

⁷ Leo X, formerly Giovanni de' Medici (1476–1521), who succeeded Julius
II as pope on 11 March 1513.

⁸ Cardinal Giovanni de' Medici made his ceremonial entrance into Florence
on 14 September 1512 in the company of Spanish troops supplied by the Holy
League. His family tradition, his avid support of Julius II, and his diplomatic
maintenance of friendly relations with his homeland during his exile all contributed
to make him the Holy League's natural choice to set up a puppet government
in Florence. Since his older brother Piero's capitulation to Charles VIII in 1494,
the Medici had been in exile from Florence. In their absence, the government
of Savonarola endured until 1498 and was succeeded by an attempt to revive
the republic in its pre-Medician form. This experiment lasted for roughly thirteen
years, until Giovanni's return, and was headed by Piero Soderini, who held
the office of Gonfalonier of Justice (see 11. 94–96 and 1. 158). After the Congress
of the Holy League, held in Mantua in 1512, had decided that Florence should
lose her independence for not having participated in the expulsion of the French,
Spanish veterans advanced on the town of Prato in the Florentine countryside
where they routed Machiavelli's citizens' militia and destroyed everything they
could lay their hands on. Panic reigned in Florence. Five representatives of
the cardinal appeared before Soderini and demanded his resignation. He not
only resigned immediately but fled to the town of Ragusa on the far shore
of the Adriatic. Giovanni had no difficulty in re-establishing the tyranny to
which his father, his grandfather, and his great-grandfather had accustomed
the citizens of Florence.

⁹ Giuliano de' Medici (1479–1516), Giovanni's younger brother, spent a great
part of his exile in Urbino at the court of Duke Guidobaldo da Montefeltro
and, after 1508, also at the court of Guidobaldo's successor, Francesco Maria
della Rovere. A wing of the palace was named the *appartamento del Magnifico*
in his honor. In Urbino, among a number of the most talented men of his
age, he acquired a mildness of temperament and a love of learning and literature
that endeared him to his contemporaries, but did not prepare him for the role
in government his family demanded of him. Although, immediately after the
restoration, he served on behalf of his brother the Cardinal as titular political
head of the family, he was soon replaced, upon Giovanni's elevation to the
papacy, by his nephew Lorenzo, the son of Piero. In 1515 on his visit to
congratulate the new king of France, Francis I, on the occasion of his coronation,
he was awarded in marriage the king's seventeen-year old aunt, Philiberte de
Savoie, and was at the same time created Duc de Nemours. Ariosto refers
to him by his French title in Satire VII, 1. 97. In *The Courtier*, Castiglione
gives Giuliano the spotlight in Book Three as the chivalrous defender of women.
Ariosto's two canzoni, "*Spirto gentil, che sei nel terzo giro . . .*," and "*Anima
eletta, che nel mondo folle . . .*," when taken together, constitute a dialogue
between Giuliano's spirit and his young widow.

¹⁰ Baldassare Castiglione (1478–1529) served the Dukes of Urbino, Guidobaldo
da Montefeltro and Francesco Maria della Rovere, on diplomatic and military
missions from 1504 until 1516. When Urbino fell under the control of Lorenzo
II de' Medici, Castiglione entered the service of Federico Gonzaga of Mantua,
for whom he managed to secure in 1520 the post of Captain General of the
Church. In 1524 he passed into the service of Clement VII as papal ambassador
to Spain. His years at the court of Emperor Charles V included the difficult
period which culminated in the sack of Rome in 1527. After Castiglione's death
in Toledo, the emperor pronounced the brief and informal, but famous, statement,
"I tell you one of the best knights in the world is dead!" Castiglione's *The*

Book of the Courtier, written between 1508 and 1518, but not published until 1528, became one of the most popular books of the Renaissance. It was at first officially dedicated to Alfonso Ariosto, a second cousin of Ludovico, but after Alfonso's death in 1525, the author rededicated it to Don Miguel da Silva. Catalano, Ariosto's modern biographer, speculates that the unfinished and now lost satire addressed to Castiglione might have been written on the occasion of Alfonso's death. Ludovico praises Castiglione in the *Orlando Furioso* as the man who formed the courtier (XXXVII, 8) and who praised Leonora Gonzaga (XLII, 86–87). In a variant canceled out of the final version of *The Courtier*, Castiglione names Ariosto, in a list of literary men who frequented the court of Urbino, as having in the person of one man presented Italy with a Homer and a Menander.

[11] For Pietro Bembo and Ariosto's relations with him, see Satire VI, preface.

[12] Giovanni de' Medici served as Papal Legate in Bologna from 1511 to 1512 just before his return to Florence.

[13] A humorous allusion to the bishop's cap lined with green.

[14] A series of typically Florentine names probably to indicate that the pope would never place the interests of a Ferrarese before those of a Florentine. After the election of Giovanni de' Medici, Rome was invaded by Florentines seeking to make their fortunes. Many of them did.

[15] Leo X's nepotism was resplendent. Among its beneficiaries were his brother Giuliano, named Captain General of the Church; his nephew Lorenzo, for whom Leo procured the Duchy of Urbino by sending a papal army against its rightful Duke, Francesco Maria della Rovere; his cousins Giulio de' Medici and Luigi de' Rossi, whom Leo made cardinals; and his nephews—Innocenzo Cybò, Giovanni Salviati, and Niccolò Ridolfi respectively, who were also made cardinals, though they had never exhibited any special merit.

[16] It was by no means a foregone conclusion that Giovanni de' Medici would be elected pope by the conclave of 1513. In the first place, he was absent from most of the proceedings due to a very serious abdominal complaint which required surgery as soon as he arrived in Rome. In the second place, he had strong competition. The older members of the conclave were backing Cardinal Alborese, while at the same time Raffaele Riario (see Satire II, 11. 206–207, and the accompanying note), a cousin of the late Julius II, was making a strong bid for the election. At length a clique of younger cardinals, whose leaders belonged to reigning houses, like Louis of Aragon, Ghismondo Gonzaga of Mantua, Ippolito d' Este of Ferrara, and Alfonso Petrucci of Siena, managed to introduce Giovanni's name. Then there was the opposition to overcome of Cardinal Francesco Soderini, brother of the deposed Gonfalonier. Bernardo Dovizi da Bibbiena (see 1. 182 and the accompanying notes), serving as Giovanni's secretary in the conclave, soothed the Florentine cardinal with a hint of the possibility of a matrimonial alliance between the young Lorenzo de' Medici and a daughter of the House of Soderini. Giovanni owed his election in large part to the many important friends he had assiduously cultivated during his years of exile and also to the propitiousness of the times. After the warlike Julius, there was a prevailing desire for a man of peaceful temperament. In any case, the first Medici pope had debts of gratitude to recognize. He did not, however, keep his promise to Soderini. And his removal of Alfonso Petrucci's brother from the governorship of Siena caused the young prelate, who had so strongly supported him in the conclave, to play the role in the Conspiracy of the Cardinals for which Leo had him hanged in the summer of 1517.

[17] The faction of the Palleschi, named after the Medici coat of arms with

its red pellets on a field of gold, had always worked secretly within Florence on behalf of the Medici during their exile. With the abrupt change in Medici fortunes after the expulsion of the French in 1513, the Palleschi grew influential enough and large enough in number to assure the smooth and bloodless return of their patrons to the position of power in Florence that the family had enjoyed during the Laurentian Age. Among the leaders of the Palleschi were the Albizzi, the Strozzi, and the Salviati families, all related to the Medici through marriage.

[18] Piero II de' Medici (1471-1503), called Il Pazzo, the older brother of Giovanni and Giuliano, succeeded to the headship of the family in 1492 upon the death of Lorenzo the Magnificent. After the Florentines expelled him in 1494 as a result of his having signed over to Charles VIII without a struggle the strongholds of Sarzana, Sarzanella, Pietrasanta, Pisa, and Livorno, he made many attempts over the years to re-enter the city by force. He frequently used the region of Casentino as a rallying point for his forces. Ariosto assumes that Leo would have felt himself especially obliged to reward anyone who had aided Piero in his violent efforts to regain Florence. But this is unlikely since the young cardinal after his exile repudiated his older brother's plots.

[19] Brandino was a tailor who lent money to Giovanni when, as an impoverished exile, he took refuge in Venice. Upon becoming pope, Leo expressed his gratitude by making him a Knight of Rhodes and by maintaining him in luxury along with a pack of other parasites.

[20] This might be Francesco Maria della Rovere, who entertained Leo's brother Giuliano at Urbino during the Medici exile. At the beginning of Leo's reign, Francesco Maria enjoyed a certain amount of favor, but very soon afterward he himself went into exile when Leo usurped the Duchy of Urbino for his nephew Lorenzo.

[21] Bernardo Dovizi da Bibbiena (1470-1520) is known to students of Italian literature for his comedy *Calandria*, produced in 1514 as part of the festivities in honor of the visit of Isabella d'Este to the court of Leo X. Castiglione contributed greatly to Bibbiena's memory by portraying him as the master of sophisticated witticism who dominates the conversation in Book Two of *The Courtier*. From 1489, when Lorenzo the Magnificent placed him in charge of the thirteen-year-old cardinal's household, until his death, he served Giovanni faithfully through all the drastic ups and downs of the Medici fortunes. Immediately upon becoming pope, Leo named Bibbiena Cardinal of Santa Maria in Portico out of gratitude for his work within the conclave of 1513 (see note 19). Ariosto had ample opportunity to become friendly with Giovanni's special secretary and remembers him in the *Orlando Furioso* (XXVI, 48) as a persecutor of vice and in his canzone "*Anima eletta, che nel mondo folle . . .*" as a close friend of Giuliano de' Medici. The present reference, however, is far less flattering to Bibbiena. The bull in question, of which Leo forgave Ariosto half the expenses, granted the poet the right of succession to the benefice of Santa Agata. Bibbiena interceded in April, 1518, to help secure Ariosto's rights only after the latter had paid out of his own pocket the registration fees which comprised the other half of the expenses involved in procuring the bull. With the repetition of the possessive in "my Bibbiena" and "at my own expense," Ariosto implies that the influential and highly successful Bibbiena was not of a mind to trouble himself when it came time to sparing an old friend an unnecessary expense.

[22] The prophet Jonah depicted by Michelangelo on the ceiling of the Sistine Chapel.

[23] The Turks shaved their entire heads, while prelates of the Roman Catholic Church submitted only to the tonsure.

[24] An allusion to Bernardino da Corte who turned over the fortress of Milan to the French after his master Ludovico Il Moro had entrusted him with its defense. Ludovico thought that the many favors he had granted his servant would insure his loyalty. Bernardino's name became synonomous with treachery.

[25] The gold chain was an accoutrement of knighthood.

[26] The identity of the bearer of this nickname is unknown, if indeed Ariosto actually had any special individual in mind. The nickname itself connotes violence.

[27] Another nickname of which the bearer's identity is unknown. It implies shadiness of character.

SATIRE IV

To Messer Sigismondo Malaguzzi

PREFACE

On 7 February 1522 Alfonso d'Este named Ariosto commissioner of the province of Garfagnana. After drawing up a will leaving all his possessions to his son Virginio, after taking leave of his beloved Alessandra, the poet set out in wintry weather to occupy his new post. He had to travel over bad roads through mountain passes infested with roving bands of thieves and murderers. He arrived on the twentieth of the month at a ravine, populated in its hollow by the inhabitants of eighty-three small towns and walled in by thickly forested mountains. For neighbors he had Florence and Lucca, both hostile to the House of Este.

The new commissioner took up residence in the fortress of the town of Castelnuovo. He found himself in a province with a complicated and turbulent history. Garfagnana had first come under Ferrarese rule as a result of the war in 1429 between Florence and Lucca which ended in the defeat within Florence of the Albizzi and the exaltation of Cosimo de' Medici to the leadership of the republic. Garfagnana had been subject to Lucca for almost two hundred years when Florence's declaration of war gave the Ghibellines of the province the chance they were waiting for to surrender their strongholds and swear submission to Niccolò III, Duke of Ferrara. Niccolò was happy to accept the friendship of a people who would add to his control of the strip of territory, including Modena and Reggio, which extended from the Adriatic to the Gulf of Genoa. The Guelphs of Garfagnana turned for their salvation to Florence. Lucca had been overly oppressive in her government, failing to respect the traditional rights of the local petty nobility. Niccolò and then his sons Leonello and Borso managed, through shrewd diplomacy with Florence and through a lenient policy toward the Garfagnanese, to solidify Ferrara's hold on the province.

Yet a number of communes continued permanently under Florentine government. And Lucca, though powerless, never gave up her claim to the territory.

Things went smoothly in Garfagnana right up to the period ending with the League of Cambrai. In 1510 Pope Julius II, as part of his program to chastise the Duke of Ferrara and deliver Italy from the French, excommunicated Alfonso, occupied Modena, and sent emissaries to Garfagnana demanding its submission. The Garfagnanese replied that they would rather die than be governed by any lord other than Alfonso d'Este. But conditions were so bad in Ferrara that Alfonso and Ippolito had already made secret arrangements to sell the province back to Lucca for twelve thousand *scudi*. The transaction would have been completed if Julius had not threatened to place Lucca under a papal interdict the moment she paid the money.

In 1512 the bellicose Pope seized Reggio and sent an army of occupation under Francesco Maria della Rovere into Garfagnana. No sooner had Francesco Maria taken the province than he set out to besiege Ferrara. He left in such haste that he neglected to leave a garrison. Lucca saw her chance and moved in. However, the reign of the Panther[1] was short-lived. In 1513 Julius II died and Giovanni de' Medici became Leo X. Lucca, fearing the new power of Florence, retreated; but it was Alfonso d'Este, and not the Medici, who filled the vacuum.

Alfonso, redeemed by the death of his enemy the Pope, remained in control until the next important move of the great powers. It came in 1521, when Leo in alliance with the Emperor, sent a papal army into Garfagnana. Because he had remained staunch in his support of the French, Alfonso found himself, for a second time, excommunicated, and in danger of losing his dukedom. The French were driven out of Milan. Then, at the height of his fortunes, Leo died. Ferrara rejoiced, and Alfonso, saved again by the death of a pope, had special coins minted to commemorate the occasion. On one side they bore Alfonso's profile and on the other a shepherd rescuing a lamb from the jaws of a lion.[2] The Garfagnanese expelled their Florentine commissioner, raised the Estensi standard, and dispatched urgent messages to the Duke requesting him to send his commissioner.

More than a month went by before the Duke appointed Ariosto to govern this battleground. Under recent tensions, old Guelph and Ghibelline feuds had revived in the opposition of the *parte italiana*, favoring Florence, against the *parte francese*, favoring the House of Este. The province was alive with brigands who sided with one party or the other for support. Homicides were committed before the very altars of the churches. Prominent families feuded, slaughtering each other with impunity. Taking advantage of the month-long vacancy in the commissariat, the Maddalena family of the *parte italiana* proceeded in an attempt to annihilate the San Donnino family of the *parte francese* down to the last man, woman, and child; and the new commissioner spent three years trying in vain to bring the assassins to justice. Added to family feuds and party strife were rivalries between whole towns, which did not hesitate to enter the field of battle against each other. And there was a chaos of border disputes, the natural outcome of almost ten years of hostility between Florence and Ferrara. Brigands hostile to Ferrara could escape pursuit by skipping over the border into Florentine territory, where they knew that far from being extradited they might perhaps be rewarded for their crimes. In fact, Florentine commissioners near the border actually employed them to harass and plunder the citizens of Ferrarese districts. The lenient policy of the House of Este only aggravated these evils. Plague and famine stalked the land.

Thirty-five years earlier Count Matteo Maria Boiardo had been appointed Captain of Reggio by Ercole I. But Reggio was a prosperous and ancient holding of the Dukes of Ferrara, and the latter part of Erocole I's reign was Ferrara's golden age. Duke Alfonso, unlike his father, was not a city builder, not an avid partron of artists and architects, and not a creator of arable lands for the improvement of his subjects' food supply. He was a forger of cannon, and needed to be. Never had the dukedom been in more danger of dissolution than during his reign. Hardships abounded for everyone including himself. At one point during the campaign of Julius II against Ferrara, Alfonso was forced to sell all the precious gems and all the gold and silver plate in his possession, including his dinnerware, in order to carry on the war. He and his family ate from majolica dishes he fashioned and decorated with his own hands. When in 1521 Leo X launched the second massive papal campaign against him, Alfonso was forced to postpone, then diminish, and finally cancel altogether his servants' salaries. He was still short of cash after Leo's death. At this time Ariosto found himself in such straitened circumstances that he might have to look elsewhere for employment. Not only had he not received his salary for the past four months, but he had been unable to collect his revenues from the Milan benefice because of the presence of French and Imperial forces there. He gave the Duke his ultimatum—pay, or farewell—and found himself unexpectedly appointed comissioner of a province. It was the very last thing he wanted, but the state of his finances forced him to accept the job.

On the surface, this appointment of a poet to govern a war-torn territory seems preposterous. But it was not altogether so. The Ariosti were members of the petty nobility, and could not avoid involvement in military and political affairs. Ariosto's first employment after his father's death had been as Captain of Canossa under Ercole I. He had remained in that position until he entered Cardinal Ippolito's household, where he saw further military service and was introduced to the hazards of the life of an emissary to hostile courts. He was almost forty-eight years of age by the time Alfonso dispatched him to Garfagnana, quick of wit, no doubt persuasive, experienced in public affairs, and the member of a family which had long dedicated itself to serving the Dukes of Ferrara and which could even claim a remote kinship through marriage with the House of Este. Here was a man not only capable of writing lucid reports, but even of some renown throughout Italy for his talents as a poet and dramatist. From Alfonso's viewpoint, the Garfagnanese should have considered themselves honored by the appointment. To top it off, Rinaldo Ariosto, Ludovico's cousin, had been the last commissioner in Castelnuovo before papal aggression commenced in the year 1510.

It was not as if the poet were being entrusted with crucial responsibilities. The commissioner of Garfagnana, as Alfonso was well aware, was severely restricted in the exercise of his powers. The Estensi had always been very attentive in their respect for the traditional liberties of the Garfagnanese. No commissioner of theirs could implement any major legal, fiscal, or military measure without the approval of elected representatives from each of the four districts of the province. In fact, no decision of the commissioner on any matter was final. Any Garfagnanese subject could go over his head and appeal directly to the Duke. Essentially, the commissioner was to serve as a mediator and a judge in local disputes too trivial for the Duke's attention. He had to be a man of discretion, prompt to transmit significant information to the Duke, and able to gain the people's consent for ducal policies. He was to play the part of a goodwill ambassador, and perhaps most important of all, he was to serve as a symbol of the prestige the citizens of Garfagnana had acquired through their association with the House of Este.

Ariosto took a nobler view of his office. In a letter complaining that the Duke had, characteristically, taken the word of a certain brigand over his own, Ariosto declared, "it is enough for me to have a clear conscience before God and in the presence of those men who can see how matters are going. For my part, I seek only that justice should be done."[3] The brigand in question had rigged an election in order to become *podestà* of one of the districts within the province. But what was Alfonso to do? In those precarious times, was he to gain the friendship of his strong and cunning subjects, or was he to stand on principle? It is fair to say that the story of Ariosto's relations with the Duke throughout the Garfagnana episode presents in miniature the age-old conflict between justice and political expediency.

Ariosto set out at once, in his high-minded way, to attack the most obvious evil—the brigands. Conditions were so bad that he felt obliged to complain that the brigands

> never cease everyday to commit murders and put ransoms on whomever they please. And they even have the audacity to send messages to certain people here in Castelnuovo to the effect that, if they fail to pay a stated sum of money, they will come and cut them to pieces, even if need be, in this very fortress. And maybe they would have the courage to do it, for they have supporters here to nourish and defend them,[4]

and he wrote again,

> . . . in truth, if some good provision is not made, this province will go from bad to worse, and your excellency will find himself lord of it in nothing but the title, for the real lordship will go to these assassins and to their leaders and supporters in this province, and especially in Castelnuovo,[5]

and again,

> . . . neither in the woods, nor in the town, nor locked up in his house is anyone in this territory safe from murderers and evil-doers. Every night I post a guard outside this house, or fortress if you will, where I live, and I always order two

crossbowmen to sleep here along with the rest of my household, because every day they threaten that they will come and remove by force the prisoner I have here.[6]

Finally, he wrote to the Elders of Lucca,

> . . . in all these mountains the assassins and men of evil ways are the real lords, and not the pope, nor the Florentines, nor my lord, nor your lordships. . . .[7]

Ariosto's 157 letters from Garfagnana comprise one long complaint on the subject of brigandry. He complained repeatedly to the Duke, but he never received a satisfactory answer. In fact, Alfonso's policy seemed designed to foster the very evil that his earnest, idealistic commissioner was trying to eradicate.

Ariosto complained to the Duke about the weakness of his forces: "these malefactors go about most of the time in greater company than the crossbowmen I have here to guard me."[8] Alfonso replied that he would send reinforcements, if the Garfagnanese agreed to pay their wages. Ariosto called a meeting of representatives from each district of the province. He requested the money and was flatly refused it. The people had had enough expenses with the twelve men presently in the commissioner's service. The representatives finally agreed to Ariosto's proposal of a citizen's militia composed of volunteers. It was cheap. And all went well until the first danger arose. The commissioner got word that if he moved quickly he could trap a gang of brigands in a house nearby. He mounted his horse, rode into the piazza, and sent out calls for his militia to assemble; by the time the men finally arrived, the brigands had been warned and had made their escape, and when the militia members found out why they had been called, they all found excuses to get away themselves. Ariosto was left twirling his thumbs. When he suggested that a price be put on the heads of the worst brigands, the representatives refused even to discuss the matter, let alone to vote on it. Ariosto did manage to publish decrees imposing heavy fines on anyone caught harboring brigands in his house, or in any way abetting their activities. The brigands, for their part, replied by putting a price on the head of Ariosto's vice-commissioner— 200 ducats alive, 100 dead. Meanwhile the Duke was trying to get out of paying any restitution money to two of Ariosto's crossbowmen who had been wounded in an attempt to capture the outlaws.

Alfonso seemed to be displaying a positive favoritism toward the brigands. In one of his earliest letters, Ariosto criticizes the Duke's leniency, complaining that

> the excessive favor your excellency grants these men of Camporgiano makes mules of them, for a more decent word I cannot find for them, and I can accomplish nothing here except by force.[9]

When the commissioner sought the Duke's permission to disarm all the men of the province, the Duke replied that it would be a violation of their liberties. Of what use to Alfonso would a completely defenseless territory have been? When Ariosto complained that public officials were selling justice, taking bribes, and otherwise conniving with brigands. Alfonso merely ignored him, or even worse, demonstrated that he believed their excuses to be truer than the advice of his own commissioner. After two years of such humiliation, Ariosto's bitterness got the better of his discretion, and he wrote,

> if your excellency does not help me to maintain the honor of my office, I, for my part, have not the strength to do so alone; for when I condemn and menace those who disobey me and then your excellency absolves them, or decides the case in such a way as to display openly that your excellency considered them to be in the right and not me, it only contributes to debase the authority of my magistracy. It would be better, if I am unsuitable here, for you to send someone else more qualified, for when you undermine everything I do, the good as well as the bad, the dignity of the commissariat diminishes . . . send someone else to take my place who has more stomach to endure these insults, for my patience is not great enough to tolerate them.[10]

Another time, when the father of a young man ransomed by brigands appealed to him for help, he was forced to tell the Duke,

> I could do nothing but try to satisfy him with words and tell him that I am waiting day by day for your excellency to take steps to bring order into this territory. When the time comes that I have nothing more to tell them and that I have lost all my credit here, I shall steal away some night and make my way

back to Ferrara . . . everyone bears ill will toward me, and speaks ill of me, but even more so of your excellency, to whose good graces I recommend myself.[11]

While Ariosto tried to appease the decent citizens of Garfagnana, Alfonso was busy granting amnesties and favors, and showing every leniency to the brigands. One wonders whether Alfonso had not planned it so.

Alfonso was a violent man. At the battle of Ravenna, while he was firing his beloved cannons round after round into the melee, he heard his men protesting that their allies, the French, were in range, and screamed, "Destroy them all, they are all our enemies!" In his heart he must have felt some kinship with the brigands of Garfagnana. Ariosto was an amusing person, and useful for the moment. Alfonso needed the support of the powerful men in Garfagnana, whether they were criminals or not. He could not openly ally himself with thieves and murderers. He needed at least the appearance of justice. Ariosto provided him with that appearance. Perhaps, for Ariosto, the ultimate humiliation of the Garfagnana experience was in being used in this manner. But Alfonso had to deal as best he could. He had no time to become absorbed in moral speculation. And he was right, politically, in trusting to men of his own sort. After Giulio de' Medici became Clement VII in 1523, Giovanni delle Bande Nere invaded Garfagnana. Ariosto was on his way back from Ferrara where he had been busy with personal affairs. On this occasion, the very brigands whom he had been endeavoring so hard to exterminate defeated and routed the invader.

By 1523, Ariosto had managed to draw up a treaty with the Elders of the Republic of Lucca for the extradition of brigands and for mutual cooperation in tracking them down. He even managed to get the Duke to ratify it. This treaty constituted for Ariosto the one important positive accomplishment of his commissariat. But he had other difficulties, of an ecclesiastical nature, with Lucca. The bishop of Lucca, as well as the bishop of Luna, retained jurisdiction over Garfagnana in all religious matters. And the priests of Garfagnana were a problem.

To any reader of that rather tiresome series of official communications Ariosto turned out during the Garfagnana period, his accounts of his problems with the priesthood must come as comic relief. On one occasion, Ariosto reported to the Duke,

While I was away these past few days in Ferrara, it befell that two sons of Messer Evangelista dal Silico came into Castelnuovo one night in disguise and entered the house of a certain young lady. Now although she is known to provide a certain gentleman of this territory with pleasure in secret, she is in no way anyone's whore, and she lives and works, without their shunning her, among all the good ladies of the province. These men laid hands on her and attempted to drag her from her house, but she screamed and people came to her rescue. The next morning she went to complain to the Captain. And for this, another son of Messer Evangelista, named Job, a priest in holy orders, searched out the mother of the aforesaid young lady and broke her skull and left her for dead. The good woman has indeed been many days in danger of dying.[12]

But Father Job went scot-free because of his clerical immunity. After expressing his displeasure over the fact, Ariosto was prompted to declare in the same letter that "the most evil and most factious men of this province are the priests" and he went on to deliver himself of the following judgment:

This case provides a bad precedent, and it displeases me greatly. If it were not that I fear ecclesiastical censure because I hold a benefice, I would take no heed of the man's priesthood, and I would punish him more severely than if he were a layman. And if I could do nothing else, I would at least exile him. Although temporal rulers do not have any authority over the clergy, still it seems to me that no cleric should be allowed to remain in the dominions of any ruler against that ruler's will.

Ariosto appealed to the bishop of Lucca for justice, but to no avail. And he reported to Alfonso, still in the same letter, two previous examples of unfair leniency on the part of Garfagnana's bishops:

. . . last summer I turned over into the hands of the bishop of Lucca that priest named Matheo who had wounded my chancellor and who was known in public to be a murderer and evil-doer; but with a sprinkling of water the bishop sent him away absolved. Before I came here, a priest named Antonio da Soraggio, who had killed a man, was in the hands of the bishop of Luna, and with a *misereatur* he was freed.

The commissioner could do nothing but tremble with exasperation. At one point he even told Alfonso that it would be a holy act to

burn down all the churches in the province.[13] Alfonso must have been
shocked, not out of piety, but because he was a feudatory of the
church and Giulio de' Medici wore the tiara. The slightest move Alfonso
made against a priest could have been used as the pretext for a papal
invasion of Ferrara. He would have been declared a rebellious vassal.

When in June, 1525, Alfonso appointed a new commissioner of
Gafagnana and relieved Ariosto of the post, he was probably glad to
be rid of his complaining poet. No doubt Ariosto himself was overjoyed
to be out of his misery. He could remember with satisfaction how
he had prohibited the export of foodstuffs from Garfagnana in order
to prevent a famine—even though part of his remuneration as commissioner had come from a percentage on the value of such exports. He
could remember the precautions he had taken to prevent an outbreak
of the plague—even though one of those precautions, the cancellation
of an annual festival, had gained him even more unpopularity than
he already had. But his frustrations were also memorable. Simple people
had stood before him and in their innocence had implored his help,
not knowing that he was as helpless as they. Vivid examples of Ariosto's
compassion are scattered through the letters. Four men from Salacagnana
had come to Castelnuovo without disclosing the matter that brought
them,

> and when they stood before me, they began to cry, nor did they
> endeavor to express anything more. I asked them what they wanted
> of me, and they answered that they could not speak because
> their lives had been threatened if they spoke, and for the love
> of God, would I please never say that they had been to see
> me.[14]

A small world of the poor, the exploited, and the victimized inhabits
the Garfagnana letters and serves as a chorus of assenting voices to
support the poet's personal complaints.

Any reader of the letters must conclude that in the *Satires* those
aristocratic references to the "vulgar" and to the "common herd"
are part of a literary pose. No case, during his commissariat, that
involved the suffering of another human being was beneath Ariosto's
consideration. He had known from the start that he was unfit to be
a governor. When finally he managed to catch some brigands, he wrote
to one of the Duke's secretaries,

I have compassion for them; yet I must place myself in the hands of those who have better judgment than I, and in whom mercy does not undermine justice. I confess it openly that I am not the sort of man to govern other men, for I am too full of pity and am not firm enough to deny any favor asked of me.[15]

Six months later he recommended the reappointment of his present Captain of the Law, because

he is virile and a man to make himself feared and obeyed, and he, with his severity, makes up for that fault of which certain people in Castelnuovo have accused me; that is, of being too kind. If another were sent here who is likewise too kind, I doubt that the two of us would make a combination of any worth. . . .[16]

Ariosto had accepted the commissariat of Garfagnana because he needed money, and not because he liked power. Consequently, he was in misery most of the time. He was neither successful in enforcing the law, nor if he had been, could it have made him happy. He simply did not like to see suffering.

When, after precisely one year of residence in Castelnuovo, Ariosto addressed the present satire to his cousin Sigismondo Malaguzzi, it was natural that he should have looked back upon his carefree, youthful years as a kind of golden age. From the window of his room in the beautiful Malaguzzi villa called the Mauriziano, where he had visited during his youth, he had had the view of a pleasant garden, a murmuring brook, gently sloping hills, and the sky. He had felt enthusiasm and inspiration, and he had been able to write. From the window of his fortress in Castelnuovo he could see only two turbulent rivers churning into each other, with harsh mountains on all sides, nothing but enemies and hatred everywhere, nothing but frustration. For an entire year he had been able to write nothing but dispatches. He longed for a tranquil life, full of the freedom to write and think.

NOTES

[1] See 1. 156.
[2] Cf. 11. 7-9.

[3] 23 January 1524.
[4] 13 September 1522.
[5] 15 April 1523.
[6] 28 May 1523.
[7] 20 June 1523.
[8] 29 May 1523. Cf. 11. 157–159.
[9] 22 June 1522.
[10] 30 January 1524.
[11] 30 August 1523. Cf. 1. 205.
[12] 17 April 1523.
[13] 8 February 1524.
[14] 20 July 1524.
[15] 2 October 1522.
[16] 16 April 1523. Cf. 11. 202–205.

Il vigesimo giorno di febraio
chiude oggi l'anno che da questi monti,
che dànno a' Toschi il vento di rovaio,
    qui scesi, dove da diversi fonti
con eterno rumor confondon l'acque
la Tùrrita col Serchio fra duo ponti;   5
    per custodir, come al signor mio piacque,
il gregge grafagnin, che a lui ricorso
ebbe, tosto che a Roma il Leon giacque;
    che spaventato e messo in fuga e morso   10
gli l'avea dianzi, e l'avria mal condotto
se non venia dal ciel iusto soccorso.
    E questo in tanto tempo è il primo motto
ch'io fo a le dee che guardano la pianta
de le cui frondi io fui già così giotto.   15
    La novità del loco è stata tanta
c'ho fatto come augel che muta gabbia,
che molti giorni resta che non canta.
    Maleguzzo cugin, che tacciuto abbia
non ti maravigliar, ma maraviglia   20
abbi che morto io non sia ormai di rabbia
    vedendomi lontan cento e più miglia,
e da neve, alpe, selve e fiumi escluso
da chi tien del mio cor sola la briglia.
    Con altre cause e più degne mi escuso   25
con gli altri amici, a dirti il ver; ma teco
liberamente il mio peccato accuso.
    Altri a chi lo dicessi, un occhio bieco
mi volgerebbe a dosso, e un muso stretto:
— Guata poco cervel! — poi diria seco   30
    — degno uom da chi esser debbia un popul retto,
uom che poco lontan da cinquanta anni
vaneggi nei pensier di giovinetto! —
    E direbbe il Vangel di san Giovanni;
che, se ben erro, pur non son sì losco   35
che 'l mio error non conosca e ch'io nol danni.

Today, the twentieth of February brings to a close
one year since, from these mountains[1] which guide
the northwind to the Tuscans, I descended into this
hollow—where with eternal uproar waters from different sources confound the Turrita with the Serchio
between two bridges[2]—in order to care for, according
to my lord's command, the flock at Garfagnana, which
had recourse to him as soon as the Lion[3] lay dead
in Rome, who till then had frightened and scattered
it, and had torn it from him, and would have brought
it to ruin if just help from heaven had not arrived.
And in all this time this is the first word I have
composed in honor of the goddesses who guard the
plant for whose garlands I was once so eager. The
strangeness of this place has been so extreme that
I have been like a bird whose cage is changed, who
goes many days without singing.

Cousin Maleguzzo, do not marvel that I have been
silent, marvel rather that I am not dead by now with
rage, seeing myself a hundred and more miles distant,
and by snow, mountains, forests, and rivers separated,
from the one[4] who alone holds the reins of my heart.
To tell you the truth, I excuse myself to my other
friends with more dignified reasons; but before you
I openly avow my sin. Another to whom I might tell
it would turn upon me a frown and pursed lips, "See
what a scarcity of brains!" Then to himself, "A worthy
man this to entrust with the government of a people!
A man not distant from his fiftieth year who revels
in the daydreams of a youth!" And he would quote
the Gospel of St John.[5] For, if indeed I err, I am
not so blind as not to recognize my error and condemn

Ma che giova s'io 'l danno e s'io 'l conosco,
se non ci posso riparar, né truovi
rimedio alcun che spenga questo tòsco?
Tu forte e saggio, che a tua posta muovi   40
questi affetti da te, che in noi, nascendo,
natura affige con sì saldi chiovi!
Fisse in me questo, e forse non sì orrendo
come in alcun c'ha di me tanta cura
chi non può tolerar ch'io non mi emendo;   45
e fa come io so alcun, che dice e giura
che quello e questo è becco, e quanto lungo
sia il cimer del suo capo non misura.
Io non uccido, io non percuoto o pungo,
io non do noia altrui, se ben mi dolgo   50
che da chi meco è sempre io mi dilungo:
perciò non dico né a difender tolgo
che non sia fallo il mio; ma non sì grave
che di via più non me perdoni il volgo.
Con manco ranno il volgo, non che lave   55
maggior macchia di questa, ma sovente
titolo al vizio di virtù dato have.
Ermilïan sì del dannaio ardente
come d'Alessio il Gianfa, e che lo brama
ogni ora, in ogni loco, da ogni gente,   60
né amico né fratel né se stesso ama:
uomo d'industria, uomo di grande ingegno,
di gran governo e gran valor si chiama.
Gonfia Rinieri, et ha il suo grado a sdegno;
esser gli par quel che non è, e più inanzi   65
che in tre salti ir non può si mette il segno.
Non vuol che in ben vestire altro lo avanzi;
spenditor, scalco, falconiero, cuoco,
vuol chi lo scalzi, chi gli tagli inanzi.
Oggi uno e diman vende un altro loco;   70
quel che in molti anni acquistar gli avi e i patri
getta a man piene, e non a poco a poco.

it. But what good is it to condemn and to be aware
of it if I cannot correct it, or find a medicine to expel
this poison?

How strong and wise you are, removing at your
leisure these passions from you, which nature makes
fast in us at birth with such firm nails! She fixed
this one in me, which is perhaps not as shocking in
me as in a certain person who is so concerned about
me that he cannot bear it that I do not reform myself.[6]
He behaves like someone I know who says, and swears
to it, that this man and that are cuckolds and fails
to measure the height of his own helmet. I commit
no murders, I do not strike or stab, I give annoyance
to no one, even though I grieve to be so far away
from the one who is always with me. I do not say,
nor do I undertake to plead, that therefore I am not
at fault, but only that my fault is not so serious but
that the vulgar might well pardon in me a much worse
one. With less whitewash the vulgar masses have not
only covered up greater stains than mine, but often
given the title of virtue to vice.

Ermilian,[7] who is as hot for money as Gianfa for
Alexis, and who lusts after it all the time, everywhere,
and from everybody, loves neither friend nor brother
nor himself. He is called a man of industry, a man
of great ingenuity, of great governance and surpassing
worth.

Rinieri[8] swells and holds his present station in
disdain. He thinks he is someone he is not, and sets
himself a mark farther ahead than he can go in three
leaps. He desires no one to surpass him in dressing
well. He needs a steward, a carver, a falconer, a
cook, and someone to take off his shoes, and someone
else to serve the meat on his plate. Today he sells
one property and tomorrow another: what his forefa-
thers acquired over many years he throws away, not
little by little, but by the handful. He is not the man

Costui non è chi morda o che gli latri,
ma liberal, magnanimo si noma
fra li volgar giudici oscuri et atri.   75
Solonnio di facende sì gran soma
tolle a portar, che ne saria già morto
il più forte somier che vada a Roma.
Tu 'l vedi in Banchi, alla dogana, al porto,
in Camera apostolica, in Castello,   80
da un ponte a l'altro a un volgier d'occhi sorto.
Si stilla notte e dì sempre il cervello,
come al Papa ognor dia freschi guadagni
con novi dazii e multe e con balzello.
Gode fargli saper che se ne lagni   85
e dica ognun che a l'util del padrone
non riguardi parenti né compagni.
Il popul l'odia, et ha di odiar ragione,
se di ogni mal che la città flagella
gli è ver ch'egli sia il capo e la cagione.   90
E pur grande e magnifico se appella,
né senza prima discoprirsi il capo
il nobile o il plebeo mai gli favella.
Laurin si fa de la sua patria capo,
et in privato il publico converte;   95
tre ne confina, a sei ne taglia il capo;
comincia volpe, indi con forze aperte
escie leon, poi c'ha 'l popul sedutto
con licenze, con doni e con offerte:
l'iniqui alzando, e deprimendo in lutto   100
li buoni, acquista titolo di saggio,
di furti, stupri e d'omicidi brutto.
Così dà onore a chi dovrebbe oltraggio,
né sa da colpa a colpa scerner l'orbo
giudizio, a cui non mostra il sol mai raggio;   105
e stima il corbo cigno e il cigno corbo;
se sentisse ch'io amassi, faria un viso
come mordesse allora allora un sorbo.

the vulgar snap or snarl at; on the contrary, he is dubbed liberal and magnanimous by vulgar judges, benighted and dismal.

Solonnio[9] undertakes to bear such a heavy load of business that the strongest pack horse bound for Rome would not fail to die beneath it. You see him now in the Banchi,[10] now at the custom-house or the gate, in the Apostolic Chamber, in the Castello, translated from one bridge to another in the twinkling of an eye. Day and night he racks his brain as to how he may bring the pope fresh earnings with new duties and fines and imposts. He rejoices in letting him know that he himself is aggrieved by them, and how everyone says that for the profit of his master he disregards his relatives and friends. The populace hates him, and has cause to hate him, if it be true that he is the sole source of every evil that lacerates the city. Nevertheless, he is proclaimed a great man and magnificent, nor without first baring their heads do nobles or plebeians ever converse with him.

Laurino[11] makes himself lord of his homeland, and converts public into private. He imprisons three and decapitates six. He begins as a fox and then with open force issues forth a lion,[12] after he has seduced the people with liberties and with gifts and donations. Raising the iniquitous and crushing down in sorrow the good, he acquires the title of sage, filthy as he is with thefts and rapes and murders.

Thus the vulgar pay homage to those whom they ought to insult. Nor can their blind judgment, to which the sun never lends a ray, distinguish between one fault and another. They think the raven is a swan, the swan a raven. If they heard that I love, they would make a face as if they had just then bitten

Dica ogniun come vuole, e siagli aviso
quel che gli par: in somma ti confesso　　　　110
che qui perduto ho il canto, il gioco, il riso.

Questa è la prima; ma molt'altre appresso
e molt'altre ragion posso allegarte,
che da le dee m'ha tolto di Parmesso.

Già mi fur dolci inviti a empir le carte　　　　115
li luoghi ameni di che il nostro Reggio,
il natio nido mio, n'ha la sua parte.

Il tuo Mauricïan sempre vagheggio,
la bella stanza, il Rodano vicino,
da le Naiade amato ombroso seggio,　　　　120

il lucido vivaio onde il giardino
si cinge intorno, il fresco rio che corre,
rigando l'erbe, ove poi fa il molino;

non mi si può de la memoria tòrre
le vigne e i solchi del fecondo Iaco,　　　　125
la valle e il colle e la ben posta tórre.

Cercando or questo et or quel loco opaco,
quivi in più d'una lingua e in più d'un stile
rivi traea sin dal gorgoneo laco.

Erano allora gli anni miei fra aprile　　　　130
e maggio belli, ch'or l'ottobre dietro
si lasciano, e non pur luglio e sestile.

Ma né d'Ascra potrian né di Libetro
l'amene valli, senza il cor sereno,
far da me uscir iocunda rima o metro.　　　　135

Dove altro albergo era di questo meno
convenïente a i sacri studi, vuoto
d'ogni iocundità, d'ogni orror pieno?

La nuda Pania tra l'Aurora e il Noto,
da l'altre parti il giogo mi circonda　　　　140
che fa d'un Pellegrin la gloria noto.

Questa è una fossa, ove abito, profonda,
donde non muovo piè senza salire
del silvoso Apennin la fiera sponda.

into a sorb-apple. Let each man say what he pleases; let each keep to his own opinion. In short, I confess to you that here I have lost song, sport, and laughter. This is the principal cause, though I can plead many, many others, that has detained me from the goddesses of Permessus.[13]

Those delightful places, where our Reggio,[14] my native nest, is situated, were once to me sweet invitations to fill pages. I constantly long for your Mauriziano,[15] the beautiful dwelling place, the Rodano[16] nearby, shady seat beloved of the Naiads, the limpid streamlet that circles the garden, the fresh brook that flows, watering the tender grasses, to the place where it turns the mill-wheel. The vines and furrows of the fertile Iaco,[17] the valley and the hill and the well-placed tower cannot be torn from my memory. Seeking there now one and now another shady retreat, in more than one language and style,[18] I called forth rivulets all the way from the Gorgonian lake.[19] My years were beautiful then, between April and May, and now, not to mention July and August, they fly beyond October. But the lovely valleys neither of Ascra nor of Libethra[20] would be able to make issue from me, without a serene heart, joyous rime or measure.

Where was there ever another lodging less suitable to sacred studies than this place, empty of every delight and full of every horror? The barren Pania between Favonius and Notus[21] surrounds me on one side, and on the other the peak that makes the glory of a pilgrim known.[22] This is a deep ditch that I inhabit, and I cannot take a single step outside without ascending the wild slopes of the sylvan Apennines. Whether

O stiami in Ròcca o voglio all'aria uscire,   145
accuse e liti sempre e gridi ascolto,
furti, omicidii, odi, vendette et ire;
    sì che or con chiaro or con turbato volto
convien che alcuno prieghi, alcun minacci,
altri condanni, altri ne mandi assolto;   150
    ch'ogni dì scriva et empia fogli e spacci
al Duca or per consiglio or per aiuto,
sì che i ladron, c'ho d'ogni intorno, scacci.
    Déi saper la licenzia in che è venuto
questo paese, poi che la Pantera,   155
indi il Leon l'ha fra gli artigli avuto.
    Qui vanno li assassini in sì gran schiera
ch'un'altra, che per prenderli ci è posta,
non osa trar del sacco la bandiera.
    Saggio chi dal Castel poco si scosta!   160
Ben scrivo a chi più tocca, ma non torna
secondo ch'io vorrei mai la risposta.
    Ogni terra in se stessa alza le corna,
che sono ottantatre, tutte partite
da la sedizïon che ci soggiorna.   165
    Vedi or se Appollo, quando io ce lo invite,
vorrà venir, lasciando Delfo e Cinto,
in queste grotte a sentir sempre lite.
    Dimandar mi potreste chi m'ha spinto
dai dolci studi e compagnia sì cara   170
in questo rincrescevol labirinto.
    Tu déi saper che la mia voglia avara
unqua non fu, ch'io solea star contento
di quel stipendio che traea a Ferrara;
    ma non sai forse come uscì poi lento,   175
succedendo la guerra, e come volse
il Duca che restasse in tutto spento.
    Fin che quella durò, non me ne dolse;
mi dolse di veder che poi la mano
chiusa restò, ch'ogni timor si sciolse.   180

I stay in the fortress or go into the open air, I always
hear quarrels, accusations, outcries, I hear of thefts,
homicides, hatreds, vendettas, rages; so that sometimes with a clear and sometimes with a troubled
countenance, I must beseech one man, threaten another, here condemn, and there dismiss absolved.
Every day I write, filling sheets of paper, dispatches
to the Duke, some for counsel and others for help,
to drive away the thieves I have around me. You
must be aware of the lawlessness into which this
territory has fallen since first the Panther and then
the Lion had it in their claws.[23] Here the evil-doers
parade in so large a troop that another troop, posted
here to capture them, dare not take its banner from
the sack. Wise is the man who ventures only a short
distance from the citadel! I write to whom it most
concerns[24] but the answer never comes that I would
like. Each district rises up in defiance, all eighty-three
of them, and all divided by the sedition that resides
here. You may now judge whether Apollo, if I invite
him here, will wish to come, leaving Delphi and
Cynthus,[25] into these caverns to hear continual strife.

You may wonder what it was that thrust me from
my sweet studies, and the company so dear to me,
into this noisome labyrinth. You must know that it
could never have been my greed, since I used to be
well contented with the stipend I drew in Ferrara.[26]
But perhaps you do not know how tardily it issued
forth after awhile with the coming of the war,[27] and
how the Duke willed then that it should stop entirely.
While the war lasted I did not complain. But later
it grieved me to see the hand still closed after every

Tanto più che l'ufficio di Melano,
poi che le leggi ivi tacean fra l'armi,
bramar gli affitti suoi mi facea invano.

Ricorsi al Duca: — O voi, signor, levarmi   185
dovete di bisogno, o non v'incresca
ch'io vada altra pastura a procacciarmi.

Grafagnini in quel tempo, essendo fresca
la lor rivoluzion, che spinto fuori
avean Marzocco a procacciar d'altra ésca,

con lettere frequenti e imbasciatori   190
replicavano al Duca, e facean fretta
d'aver lor capi e lor usati onori.

Fu di me fatta una improvisa eletta,
o forse perché il termine era breve
di consigliar chi pel miglior si metta,   195

o pur fu appresso il mio signor più leve
il bisogno de' sudditi che il mio,
di ch'obligo gli ho quanto se gli deve.

Obligo gli ho del buon voler, più ch'io
mi contenti del dono, il quale è grande,   200
ma non molto conforme al mio desio.

Or se di me a questi omini dimande,
potrian dir che bisogno era di asprezza,
non di clemenzia, a l'opre lor nefande.

Come né in me, così né contentezza   205
è forse in lor; io per me son quel gallo
che la gemma ha trovata e non l'apprezza.

Son come il Veneziano, a cui il cavallo
di Mauritania in escellenzia buono
donato fu dal re di Portogallo;   210

il qual, per aggradir il real dono,
non discernendo che mistier diversi
volger temoni e regger briglie sono,

sopra vi salse, e cominciò a tenersi
con mani al legno e co' sproni a la pancia: 215
— Non vuò' — seco dicea — che tu mi versi. —

fear was vanquished, and so much the more since
the benefice of Milan made me long for its revenues
in vain while the laws kept silence there among the
armies.[28] I spoke then to the Duke, "Either you, my
lord, must relieve me of my need, or else let it not
displease you if I go to find myself another pasture."
Meanwhile, their revolution being fresh, the people
of Garfagnana, who had driven the Marzocco out to
forage elsewhere for his food, were soliciting the Duke
with envoys and with frequent letters and were making
haste to regain their governors and their accustomed
honors. An unexpected choice was made of me, either
because the time was short for taking counsel as to
who might best be placed here, or because my lord
held the distress of his subjects at a lower price than
mine—for which consideration I am as much obliged
to him as he deserves.

I am more grateful to him for his good intention
than I am content with his gift, which is great, but
not highly consonant with my desire. Now if he were
to ask these citizens about me, they would tell him
there is need of harshness, and not clemency, for
their nefarious deeds. Just as I am not content with
them, so perhaps they are not with me. As for me,
I am that cock who found the jewel and did not value
it.[29]

I am like the Venetian[30] to whom the King of
Portugal gave a Moroccan stallion of surpassing excel-
lence. To show his gratitude for the royal gift, and
unaware that the skill of the bridle is quite other than
the skill of the helm, he leaps aboard the horse and
secures himself by clutching the reins with his fist
and the paunch with his spurs. "I do not want you
to throw me," he whispers. The horse feels himself

Sente il cavallo pungersi, e si lancia;
e 'l buon nocchier più allora preme e stringe
lo sprone al fianco, aguzzo più che lancia,
    e di sangue la bocca e il fren gli tinge: 220
non sa il cavallo a chi ubedire, o a questo
che 'l torna indietro, o a quel che l'urta e spinge;
    pur se ne sbriga in pochi salti presto.
Rimane in terra il cavallier col fianco,
co la spalla e col capo rotto e pesto.   225
    Tutto di polve e di paura bianco
si levò al fin, dal re mal satisfatto,
e lungamente poi si ne dolse anco.
    Meglio avrebbe egli, et io meglio avrei fatto,
egli il ben del cavallo, io del paese,   230
a dir: — O re, o signor, non ci sono atto;
    sie pur a un altro di tal don cortese.

EX CASTRO NOVO CARFIGNANAE

pricked and leaps forward, and the good helmsman tightens his grip and striking his spurs, sharper than spears, into the horse's sides, tinges his muzzle and the reins with blood. The horse does not know which to obey, the reins that hold him back or the driving spurs that hurl him forward. Yet he soon frees himself in a few leaps, and the cavalier finds himself on the ground with his ribs and shoulder smashed, and his head broken. All white with dust and fear, he gets up at last, ill-satisfied with the king's gift, and complains long afterwards of his injustice.

He would have done better, and so would I, he with his horse and I with my territory, to have said, "O king, O lord, this is not for me. I beg you to be gracious to someone else with such a gift.

NOTES

[1] The Apennines to the north of Tuscany.

[2] At Castelnuovo, situated at the foot of the Apennines, the waters of the Serchio join with those of the swifter flowing Turrita, precisely at the foot of the spur upon which rises the fortress, now called *Rocca Ariostea*, where Ariosto resided during his governorship. The Ponte di S. Lucia, constructed by Castruccio Castracani, whose biography Machiavelli wrote, crosses the Serchio; the Ponte della Madonna, constructed by Borso d'Este, crosses the Turrita.

[3] Pope Leo X.

[4] Alessandra Benucci. See Satire V, preface.

[5] He would be speaking a sacred verity.

[6] We do not know if Ariosto had a particular person in mind.

[7] Francesco Armellini of Perugia served Leo X and his successors. He made himself especially disliked by the Roman people on account of the heavy taxes he levied against them. He was a victim of frequent pasquinades. Leo made him first a cardinal and then Treasurer of the Holy See. According to Ariosto, he loved money as fervently as a certain Gianfa, possibly the humanist Gianfrancesco Fortunio, desired to have homosexual love affairs. The literary allusion is to the opening line of Vergil's second eclogue, "*Formosum pastor Corydon ardebat Alexim. . . .*"

[8] Perhaps Niccolò Ridolfi, one of the nephews whom Leo X elevated to the rank of cardinal. His vanity and prodigality marked him as a target for pasquinades.

[9] Perhaps Cardinal Lorenzo Pucci, Bursar of the Vatican under Leo X.

[10] See Satire II, note 20.

[11] Probably Lorenzo II de' Medici (1492-1519), son of Piero, who assumed the political leadership of Florence in August 1513 after his uncle Giovanni had become Pope Leo X. Leo made him Duke of Urbino in August, 1516. Lorenzo had been raised by an aristocratic mother to care more for personal luxuries and the pomp of nobility than for the welfare of Florence. When in June, 1515, he had himself named Captain General of the Republic for a term of four years, his uncle the pope judged him to be without any experience at all, and charged him with attempting to subvert the traditional posture of the Medici family in Florence, that tacit assumption of power without titles and public dignities. See Satire III, preface, for Ariosto's attendance at Lorenzo's funeral, and Satire VII, 1. 96.

[12] Ariosto probably had Dante or Cicero in mind rather than Machiavelli. In the *Inferno* (XXVII, 11. 73-75), Guido da Montefeltro tells Dante that during his life his works were not those of the lion, but those of the fox. In *De Officiis* (I, 13), Cicero, employing the fox and lion metaphor, points out that the two major sources of injury and injustice are force and fraud. It is possible, however, that Ariosto may have seen a manuscript copy of *The Prince*, or at least gained knowledge by word of mouth of Machiavelli's use of the expression. Certainly when we see it used to describe Lorenzo de' Medici, the dedicatee of *The Prince*, we are entitled to suspect that Ariosto was aware of Machiavelli's little book.

[13] A rivulet which flowed at the foot of Mt. Helicon.

[14] Reggio was Ariosto's birthplace (see Satire III, 1. 13) and the ancient home of his mother's family, the Malaguzzi.

[15] A villa which belonged to the Malaguzzi family. It is situated only a short

distance from the city of Reggio. Students of Ariosto believe that either a large room on the ground floor or another above overlooking the garden served as Ariosto's study during his sojurns at the home of his mother's relatives. Ariosto must have paid the majority of his visits to the Mauriziano during the comparatively blissful years before his father's death in 1500.

[16] A rivulet which flows past the villa.

[17] An allusion to another villa of the Malaguzzi, which they called the Albinea. It was situated very near the Mauriziano on Mt. Iaco, now known as Monteiatico.

[18] In his youth Ariosto wrote Latin as well as Italian verse.

[19] The fountain Hippocrene was produced by a stamp of the hoof of Pegasus, the winged horse that sprang from the blood of Medusa.

[20] Hesiod was born and lived his farmer's life in Ascra in Boeotia near Mt. Helicon. Libethra was a fountain, sacred to the Muses, near Magnesia in Macedonia.

[21] The Pania is a large twin-peaked mountain to the southwest of Castelnuovo di Garfagnana. Favonius is the westwind, and Notus, the southwind. Here, and only here, have I chosen to depart in my translation from Debenedetti's text of the Satires. MS. F contains a revision, in Ariosto's hand, of "Favonio" to "Aurora." Debenedetti follows this text. However, this reading places the mountain to the southeast of Castelnuovo, when it is, in fact, to the southwest. I suspect that, when Ariosto made this revision, he intended to rewrite the entire tercet. Whatever the case may be, there is certainly no virtue in perpetuating an error, unless one's faith in the text is of the sort that moves mountains.

[22] In the tercet as a whole, Ariosto is stating periphrastically—as usual—that he is surrounded by mountains. On one side he has the Apuan Alps, represented by the "barren Pania," and on the other the Apennines, represented by the Monte di san Pellegrino.

[23] Lion is probably a reference to the Marzocco—although Ariosto may specifically have had Leo X in mind, and not Florence in general. A panther served as the insignia of the Republic of Lucca.

[24] Duke Alfonso.

[25] Cynthus, a mountain of Delos, was celebrated as the birthplace of Apollo and Diana.

[26] His salary as a servant of the Duke.

[27] Between France and the Empire. See the preface to the present satire.

[28] The French and Imperial armies.

[29] An allusion to the fable Pullus ad margaritam of Phaedrus (III, xii).

[30] The bad horsemanship of Venetians was a stock joke in Ariosto's time.

SATIRE V

To Messer Annibale Malaguzzi

PREFACE

Sometime in July or August of 1521 Ariosto arrived in Reggio on one of his frequent visits. The first important news to come his way was of the imminent marriage of his cousin Annibale Malaguzzi to Lucrezia Pio, a daughter of the ruling family of Carpi.[1] Ariosto soon discovered that he was the last among all of Annibale's friends and relatives to be informed of the event. Perhaps Annibale had wished to practice discretion in concealing his engagement from his witty, forty-seven-year-old bachelor cousin, the poet known for his protestations that he would never, for marriage or the priesthood, sacrifice his freedom.[2] Or perhaps Annibale had merely neglected to make any personal announcements. Whatever the case, Ariosto felt himself offended, and felt obliged to devise a clever revenge, so he composed the present satire as a piece of ironic advice to his cousin the bridegroom on the subject of marriage. Satire V, a facetious treatise in miniature on the pitfalls of wedded bliss, comes amidst its neighbors as a welcome example of comic relief, fraught with the sensuous and ironic wit to be expected of the author of the *Orlando Furioso*.

Although this appraisal of womanhood, in the tradition of the *querelle des femmes*, is the least autobiographical of all the satires, its humor can only be enhanced by a knowledge, such as remains to us, of the actual women with whom Ariosto consorted during his lifetime. We know very little about Ariosto's amorous involvements, mainly because Ariosto was scrupulously secretive. According to tradition, he had, etched upon the lid of his inkwell, a little cupid with his index finger to his lips. Nevertheless, the relentless research of Michele Catalano, Ariosto's twentieth-century biographer, into every available document relating to the poet's life has made it possible for interested students to form a shadowy picture of the poet's encounters with women. In

Satire V, Ariosto may have intended the joke to be on his cousin, but Annibale probably had the last laugh.

We cannot know, of course, the extent of Ariosto's casual affairs. However, thanks to Annibale Malaguzzi himself, we do have possession of a single anecdote involving a certain Madonna Vinea. In March of 1508, Annibale wrote to his cousin Alessandro Malaguzzi that he had passed by Madonna Vinea's house and seen her sitting by the window. As one of her former lovers, he stopped to pass the time of day, and she gave every indication that she would have liked to welcome him in, but she found herself unable since Ariosto was already inside.[3] Ariosto, a tall, amply bewhiskered gentleman, with large, brilliant, ingratiating eyes,[4] and a good sense of humor and much experience of the world, may well have enjoyed the favors of numerous consenting dames.

About his less casual affairs we have more information. In the present satire, Ariosto deplores the fact that many noblemen of Ferrara were bestowing their attentions upon servant girls and peasant wenches, and begetting bastard children by them. When forced to legitimate their children, those noblemen tainted their lineages by the admission of vulgar stock.[5] While he was writing, Ariosto should have remembered the saying about people who live in glass houses. After his father's death in 1500, he had gone to Canossa to occupy the post of captain, and had taken with him a maidservant named Maria to attend to his personal needs. By 1503, she had given birth to his first illegitimate son. Although Ariosto never formally acknowledged his paternity, other members of his family accepted the boy Giambattista as one of their number. In 1538, five years after his father's death, Giambattista's uncles Galasso and Alessandro had him legitimated, perhaps in anger with Virginio, the poet's second son, against whom they were carrying on a legal action.

Maria was not the only girl of the lower classes to catch Ariosto's eye. There was also Orsolina Sassomarino, the daughter of a humble nailmaker of Ferrara. In 1509, she gave birth to Virginio, the beloved son for whom Ariosto provided an expensive education, an annual income for life, and two documents securing legitimacy. Ariosto enjoyed Orsolina's company until 1514, when he found a husband for her from among the members of his own household. He paid the young man's father a sizable sum of money, and provided the couple with a house and furnishings. He continued to have dealings with Orsolina, though of a business nature, for the rest of his life. She kept the accounts for her husband, who managed some of Ariosto's holdings in Ferrara. As late as 1530, in the second legitimacy proceedings, Ariosto named Orsolina as Virginio's mother.

Ariosto must have taken a serious view of his relationship with Orsolina; but not so serious that she could not be replaced in his affections by another lady who exerted a far more enduring attraction. By 1513 Ariosto had discovered that his secret love for Alessandra Benucci might be returned; consequently, he dissolved his relationship with the docile Orsolina as gracefully as he could. He must have felt genuine affection for Virginio's mother, the nail-maker's daughter. He provided for her welfare, and cared for their son, as scrupulously as could be expected of the best of benefactors and fathers. His aristocratic airs in the present satire should be viewed with suspicion. Ariosto may have intended to give Annibale, his close friend, a laugh at his own expense. When the sun set, and the hour drew near for romance of a tangible nature, Ariosto had proved himself more than once to be a democrat.

In Florence, in the year 1513, on the twenty-fourth of June, the feast day of St. John the Baptist, Ariosto was taken prisoner once and for all by the beauty of the lady of his *Canzoniere*—Alessandra Benucci.[6] He had come to Florence not only to participate in the festivities, but also to seek out among his Florentine friends a spokesman to advance his interests at the court of the new pope, Leo X. His recent disappointment in Rome had not been enough to resign him to failure.[7] Perhaps he encountered Alessandra in the house of his friend Niccolò Vespucci, who was related to her through marriage. According to Ariosto's own description, her long blond hair, adorned with a jewel-studded clasp in the shape of a laurel sprig, fell upon her shoulders, and made a striking contrast with the black silk of her dress, which was embroidered with two vine shoots intertwined. It was not as if he were seeing or admiring her for the first time; however, she had always seemed far beyond his reach. She had lived in Ferrara since the year 1498, when her husband Tito Strozzi, a member of the great family of Florentine bankers, had moved there to serve, at the court of Ercole I, as agent for his wealthy cousins. Ariosto had been forced, for many years, to hold his passion in check. Meanwhile, Alessandra had given birth to six children by her husband and attended to all the duties of a good wife. By 1513, however, Tito Strozzi, who

was more than twice as old as his wife when he had married her
in 1497, had aged rapidly and grown ill. Far from her husband's house
and intoxicated by the carnival atmosphere of Florence, where the
celebrations of the Baptist's day were unusually jubilant that summer
due to the recent exaltation of Giovanni de' Medici, Alessandra, still
comparatively youthful, must have seen no harm in encouraging for
the moment Ariosto's passion, of which she may well have been long
aware. From that day when he first saw a look of consent in her
eyes, Ariosto remained faithful to Alessandra until his death.

In 1515, Tito Strozzi died, leaving his widow with the responsibility
for their six children. He had named her in his will as their guardian,
and given her the usufruct of their patrimony until they came of age—on
the one condition that she decided to remain single. Consequently,
there was to be no marriage in the near future between herself and
Ariosto. Had she remarried, what was left of her dowry would not
have been enough to support her in the style of life to which she
had become accustomed in her late husband's house. Ariosto's finances
were continually on the decline. He could not have supported a wife
used to luxuries that went with a good income, nor could he have
supported her children. Nor did matters improve when he left Cardinal
Ippolito's service in 1517 and entered Duke Alfonso's. In 1522, he wound
up as commissioner of Garfagnana, and he stayed in the post until
1525. Also, until he signed Santa Agata over to Virginio in 1524, Ariosto
could not have married without risking the loss of its income. After
1524, when he no longer held any benefices except the Milan chancellory,
he was finally free to marry, and he did marry Alessandra, though
we cannot determine the date. It was probably after 1525, when he
was in his early fifties and she in her early forties. They kept their
marriage a secret, because of the Strozzi patrimony, and lived in separate
houses.

In the present satire, Ariosto advises his cousin not to marry a woman
accustomed to wealth, because she will bring expenses greater than
he can afford.[8] Of course, Lucrezia Pio's family was far wealthier
than the Malaguzzi family, so Ariosto's barb may well have struck
home. Ironically, however, one of the few letters we possess of
Alessandra's includes a charming request of her wealthy in-laws in
Florence for two beautiful tassels for a belt and a pair of expensive
gloves.[9] She begs them not to mention the purchase to her husband
Tito, because he is always grumbling about her expenditures. Alessandra

appreciated money and the things it could buy. In the same letter, she also requests more gold thread for a lucrative trade she was carrying on with the Jews of Ferrara. Later in life, she was even to take up money-lending, and not to balk at having debtors imprisoned when they could not pay. Alessandra was parsimonious when it came to spending on her children. Her daughters threatened to run away from the convent where she had placed them. It had a bad reputation. Alessandra replied that she would have them thrown in jail if they dared do such a thing, and complained that she could not afford a better convent, nor could she amass dowries for them. Meanwhile, she was busy buying and selling farms and houses with the money from their patrimoney.

Ariosto also advises Annibale to marry a simple girl raised at the distaff in her father's house, and not a society dame raised at the court.[10] It is doubtful that Alessandra could have met this requirement. She enjoyed banquets and festivities and the company of society people. In 1507, she was a member of Laura d'Este's bridal party, and she stayed away from home for a month while the bride was getting installed in her husband's house. In a letter to one of his cousins, Tito Strozzi complained about having to sleep alone.[11] Alessandra also attended the many banquets given by Diana d'Este, and one in particular in honor of Fabrizio Colonna after his capture by Alfonso at the battle of Ravenna. Ariosto attended this banquet, and perhaps, during a game of "secrets," attempted to reveal his love to Alessandra.

The Alessandra Benucci of Ferrara was probably very different from the ideal lady of the Canzoniere. She had not had an easy life; consequently, she made the most of her pleasures, and counted her money while doing so. She had been married in adolescence to a man more than twice her age, and had soon given birth to six children. One cannot help but think that, as a result, she aged more swiftly than was necessary. After her first husband's death, circumstances forced her to carry on, for more than ten years, an affair in secret with the second man in her life, whom she had chosen of her own free will. She suffered the opprobrium of relatives and neighbors. Even when her marriage with Ariosto was finally consummated, she had to keep it secret to protect her income. She could not publicly declare that she had ever been married a second time until three years after Ariosto's death. She lived to be very old, and so alone that she had no one but the church to turn to for comfort. She died in 1552, having willed most of her estate to the monks of San Rocco.

It is generally agreed that Alessandra is the lady to whom Ariosto alludes in the prologue of the *Orlando Furioso* as she who is driving him as mad as Angelica drove Orlando.[12] She must also be the tall, mysterious lady of the Fountain of Dames, and Ariosto her anonymous poet.[13] Although the tradition is false that Alessandra was constantly at Ariosto's side helping him to prepare the final draft of the *Orlando Furioso* for publication in 1516, she could not have commanded the respect and fidelity of a man of Ariosto's acuteness and independence of nature unless she had much to offer in spiritual ways. She had no more than the rudiments of an education. She was no Isabella d'Este; yet one suspects that she would not have been uncomfortable in that great lady's company.

NOTES

[1]For a reasonable estimate of the date of composition for the present satire and the date of Annibale Malaguzzi's wedding, see Catalano, I, 527–529.

[2]See Satire II, 11. 113–123.

[3]Catalano, II, 84.

[4]See Dosso Dossi's portrait.

[5]L1. 55–72.

[6]See the canzone "*Non so s'io potro . . . .*"

[7]See Satire III, preface, and 11. 82–186.

[8]L. 118–144.

[9]Catalano, II, 403.

[10]L. 115–117.

[11]Catalano, II, 404.

[12]I, 2.

[13]XLII, 93–95.

Da tutti li altri amici, Annibale, odo,
fuor che da te, che sei per pigliar moglie:
mi duol che 'l celi a me, che 'l facci lodo.

    Forse mel celi perché alle tue voglie
pensi che oppor mi debbia, come io danni,   5
non l'avendo tolta io, s'altri la toglie.

    Se pensi di me questo, tu te inganni:
ben che senza io ne sia, non però accuso
se Piero l'ha, Martin, Polo e Giovanni.

    Mi duol di non l'avere, e me ne iscuso   10
sopra varii accidenti che lo effetto
sempre dal buon voler tennero escluso;

    ma fui di parer sempre, e così detto
l'ho più volte, che senza moglie a lato
non puote uomo in bontade esser perfetto.   15

    Né senza si può star senza peccato;
che chi non ha del suo, fuor accattarne,
mendicando o rubandolo, è sforzato;

    e chi s'usa a beccar de l'altrui carne,
diventa giotto, et oggi tordo o quaglia,   20
diman fagiani, uno altro dì vuol starne;

    non sa quel che sia amor, non sa che vaglia
la caritade: e quindi avien che i preti
sono sì ingorda e sì crudel canaglia.

    Che lupi sieno e che asini indiscreti   25
mel dovreste saper dir voi da Reggio,
se già il timor non vi tenesse cheti.

    Ma senza che 'l dicate, io me ne aveggio;
de la ostinata Modona non parlo,
che, tutto che stia mal, merta star peggio.   30

    Pigliala, se la vuoi; fa, se déi farlo;
e non voler, come il dottor Buonleo,
a la estrema vecchiezza prolungarlo.

    Quella età più al servizio di Lieo
che di Vener conviensi: si dipinge   35
giovane fresco, e non vecchio, Imeneo.

Annibale, I hear from all my other friends, but not from you, who are about to take a wife. It grieves me that you hide it from me, for I praise this act of yours. But perhaps you conceal it because you think I might oppose your wish, as if, not having taken a wife myself, I am bound to disapprove of everyone who marries. If this is what you think of me, you much deceive yourself. Although I have no wife, I do not therefore reproach Piero, Paolo, Martin, and Giovanni for being married. It pains me not to have a wife, and my only excuse is that assorted circumstances always separated the accomplishment from my good intentions.

But I was always of the opinion, and I have openly declared it on many occasions, that no man can perfect himself in all good qualities without a wife to help him. Nor, wifeless, can one live without sin. The man who does not have his need is forced, begging or stealing, to go foraging elsewhere And he who grows accustomed to pecking at someone else's meat becomes gluttonous, lusting for thrush or quail today, pheasant tomorrow, and the next day, partridge. He knows not what love is, nor does he know the worth of charity. And that is why it happens that priests are such a cruel and ravenous rabble. That they are wolves and impertinent asses you at Reggio[1] would know well how to inform me, if indeed fear did not keep you silent. But I know without your telling me. And I pass over stubborn Modena, in an evil way and meriting worse.

Take a wife if you want one. By all means, if you must. Do not endeavor, like Doctor Buonleo,[2] to delay the decision till your extreme old age. Age is more suitable to the service of Lyaeus[3] than of Venus. Hymen is pictured as a fresh youth, not as an old

Il vecchio, allora che 'l desir lo spinge,
di sé prosume e spera far gran cose;
si sganna poi che al paragon si stringe.

Non voglion rimaner però le spose   40
nel danno; sempre ci è mano adiutrice
che soviene a le pover' bisognose.

E se non fosse ancor, pur ognun dice
che gli è così: non pòn fuggir la fama,
più che del ver, del falso relatrice,   45

la qual patisce mal chi l'onor ama;
ma questa passïon debole e nulla,
verso un'altra maggior, ser Iorio chiama.

— Peggio è — dice — vedersi un ne la culla,
e per casa giocando ir duo bambini,   50
e poco prima nata una fanciulla:

et esser di sua età giunto a' confini,
e non aver che doppo sé lor mostri
la via del bene, e non li fraudi e uncini. —

Pigliala, e non far come alcuni nostri   55
gentiluomini fanno, e molti féro,
ch'or giaccion per le chiese e per li chiostri:

di mai non la pigliar fu il lor pensiero,
per non aver figliuoli che far pezzi
debbian di quel che a pena basta intiero.   60

Quel che acerbi non fér, maturi e mézzi
fan poi con biasmo: truovan ne le ville
e ne le cucine anco a chi far vezzi.

Nascono figli e crescon le faville,
et al fin, pusillanimi e bugiardi,   65
s'inducono a sposar villane e ancille,

perché i figli non restino bastardi.
Quindi è falsificato di Ferrara
in gran parte il buon sangue, se ben guardi;

quindi la gioventù vedi sì rara   70
che le virtudi e li bei studi, e molta
che degli avi materni i stili impara.

man. Old men, when desire pricks them, plume themselves and hope to perform great deeds. They undeceive themselves afterward when they face the test. But their spouses do not wish in consequence to remain deprived. And there is always a helping hand to assist poor women in need. And even if it does not happen, yet everyone will say it has. It is harder for old men to escape false rumors than a true report.

The man who prizes honor ill endures this shame. But Master Iorio[4] calls this torment trivial, or none at all, by comparison with another greater one. "Worse it is," says he, "to see a baby in the cradle, and two little boys run playing through the house, and the eldest child a girl born not long before, when you have arrived at the end of your years and there is no one who afterward will show them the way to security and not cheat and rob them."

Take a wife, and do not live as some of our petty noblemen do, and many did who now repose in churches and cloisters. Their thought was never to take a wife, in order not to have sons, who would divide among many property that scarcely sufficed for one. What these great men abstain from when they are green they do with shame when they are ripe and rotten. They find in huts and kitchens girls to fondle. Sons are born and sparks begin to fly, and at last, faint-hearted and false, they are persuaded to marry country girls and chamber maids, so that their sons will not be bastards. And this is why, if you take a close look, a great part of the good blood of Ferrara is adulterated. This is why you see so few among the younger generation who put their minds to virtue and the beautiful studies, and so many who adopt the style of their maternal ancestors.

Cugin, fai bene a tòr moglier; ma ascolta:
pensaci prima; non varrà poi dire
di non, s'avrai di sì detto una volta.   75

In questo il mio consiglio proferire
ti vuo', e mostrar, se ben non lo richiedi,
quel che tu déi cercar, quel che fuggire.

Tu ti ridi di me forse, e non vedi
come io ti possa consigliar, ch'avuto   80
non ho in tal nodo mai collo né piedi.

Non hai, quando dui giocano, veduto
che quel che sta a vedere ha meglio spesso
ciò che s'ha a far, che 'l giocator, saputo?

Se tu vedi che tocchi, o vada appresso   85
il segno il mio parer, dàgli il consenso;
se non, riputal sciocco, e me con esso.

Ma prima ch'io ti mostri altro compenso,
t'avrei da dir che, se amorosa face
ti fa pigliar moglier, che segui il senso.   90

Ogni virtude è in lei, s'ella ti piace:
so ben che né orator latin, né greco,
saria a dissuadertilo efficace.

Io non son per mostrar la strada a un cieco;
ma se tu il bianco e il rosso e il ner comprendi,   95
essamina il consiglio ch'io te arreco.

Tu che vuoi donna, con gran studio intendi
qual sia stata e qual sia la madre, e quali
sien le sorelle, s'a l'onore attendi.

S'in cavalli, se 'n boi, se 'n bestie tali   100
guardian le razze, che faremo in questi,
che son fallaci più ch'altri animali?

Di vacca nascer cerva non vedesti,
né mai colomba d'aquila, né figlia
di madre infame di costumi onesti.   105

Oltre che il ramo al ceppo s'assimiglia,
il dimestico essempio, che le aggira
pel capo sempre, ogni bontà sgombiglia.

Cousin, you do well to take a wife. But mark this
well. Think carefully before you do. It will avail you
nothing to say no later, if you have once said yes.
In this matter, I wish to offer you my advice, even
though you do not ask for it, and to show you what
you should look for and what you should avoid. But
perhaps you laugh at me, and do not see how I can
counsel you, since I have not put my own feet, or
neck, into the noose. Have you not seen that, when
two are playing, the observer often knows better than
the players what should be done? If you see that
my opinion hits the mark or comes close to it, give
it your agreement; if it does not, call it foolish and
me along with it. But before I show you any remedy,
I should tell you first of all to follow the lead of
your senses if the torch of love makes you take a
wife. She has every virtue if she gives you pleasure.
I am well aware that in this case neither a Latin orator
nor a Greek could say aught to discourage you. I
cannot light the way for a blind man. But if you can
tell white from black and red, study well the counsel
I offer you.

You who want a woman, if you have any consideration for your honor, examine with great care her
mother's past and present behavior, and how her
sisters behave. If with horses and cattle and like beasts
we have regard to the stock they come from, what
should we think of these creatures, who are more
deceiving than other animals?[5] You never saw a cow
give birth to a doe, nor an eagle to a dove, nor a
disgraceful mother to a daughter with honest habits.
Besides the natural resemblance of branches to their
trunks, her mother's familiar example, continually
revolving through her head, will throw every good

Se la madre ha duo amanti, ella ne mira
a quattro e a cinque, e spesso a più di sei,   110
et a quanti più può la rete tira:
  e questo per mostrar che men di lei
non è leggiadra, e non le fur del dono
de la beltà men liberali i dèi.
  Saper la balia e le compagne è buono: 115
se appresso il padre sia nodrita o in corte,
al fuso, a l'ago, o pur in canto e in suono.
  Non cercar chi più dote, o chi ti porte
titoli e fumi e più nobil parenti
che al tuo aver si convenga e alla tua sorte;   120
  ché difficil sarà, se non ha venti
donne poi dietro e staffieri e un ragazzo
che le sciorini il cul, tu la contenti.
  Vorrà una nana, un bufoncello, un pazzo,
e compagni da taola e da giuoco   125
che tutto il dì la tengano in solazzo.
  Né tòr di casa il piè, né mutar loco
vorrà senza carretta; ben ch'io stimi,
fra tante spese, questa spesa poco:
  che se tu non la fai, che sei de' primi   130
e di sangue e d'aver ne la tua terra,
non la farà già quei che son degli imi.
  E se mattina e sera ondeggiando erra
con cavalli a vettura la Giannicca,
che farà chi del suo li pasce e ferra?   135
  Ma se l'altre n'han dui, ne vuol la ricca
quattro; se le compiaci, più che 'l conte
Rinaldo mio la te aviluppa e ficca;
  se le contrasti, pon la pace a monte,
e come Ulisse al canto, tu l'orecchia   140
chiudi a pianti, a lamenti, a gridi et onte;
  ma non le dir oltraggio, o t'apparecchia
cento udirne per uno, e che ti punga
più che punger non suol vespe né pecchia.

quality into confusion. If her mother has two lovers,
she will aim at four, or five, and perhaps at more
than six, and she will haul in the net over as many
more as she can. And all this to show that she is
no less alluring than her mother, and that the gods
were to her no less liberal with the gift of beauty.

It is also good to know her nurse and her companions, and to learn whether she was raised in her father's
house or at the court, at the distaff and the needle,
or in singing and playing. Do not look for the wife
who will bring you the richest dowry, with titles and
vanities, and relatives more noble than befit your rank;
because it will be hard for you to please her unless
you give her twenty dames in waiting to follow her
about, and footmen, and a boy to air out her posterior.[6]
She will desire a she-dwarf, a midget buffoon, a fool,
and companions at table and play to keep her amused
from dawn to dusk. Nor will she wish to set foot
outside the house, nor to move from one place to
another, without a carriage, even though I attach small
importance to this cost among so many others. For
if you, who are among the first in your district in
both blood and wealth, will not make this expense,
they will not make it either who are among the last.
And if Gianicca[7] goes tossing about from morning
to night with hired horses, what will the person do
who must feed horses and shoe them at his own cost?
But if other women have two horses, the rich wife
will desire four. And if you humor her, she will snare
you and impale you more cleverly than the wife of
my Count Rinaldo;[8] but if you oppose her, then scatter
your peace to the winds, and like Ulysses with the
sirens, stop up your ears to weeping and wailing and
screams and abuses. Dare not affront her, or prepare
yourself to hear a hundred insults in return for one,
and be assured that they will sting you harder than

Una che ti sia ugual teco si giunga,   145
che por non voglia in casa nuove usanze,
né più del grado aver la coda lunga.

Non la vuo' tal che di bellezze avanze
l'altre, e sia in ogni invito, e sempre vada
capo di schiera per tutte le danze.   150

Fra bruttezza e beltà truovi una strada
dove è gran turba, né bella né brutta,
che non t'ha da spiacer, se non te aggrada.

Che quindi esce, a man ritta truova tutta
la gente bella, e dal contrario canto   155
quanta bruttezza ha il mondo esser ridutta.

Quinci più sozze, e poi più sozze quanto
tu vai più inanzi; e quindi truovi i visi
più di bellezza e più tenere il vanto.

S'ove déi tòr la tua vuoi ch'io te avisi,   160
o ne la strada, o a man ritta nei campi
dirò, ma non di là troppo divisi.

Non ti scostar, non ir dove tu inciampi
in troppo bella moglie, sì che ognuno
per lei d'amor e di desire avampi.   165

Molti la tenteranno, e quando ad uno
repugni, o a dui, o a tre, non star in speme
che non ne debbia aver vittoria alcuno.

Non la tòr brutta; che torresti insieme
perpetua noia; medïocre forma   170
sempre lodai, sempre dannai le estreme.

Sia di buona aria, sia gentil, non dorma
con gli occhi aperti; che più l'esser sciocca
d'ogni altra ria deformità deforma.

Se questa in qualche scandalo trabocca,   175
lo fa palese in modo che dà sopra
li fatti suoi facenda ad ogni bocca.

L'altra, più saggia, si conduce all'opra
secretamente, e studia, come il gatto,
che la immondïzia sua la terra copra.   180

wasps and bees. Let a wife be joined to you who
is your equal, a wife who will not endeavor to start
new customs in your house, and who will not have
a tail lengthier than befits your rank.

Do not desire her to be such that she surpasses
all others in beauty and is invited everywhere and
leads the troop through all the dances. Between
ugliness and beauty find the path where the great
multitude resides, those who are neither beautiful nor
ugly, and do not much displease you even though
they may not be very welcome. The man who leaves
this path finds on the right only the beautiful and
on the left as much ugliness gathered as the world
embraces. On the left they become fouler and fouler
the farther you advance; on the right you behold their
faces increase in loveliness more and more. If you
wish me to tell you where you should choose your
wife, I will say, either on the path or on the right
side in the fields, but not too far from the path. Do
not stray too far, do not go where you may stumble
upon too fine a wife, so that everyone erupts in flames
of love and longing for her. Many will attempt her,
and even if she repulses one or two or three, do
not rest in hope that no one will win a victory. Do
not choose an ugly wife, either, for with her you
would take on perpetual annoyance. For my part,
I have always praised the mean and mistrusted the
extremes.

Let her be gracious and gentle. Let her not fall
asleep open eyed, for stupidity warps a woman worse
than any other disgusting disfigurement. If a stupid
woman slips into a scandal, she makes it public, giving
every tongue something to work with concerning her
affairs. But a wise wife manages her business secretly
and makes sure like a cat that the earth covers up

Sia piacevol, cortese, sia d'ogni atto
di superbia nimica, sia gioconda,
non mesta mai, non mai col ciglio attratto.

Sia vergognosa; ascolti e non risponda
per te dove tu sia; né cessi mai,
né mai stia in ozio; sia polita e monda. 185

De dieci anni o di dodici, se fai
per mio consiglio, fia di te minore;
di pare o di più età non la tòr mai:

perché passando, come fa, il megliore
tempo e i begli anni in lor prima che in noi, 190
ti parria vecchia, essendo anco tu in fiore.

Però vorrei che 'l sposo avesse i suoi
trent'anni, quella età che 'l furor cessa
presto al voler, presto al pentirse poi. 195

Tema Dio, ma che udir più d'una messa
voglia il dì non mi piace; e vuo' che basti
s'una o due volte l'anno si confessa.

Non voglio che con gli asini che basti
non portano abbia pratica, né faccia 200
ogni dì tórte al confessore e pasti.

Voglio che se contenti de la faccia
che Dio le diede, e lassi il rosso e il bianco
a la signora del signor Ghinaccia.

Fuor che lisciarsi, uno ornamento manco
d'altra ugual gentildonna ella non abbia; 205
liscio non vuo', né tu credo il vogli anco.

Se sapesse Erculan dove le labbia
pon quando bacia Lidia, avria più a schivo
che se baciasse un cul marzo di scabbia. 210

Non sa che 'l liscio è fatto col salivo
de le giudee che 'l vendon; né con tempre
di muschio ancor perde l'odor cattivo.

Non sa che con la merda si distempre
di circoncisi lor bambini il grasso 215
d'orride serpi che in pastura han sempre.

her filth. Let your wife be pleasant and courteous. May she be an enemy of every haughty act, joyous, never melancholy, and never with a knitted brow. Let her be modest. May she listen and never speak for you when you are present. May she never cease to be busy, nor ever stand idle. Let her be clean and pure.

If you follow my advice, she ought to be ten or twelve years younger than you. Never take a wife your own age or older. Since the best season and the beautiful years pass, as they do, earlier in women than in us, she will seem old to you while you are still in flower. Therefore, I should desire that the husband had reached his thirtieth year, that age when furor, quick to desire, and quick to repent, has ceased.

May she fear God, but if she wished to attend more than one mass a day I should be displeased, and I would have it suffice if she confessed herself once or twice a year. I should not wish her to have business with those asses who bear no burdens, or to be making tarts and repasts every day for her confessor.

And I prefer that she be contented with the face God gave her, and that she leave the red and the white to Signor Ghinaccia's lady.[9] Except for make-up, may she never have a single ornament less than any other gentlewoman of her rank. I dislike cosmetics and I am sure that you agree. If Erculano[10] knew where he sets his lips when he kisses his Lidia, he would be more disgusted than if he had kissed an arse-hole rotten with scabs. He is not aware that make-up is made with the saliva of the Jews who sell it. Nor does it lose its filthy odor when it is tempered with musk. He does not know that with the dung of their circumcised babies they mix the fat of horrid serpents they always keep in sustenance.

Oh quante altre spurcizie a dietro lasso,
di che s'ungono il viso, quando al sonno
se acconcia il steso fianco, e il ciglio basso!
Sì che quei che le baciano, ben ponno   220
con men schivezza e stomachi più saldi
baciar lor anco a nuova luna il conno.
Il sollimato e gli altri unti ribaldi,
di che ad uso del viso empion gli armari,
fan che sì tosto il viso lor s'affaldi;   225
o che i bei denti, che già fur sì cari,
lascian la bocca fetida e corrotta,
o neri e pochi restano, e mal pari.
Segua le poche, e non la volgar frotta;
né sappia far la tua bianco né rosso,   230
ma sia del filo e de la tela dotta.
Se tal la truovi, consigliar ti posso
che tu la prenda; se poi cangia stile,
e che se tiri alcun gallante a dosso,
o faccia altra opra enorme, e che simìle   235
il frutto, in tempo del ricor, non esca
ai molti fior ch'avea mostrato aprile;
de la tua sorte, e non di te t'incresca,
che per indiligenza e poca cura
gusti diverso a l'apetito l'ésca.   240
Ma chi va cieco a prenderla a ventura,
o chi fa peggio assai, che la conosce,
e pur la vuol, sia quanto voglia impura,
se poi pentito si batte le cosce
altro che sé non de' imputar del fallo,   245
né cercar compassion de le sue angosce.
Poi ch'io t'ho posto assai bene a cavallo,
ti voglio anco mostrar come lo guidi,
come spinger lo déi, come fermallo.
Tolto che moglie avrai, lascia li nidi   250
degli altri, e sta sul tuo; che qualche augello,
trovandol senza te, non vi si annidi.

O how many other filthy ointments do I leave unmentioned, with which the women grease their faces before
they stretch their bodies out and lower their lids in
sleep! Those who kiss them could indeed with less
revulsion and calmer stomachs kiss their privates under
the new moon. The sublimate and the other pernicious
ointments, with which they stuff their wardrobes for
the benefit of their faces, are what cause their skin
to wrinkle up so quickly and cause their beautiful
teeth, so precious once, to rot and defile their mouths
and to become black and scarce and uneven.

May she imitate the few, and not the vulgar herd.
Nor should your wife know how to paint with red
and white. Better if she is skilled with cloth and thread.
If you find such a woman, I advise you to take her.
If afterward she changes her style and hoists some
gallant on her back, or involves herself in some other
enormity, if in the season of plenty, fruit does not
issue from the many blossoms that were displayed
in April, curse your misfortune. Do not reproach
yourself, for it is not on account of your own negligence
or lack of care that you taste food disagreeable to
your appetite. It is for the man who blindly takes
his chances on a wife, or for him who does much
worse, knowing her and still desiring her, however
impure the desire, to slap his thighs in repentance,
and to blame no one but himself for his mistake,
and in his agony to look nowhere for sympathy.

Now that I have mounted you so tidily on your
mare, I must show you how to guide her, how to
urge her on and how to halt her. Once you have
taken a wife, forsake the nests of others and roost
in your own, or some other bird, finding it empty,
will settle there himself. Caress your wife and compli-

Falle carezze, et amala con quello
amor che vuoi ch'ella ami te; aggradisci,
e ciò che fa per te paiati bello.   255
   Se pur tal volta errasse, l'ammonisci
sanza ira, con amore; e sia assai pena
che la facci arrossir senza por lisci.
   Meglio con la man dolce si raffrena
che con forza il cavallo, e meglio i cani   260
le lusinghe fan tuoi che la catena.
   Questi animal, che son molto più umani,
corregger non si dén sempre con sdegno,
né, al mio parer, mai con menar de mani.
   Ch'ella ti sia compagna abbi disegno;   265
non come in comperata per tua serva
reputa aver in lei dominio e regno.
   Cerca di sodisfarle ove proterva
non sia la sua domanda, e, compiacendo,
quanto più amica puoi te la conserva.   270
   Che tu la lasci far non te commendo,
senza saputa tua, ciò ch'ella vuole;
che mostri non fidarti anco riprendo.
   Ire a conviti e publiche carole
non le vietar, né, a li suoi tempi, a chiese,   275
dove ridur la nobiltà si suole:
   gli adùlteri né in piazza né in palese,
ma in case de vicini e de commatri,
balie e tal genti, han le lor reti tese.
   Abbile sempre, ai chiari tempi e agli atri,   280
dietro il pensier, né la lasciar di vista:
che 'l bel rubar suol far gli uomini latri.
   Studia che compagnia non abbia trista:
a chi ti vien per casa abbi avvertenza,
che fuor non temi, e dentro il mal consista;   285
   ma studia farlo cautamente, senza
saputa sua; che si dorria a ragione
s'in te sentisse questa diffidenza.

ment and love her as you would have her love you.
Let all she does for you be welcome and agreeable
to you. If, however, she errs sometimes, admonish
her, not with anger, but with love. And consider it
sufficient penance, if you make her blush without
her cosmetics. Better to rein in a horse with a gentle
hand than forcibly; coaxing makes you master of a
dog sooner than the chain. Creatures which are much
more human than these should not be corrected all
the time with anger, nor, in my opinion, ever with
a slap of the hand. Plan for your wife to be your
companion, and do not boast that you have dominion
and sway over her as if you had bought a slave. Try
to satisfy her when her demands are not exorbitant,
and by complying with them, preserve her friendship
as much as you can.

I find it unadvisable that you should let her do
as she pleases without your knowledge. But I warn
you not to show signs of mistrust. Do not forbid her
to go to banquets and to public dances, nor, when
she pleases, to churches where the nobility are accustomed to gather. Adulterers, neither in the market-
place nor in the open, but in the houses of neighbors,
gossips, nurses, and such rabble, spread their nets.
Keep her always in mind, during the light hours and
the dark, and do not let her out of your sight. Easy
pickings make men thieves. Make sure she keeps no
evil company. Be aware of all who come to visit her
at your house, so that you do not fear what is outside
while the disease rages within. But above all carry
on your surveillance stealthily, without her knowing.
She would have a right to sorrow if she sensed in
you this uncertainty. Shield her as much as possible

Lievale quanto puoi la occasïone
d'esser puttana, e pur se avien che sia,   290
almen che ella non sia per tua cagione.

Io non so la miglior di questa via
che già t'ho detta, per schivar che in preda
ad altri la tua donna non se dia.

Ma s'ella n'avrà voglia, alcun non creda   295
di ripararci: ella saprà ben come
far ch'al suo inganno il tuo consiglio ceda.

Fu già un pittor, Galasso era di nome,
che dipinger il diavolo solea
con bel viso, begli occhi e belle chiome;   300
né piei d'augel né corna gli faccea,
né faccea sì leggiadro né sì adorno
l'angel da Dio mandato in Galilea.

Il diavol, riputandosi a gran scorno
se fosse in cortesia da costui vinto,   305
gli apparve in sogno un poco inanzi il giorno,
e gli disse in parlar breve e succinto
ch'egli era, e che venia per render merto
de l'averlo sì bel sempre dipinto;
però lo richiedesse, e fosse certo   310
di subito ottener le sue domande,
e di aver più che non se gli era offerto.

Il meschin, ch'avea moglie d'admirande
bellezze, e ne vivea geloso, e n'era
sempre in sospetto et in angustia grande,   315
pregò che gli mostrasse la maniera
che s'avesse a tener, perché il marito
potesse star sicur de la mogliera.

Par che 'l diavolo allor gli ponga in dito
uno annello, e ponendolo gli dica: 320
— Fin che ce 'l tenghi, esser non puoi tradito. —

Lieto ch'omai la sua senza fatica
potrà guardar, si sveglia il mastro, e truova
che 'l dito a la moglier ha ne la fica.

from all occasion to play the whore, and if nevertheless it happens that she does, at least let it not be through your fault. I am acquainted with no method, better than this which I have shown you, to prevent your lady from giving herself in prey to others. But if she really desires to do so, there is no way to prevent her. Full well she knows how to arrange it so that your prudence yields to her deception.

There once was a painter by the name of Galasso[11] who used to paint the devil with a beautiful face, with brilliant eyes, and lovely hair. He never gave him horns and the claws of a hawk. Nor did he make the angel sent by God into Galilee so graceful and lustrous. The devil, who would have held himself greatly shamed if he were surpassed in courtesy by this man, appeared to him in a dream just before dawn, and told him in words both brief and succinct who he was and that he had come to reward him for having always depicted his person with such allure. Galasso might ask him for anything he wished and be certain to obtain his desire immediately, and perhaps even more than he hoped for. The poor wretch, who had a wife of wondrous beauty, and who lived in constant jealousy, forever suspicious of her and in dire distress, prayed the devil to show him the course a husband must take if he wished to rest assured of his wife. Then the devil seemed to slip a ring on his finger, and while securing it there, seemed to say, "As long as you wear this ring, you cannot be betrayed." Glad that henceforth he would be able to guard his wife without toil, the master woke up and found his finger in her vagina.

Questo annel tenga in dito, e non lo muova   325
mai chi non vuol ricevere vergogna
da la sua donna; e a pena anco gli giova,
    pur ch'ella voglia, e farlo si dispogna.

Let the man who does not wish to be disgraced
by his wife wear this ring on his finger, and never
remove it. But even that will scarce avail him, if once
the desire comes upon her and she disposes herself
to action.

NOTES

[1] Reggio fell to the troops of Julius II in 1512, and Alfonso did not retake the province until 1523. Papal forces had already conquered Modena in 1510, and only with the sack of Rome in 1527 did Alfonso have the opportunity to reoccupy it. Lines 29-30 may refer specifically to the Duke's arrival in July, 1521, before the gates of Modena with some artillery and a small army, only to be repulsed after having successfully retaken the towns of Finale and San Felice. Catalano argues that this is the case and that Satire V must have been written shortly after the event.

[2] This is probably Scipione Bonlei, a doctor in the service of Cardinal Ippolito.

[3] Lyaeus was another name for Bacchus.

[4] An unidentified person.

[5] Cf. Horace, *Carmina*, IV, iv, 29: "*Fortes creantur fortibus et bonis;/est in iuvencis, est in equis patrum/virtus, neque imbellem feroces/progenerant aquilae columbam.*" The idea goes back to Plato's Republic.

[6] The boy is a page to bear up the lady's train.

[7] Another unidentified person.

[8] Rinaldo was Ludovico's cousin on his father's side of the family. He was slightly older than the poet and shared a very close friendship with him. After having entered the service of Ercole I in 1499, he rose swiftly to become the leader of the Ariosto family of Ferrara. He was captain of Reggio from 1505 to 1506, commissioner of Garfagnana from 1507 to 1509, of Montagnana in 1510, and of the Romagna from 1514 to 1516. He accompanied Alfonso I to the court of Julius II in 1512, and was at his master's side during the fortunate flight from Rome. He served as ambassador to the Medici, and in 1518, was sent to the French court as orator for the Estensi. Rinaldo frequently helped Ludovico out of financial difficulties. He also enjoyed the company of his younger cousin at the banquets and festivities of Ferrarese society. Although Rinaldo married three times, he so delighted in philandering that he contracted syphilis. He carried on a steady correspondence with his fellow sufferer, Isabella d'Este, in order to obtain the latest cures; but to no avail, for the disease finally killed him in 1519. Immediately, Ludovico found himself embroiled in a bitter litigation with the Duke and the Cardinal over Rinaldo's inheritance, which should have brought him considerable wealth. However, the case was not closed until long after his death. The reference in the lines above is to Rinaldo's third wife, Contarina Farnese, who spent money recklessly in order to take a position of prominence among the great ladies of Ferrarese high society.

[9] The name suggests one who smirks, sneers, or makes ugly faces.

[10] A third unidentified person.

[11] Galasso might be Ariosto's contemporary, the Ferrarese painter Galasso Galassi. The following salacious story was quite popular during the Renaissance. Ariosto's source was Poggio's *Facetiae*, cxxxii, in which the Milanese humanist Francesco Filelfo served as protagonist. Rabelais also used the story in his *Tiers Livre*, ch. xxviii.

SATIRE VI

To Messer Pietro Bembo

PREFACE

To the Most Reverend Monsignor Pietro Bembo.

Magnificent and Most Reverend Messer Pietro, my very distinguished patron. My son Virginio is on his way to Padua to take up a course of studies. I have directed him, before he does anything else, to go pay reverence to Your Lordship, and to make himself known to you as your servant. I pray Your Lordship to be content to lend him, when necessary, your favor, and to admonish him whenever you see him, and to urge him not to waste his time. I shall ever commend myself to you and my services will always be at your command.

I am almost finished revising my *Furioso*.[1] When I am, I shall come to Padua to confer with Your Lordship, and to learn from you whatever I am incapable of understanding by myself. May God always preserve you.

Ferrara, xxiii February MDXXXI.
Your Lordship's
Servant Ludovico Ariosto.

This famous letter from the reigning poet of Italy to the literary arbiter of the age was written approximately five years after the estimated date of composition for Satire VI. In this satire, written toward the end of the year 1524 or the beginning of 1525, Ariosto requests Bembo's advice as to who might best serve as Greek tutor to his fifteen-year-old son. By 1531, the date of the letter, Virginio was a young man, ready to begin a course of professional studies in canon law at the University of Padua. More interesting to students of literature than Virginio's education, however, is the intimacy between Ariosto and Bembo which permitted Ariosto twice to request the great man's personal intervention in a family matter.

By the time Ariosto addressed the present satire to Bembo, the two men must have known each other for almost twenty-six years. From 1498 to 1500 Bernardo Bembo resided in Ferrara as Venetian envoy, and his son Pietro lived with him. It would have been difficult for a talented young writer and scholar with connections at the Estensi court to avoid attending the very popular performances of Latin comedies in Italian translation produced there. One of the more ingenious actor-director-translators in Duke Ercole I's theatre company happened to be Ludovico Ariosto. No doubt, the two young poets must have found in each other much that was attractive.[2] Ariosto must have taken a particularly sharp interest in Bembo's early lyrics in the vernacular, and may have seen in their pure Petrarchan style a promise that the Italian vernacular had a future in literature as bright as the golden past of the Latin language.

By the time of Bembo's second lengthy stay in Ferrara from 1502 to 1503, the relationship had not only progressed to a sharing of intimacies, but had become portentous for literature. Bembo had just finished preparing his Aldine editions of Petrarch's *Canzoniere* and Dante's *Divine Comedy*, and was in the act of writing the *Asolani*. It is believed that Ariosto was privy from the start to the infatuation Bembo felt for Lucrezia Borgia, the dedicatee of the *Asolani*, and that he, personally, in the author's absence, was entrusted with conveying to Lucrezia a copy of the manuscript as soon as the work was completed.[3] As a result of his friendship with Bembo, and as a result of Bembo's theories about, and practice in, the vernacular, Ariosto decided during this period to turn once and for all from Latin to Italian. In the *Asolani*, Bembo had imitated the language of the Tuscan masters of the *trecento*, in particular Boccaccio, with the same reverence and application to detail traditionally reserved for the imitation of Cicero and Vergil in modern Latin. He had proved that Italian could be approached with the seriousness customarily reserved only for classical languages.

A famous anecdote dates from this period. Ariosto is supposed to have informed Bembo of his decision to devote himself to writing Italian, and Bembo is supposed to have responded by urging the poet not to be rash, and by suggesting that he would succeed better with Latin. Ariosto replied tartly that he would rather be first among writers of Italian than in the second rank among Latinists, and that he well knew the bent of his own genius. If the anecdote is true, we would be unfair to blame Bembo for his misjudgment. By 1503, Ariosto had very little to show for himself in Italian, while he had in fact demonstrated considerable facility in Latin.

Bembo spent the years from 1506 to 1511 at the court of Urbino where Ariosto may have had ample opportunity to continue his friendship with him. No doubt Bembo was among the group of Ariosto's friends there who served as an audience for readings from early drafts of the *Orlando Furioso*. With the election of Leo X in 1512, Bembo moved to Rome to take up a long residence. Leo made him a papal secretary in 1513. Perhaps he was present for the splendid production of *I Suppositi* in the Vatican Palace in 1519. Certainly Ariosto, on his frequent missions to the papacy on behalf of Cardinal Ippolito, found time to spend with Bembo and his other friends in Rome. Bembo, in his new post as papal secretary, was given the opportunity to make up for the doubts he might once have expressed about Ariosto's future as a poet in Italian. In the praise accorded Ariosto in the papal privilege of 20 June 1515 granting the poet literary rights to his poem, Bembo, along with Sadoleto, showed his official admiration for the *Orlando Furioso*.[4]

In 1521, Bembo retired from Rome to Padua in ill health. In 1525, the *Prose della volgar lingua*, his most explicit statement of his theories about the vernacular, was published. As one might conclude from the letter of 1531, Ariosto allowed himself to be guided by Bembo's precepts in his revisions for the third edition of the *Orlando Furioso*. However, it was not in Ariosto's character to submit slavishly to anyone's precepts. Bembo may have been the most revered critic of his day, but Ariosto was first among poets. He deferred to Bembo in questions of grammar but remained eclectic in his choice of vocabulary, using modern words and dialectal spellings whenever they best expressed his meaning and mood, or lent grace to his stanza. Ariosto must have been deeply impressed by Bembo's erudition, and no doubt felt himself to be very much the inferior classicist in an age when the classics reigned supreme; but he gave no indication that he considered Bembo his master in Italian.

Apart from the castigation of humanists, and the request for a tutor for Virginio, the present satire comprises in the main Ariosto's excuse for never having learned Greek: he never had the time. At his father's insistence, he had spent his adolescence, from fifteen years of age to twenty, studying civil law at the University of Ferrara. When finally by 1494, his father had given him up as hopeless for the law, and he had managed by himself to find a tutor in humanist studies, Gregorio da Spoleto, he realized that he would have to concentrate all his time on the Latin classics he had so long neglected. However, even these relatively elementary studies were cut short. By 1497, his father had suffered his final disgrace and been forced to resign as Commissioner of the Romagna.[5] The family income needed supplementing. The elder Ariosto managed to secure his son a place on Duke Ercole I's payroll. With his new responsibilities as courtier, Ariosto could not have had very much time to devote to his studies under Gregorio. In any case, Gregorio was off to France in 1499, and died there in the employ of his new pupil Francesco Sforza. Then came the worst hardship. Ariosto's father died in 1500, and the poet found himself in the role of *pater-familias* with nine brothers and sisters to support and an aged mother. From the time he set off to occupy the captaincy of Canossa in 1500, through his years of service under Cardinal Ippolito and Duke Alfonso, up to the last years of his life, Ariosto was loaded down with duties attaching to his position at the court. What time he had left over for literature he devoted to more important projects than learning Greek.

It seems a little amusing in retrospect that one of the greatest poets in the history of literature should have adopted such an apologetic posture with respect to his ignorance of Greek. Of course, he was addressing Bembo, the great classicist, and of course, the age he lived in held the classics in the highest esteem; but one suspects that Ariosto did not feel quite as culturally deprived by his lack of Greek as he leads us to believe in the present satire. Perhaps in this connection, we should keep in mind Ariosto's Horatian model for the *Satires*. Possibly, Ariosto is requesting his cultured reader to see the similarity between Horace's father and himself, intent upon procuring the best possible education for his son. No doubt he also intended the reader to contrast Horace's good fortune in having a father sympathetic to his intellectual needs, with his own bad fortune in having a father who drove him remorselessly to work at a course of studies he hated. In the present satire, Ariosto makes reference to his lack of Greek only to reinforce the contrast he has been drawing throughout the *Satires* between Horace's good life in the Rome of Maecenas and Augustus and his own misfortunes in the Italy of the Medici and the Estensi. As to whether or not Ariosto would in actuality have taken up Greek had circumstances been more favorable, perhaps we should reserve judgement. And in any case, it does not matter.

When Ariosto was composing the present satire, he did not need to remind his friend in Padua that he was still Commissioner of Garfagnana. He had been Commissioner for almost three years. By then, Bembo and all of Ariosto's other friends must have grown so used to his complaints that he would have been presuming upon their patience had he said anything more about the matter. The mere unstated fact must have served in Bembo's mind to arouse sympathy for Ariosto, as he read in the epistle that lay before him the poet's reminiscences of hardships that had begun more than a quarter of a century in the past.

NOTES

[1] For the third edition, published in 1532.

[2] We have a literary document from this period attesting to a relationship between the two: *Lirica Latina*, VII.

[3] Catalano publishes a letter (I, 463) from Bembo to Lucrezia, and argues that the Ludovico mentioned repeatedly in it is indeed the poet.

[4] See Catalano, II, 149.

[5] See Satire III, n. 2.

Bembo, io vorrei, come è il commun disio
de' solliciti padri, veder l'arti
che essaltan l'uom, tutte in Virginio mio;
    e perché di esse in te le miglior parti
veggio, e le più, di questo alcuna cura   5
per l'amicizia nostra vorrei darti.

Non creder però ch'esca di misura
la mia domanda, ch'io voglia tu facci
l'ufficio di Demetrio o di Musura
    (non si dànno a' par tuoi simili impacci),   10
ma sol che pensi e che discorri teco,
e saper dagli amici anco procacci
    s'in Padova o in Vinegia è alcun buon greco,
buono in scïenzia e più in costumi, il quale
voglia insegnarli, e in casa tener seco.   15

Dottrina abbia e bontà, ma principale
sia la bontà: che, non vi essendo questa,
né molto quella alla mia estima vale.

So ben che la dottrina fia più presta
a lasciarsi trovar che la bontade: 20
sì mal l'una ne l'altra oggi s'inesta.

O nostra male aventurosa etade,
che le virtudi che non abbian misti
vici nefandi si ritrovin rade!

Senza quel vizio son pochi umanisti   25
che fe' a Dio forza, non che persüase,
di far Gomorra e i suoi vicini tristi:
    mandò fuoco da ciel, ch'uomini e case
tutto consumpse; et ebbe tempo a pena
Lot a fugir, ma la moglier rimase.   30

Ride il volgo, se sente un ch'abbia vena
di poesia, e poi dice: — È gran periglio
a dormir seco e volgierli la schiena. —

Et oltra questa nota, il peccadiglio
di Spagna gli dànno anco, che non creda   35
in unità del Spirto il Padre e il Figlio.

Bembo, in keeping with the usual desire of attentive fathers, I would like to see in my Virginio all the arts that ennoble a man; and since I see in you their best features and greatest number, I, in the name of our friendship, would like to give you some care of this matter. Do not conclude, however, that my request is out of measure, that I desire you to perform the offices of a Demetrius or a Musurus[1] (such annoyances are not for people like you); I only wish you to reflect and take counsel, and to inquire among your friends, whether there is a good Greek in Padua or Venice, good in his knowledge and better in his behavior, who would teach my son and lodge him in his house.

Make sure he is learned and good, but first of all good, for without goodness learning, in my opinion, is worth little. I know indeed that learning is much more quickly to be found than goodness, since these days the one agrees so poorly with the other. O infelicitous age of ours when virtues that nefarious vices have not polluted are so rarely to be found!

Few humanists[2] are without that vice which did not so much persuade, as forced, God to render Gomorrah and her neighbor wretched! He sent down fire from heaven that consumed men and houses all, and Lot had scarcely time to flee, while his wife remained behind. The vulgar laugh when they hear of someone who possesses a vein of poetry, and then they say, "It is a great peril to turn your back if you sleep next to him."

And beyond this blemish, the peccadillo of Spain[3] damns him as well, which does not concede belief in the Father, the Son, and the Holy Ghost; but he

Non che contempli come l'un proceda
da l'altro o nasca, e come il debol senso
ch'uno e tre possano essere conceda;
    ma gli par che non dando il suo consenso   40
a quel che approvan gli altri, mostri ingegno
da penetrar più su che 'l cielo immenso.
Se Nicoletto o fra Martin fan segno
d'infedele o d'eretico, ne accuso
il saper troppo, e men con lor mi sdegno: 45
    perché, salendo lo intelletto in suso
per veder Dio, non de' parerci strano
se talor cade giù cieco e confuso.
Ma tu, del qual lo studio è tutto umano
e son li tuoi suggetti i boschi e i colli,   50
il mormorar d'un rio che righi il piano,
    cantar antiqui gesti e render molli
con prieghi animi duri, e far sovente
di false lode i principi satolli,
    dimmi, che truovi tu che sì la mente   55
ti debbia aviluppar, sì tòrre il senno,
che tu non creda come l'altra gente?
Il nome che di apostolo ti denno
o d'alcun minor santo i padri, quando
cristiano d'acqua, e non d'altro ti fenno,   60
    in Cosmico, in Pomponio vai mutando;
altri Pietro in Pïerio, altri Giovanni
in Iano o in Iovïan va riconciando;
    quasi che 'l nome i buon giudici ingannì,
e che quel meglio t'abbia a far poeta   65
che non farà lo studio de molti anni.
Esser tali dovean quelli che vieta
che sian ne la republica Platone,
da lui con sì santi ordini discreta;
    ma non fu tal già Febo, né Anfïone,   70
né gli altri che trovaro i primi versi,
che col buon stile, e più con l'opre buone,

does not trouble to contemplate how one proceeds
or is born from the other, or how our weak minds
may comprehend the unity of one and three. He thinks
that, in not giving his consent to what others approve,
he demonstrates such intelligence as must penetrate
beyond the vastness of the heavens. If Nicoletto[4]
and Brother Martin[5] show signs of unbelief or heresy,
I accuse their excessive knowledge and am less angry
with them; when the intellect ascends on high to see
God, we must not think it strange if sometimes it
falls down blind and bewildered.

But you, whose study is entirely human, and whose
subjects are the woods and the hills, and the murmuring
of a brook that waters the plain, and whose task it
is to sing of ancient deeds, and to soften with prayers
inexorable spirits, and to satiate princes with false
praises, tell me, what have you found that so confuses
your minds and so deprives you of your sense that
you do not believe as others do? The names your
fathers gave you of apostles and lesser saints, and
of no one else, when they made you Christians with
water, you change to Cosmicus[6] and to Pomponius.[7]
One of you spoils Pietro with Pierius,[8] while another
ruins Giovanni with Janus[9] or Jovian,[10] as if names
could deceive good judges and could make you better
poets than years and years of labor and learning.

Such must have been those poetasters to whom
Plato denied entrance to that republic, which he
invested with such saintly laws. But Phoebus was
not so, nor Amphion,[11] nor the others who found
the first verses. With their good style and more with
their good works, they persuaded men to join together

persuasero agli uomini a doversi
ridurre insieme, e abandonar le giande
che per le selve li traean dispersi;   75
   e fér che i più robusti, la cui grande
forza era usata alli minori tòrre
or mogli, or gregge et or miglior vivande,
   si lasciaro alle leggi sottoporre,
e cominciar, versando aratri e glebe,   80
del sudor lor più giusti frutti accòrre.

Indi i scrittor féro all'indotta plebe
creder ch'al suon de le soavi cetre
l'un Troia e l'altro edificasse Tebe;
   e avesson fatto scendere le petre   85
dagli alti monti, et Orfeo tratto al canto
tigri e leon da le spelonche tetre.

   Non è, s'io mi coruccio e grido alquanto
più con la nostra che con l'altre scole,
ch'in tutte l'altre io non veggia altretanto,   90
   d'altra correzïon che di parole
degne; né del fallir de' suoi scolari,
non pur Quintilïano è che si duole.

   Ma se degli altri io vuo' scoprir gli altari,
tu dirai che rubato e del Pistoia   95
e di Petro Aretino abbia gli armari.

   Degli altri studi onor e biasmo, noia
mi dà e piacer, ma non come s'io sento
che viva il pregio de' poeti e moia.

   Altrimenti mi dolgo e mi lamento   100
di sentir riputar senza cervello
il biondo Aonio e più leggier che 'l vento,
   che se del dottoraccio suo fratello
odo il medesmo, al quale un altro pazzo
donò l'onor del manto e del capello.   105

   Più mi duol ch'in vecchiezza voglia il guazzo
Placidïan, che gioven dar soleva,
e che di cavallier torni ragazzo,

and to give up eating acorns, which forced them to
live dispersed throughout the forests. They persuaded
the more robust, whose strength had been thus far
employed in stealing wives and flocks and food from
weaker men, to submit to laws and to begin with
their plows to turn the soil and to harvest with the
sweat of their brows the fruits of justice. Thus writers
convinced the unlearned populace that, with the sound
of their sweet lyres, Phoebus built Troy, and Amphion,
Thebes, and that they caused stones to tumble down
from lofty mountains, and that with his song Orpheus
lured tigers and lions from their gloomy lairs.

Though I cry out and become angered somewhat
more with our school than with the others, I see in
all of them quite as much that merits a correction
beyond what words can give. Quintilian is not alone
in lamenting the sins of his disciples. But if I strive
to lay bare the altars of the others, you will tell me
I am rifling the closets of Il Pistoia[12] and Pietro
Aretino.[13] Honor and blame accorded to the other
studies bring me pleasure and pain, but not as much
of either as when I hear that the reputation of poets
lives or dies.

If I hear that blond Aonius[14] is said to be without
a brain and more unstable than the wind, I sorrow
and I lament far more than if I hear the same said
of his brother[15] the dimwitted doctor to whom another
madman gave the honor of the cloak and the cap.
I am more dismayed that Placidianus[16] in his age craves
the candied fruits which in his youth he used to give
away and that from a knight he is become a child,

che di sentir che simil fango aggreva
il mio vicino Andronico, e vi giace   110
già settant'anni, e ancor non se ne lieva.

Se mi è detto che Pandaro è rapace,
Curio goloso, Pontico idolatro,
Flavio biastemator, via più mi spiace
che se per poco prezzo odo Cusatro   115
dar le sentenzie false, o che col tòsco
mastro Battista mescole il veratro;

o che quel mastro in teologia ch'al tósco
mesce il parlar fachin, si tien la scroffa,
e già n'ha dui bastardi ch'io conosco;   120

né per saziar la gola sua gaglioffa
perdona a spesa, e lascia che di fame
langue la madre e va mendica e goffa;

poi lo sento gridar, che par che chiame
le guardie, ch'io digiuni e ch'io sia casto,   125
e che quanto me stesso il prossimo ame.

Ma gli error di questi altri così il basto
di miei pensier non gravano, che molto
lasci il dormir o perder voglia un pasto.

Ma per tornar là donde io mi son tolto,   130
vorrei che a mio figliuolo un precettore
trovassi meno in questi vizii involto,

che ne la propria lingua de l'autore
gli insegnasse d'intender ciò che Ulisse
sofferse a Troia e poi nel lungo errore,   135

ciò che Apollonio e Euripide già scrisse,
Sofocle, e quel che da le morse fronde
par che poeta in Ascra divenisse,

e quel che Galatea chiamò da l'onde,
Pindaro, e gli altri a cui le Muse argive   140
donar sì dolci lingue e sì faconde.

Già per me sa ciò che Virgilio scrive,
Terenzio, Ovidio, Orazio, e le plautine
scene ha vedute, guaste e a pena vive.

than when I hear that my neighbor Andronicus[17] is buried under the same slime and has been lying there for seventy years and still has not arisen. If it is said to me that Pandarus[18] is rapacious, Curius[19] gluttonous, Ponticus[20] idolatrous, and Flavius[21] blasphemous, I am far more displeased, than if I hear that Cusatro[22] hands down false judgments for a small fee, or that Master Battista[23] mixes his white hellebore with poison, or that a certain master of theology[24] who mixes his Tuscan with Bergamasque cohabits with a sow and has already had two bastards by her that I know of. Nor does he spare expense to stuff his worthless gut while he lets his own mother grow feeble with hunger and go begging and limping. I hear him scream out as if he were calling the guard, because I fast and am chaste and love my neighbor as I do myself. Yet the sins of this rabble do not so very much weigh down the sack of my thoughts that I lose much sleep or am inclined to miss a meal.

But to return to the place whence I digressed, Bembo, I would like you to find my son a preceptor less enveloped in these vices, who in the actual language of the author can teach him to understand what Ulysses suffered at Troy and afterwards during his long wandering, what Apollonius and Euripides once wrote, and Sophocles, and he who having eaten laurel seems in Ascra to have become a poet,[25] and he who called Galatea from the waves,[26] and Pindar, and the others to whom the Argive Muses gave tongues so sweet and eloquent. He already knows from my instruction what Vergil and Terence wrote, and Ovid and Horace, and he has seen the plays of Plautus, though they were maimed and scarce alive. Henceforth

Omai può senza me per le latine   145
vestigie andar a Delfi, e de la strada
che monta in Elicon vedere il fine;
    ma perché meglio e più sicur vi vada,
desidero ch'egli abbia buone scorte,
che sien de la medesima contrada.   150
    Non vuol la mia pigrizia o la mia sorte
che del tempio di Apollo io gli apra in Delo,
come gli fei nel Palatin, le porte.
    Ahi lasso! quando ebbi al pegàseo melo
l'età disposta, che le fresche guancie   155
non si vedeano ancor fiorir d'un pelo,
    mio padre mi cacciò con spiedi e lancie,
non che con sproni, a volger testi e chiose,
e me occupò cinque anni in quelle ciancie.
    Ma poi che vide poco fruttüose   160
l'opere, e il tempo invan gittarsi, dopo
molto contrasto in libertà mi pose.
    Passar venti anni io mi truovavo, et uopo
aver di pedagogo: che a fatica
inteso avrei quel che tradusse Esopo.   165
    Fortuna molto mi fu allora amica
che mi offerse Gregorio da Spoleti,
che ragion vuol ch'io sempre benedica.
    Tenea d'ambe le lingue i bei secreti,
e potea giudicar se meglior tuba   170
ebbe il figliuol di Venere o di Teti.
    Ma allora non curai saper di Ecuba
la rabbiosa ira, e come Ulisse a Reso
la vita a un tempo e li cavalli ruba;
    ch'io volea intender prima in che avea offeso   175
Enea Giunon, che 'l bel regno da lei
gli dovesse d'Esperia esser conteso;
    che 'l saper ne la lingua de li Achei
non mi reputo onor, s'io non intendo
prima il parlar de li latini miei.   180

he can follow the traces of the Latins to Delphi without
my help and see the end of the path that rises to
Helicon. But so he may walk there better and more
securely, I desire him to have a good escort of men
who were born in that country.

My indolence or my fate does not permit me to
open to him on Delos, as I have on the Palatine,
the gates to the temple of Apollo. Alas! When I was
of an age inclined to the Pegasian melody,[27] when
my vernal cheeks had not as yet blossomed with a
single hair, my father[28] drove me, not with spurs,
but with swords and lances, to leaf through legal texts
and glosses, and for five years employed me in that
nonsense. But when he saw how fruitless were those
labors and how the time was thrown away, after much
bickering he set me free.

I found myself past twenty years of age and in
great need of a tutor, for I would have been at pains
to understand the writer who translated Aesop.[29] In
those days Fortune was very much my friend, for
she provided me with Gregorio da Spoleto,[30] whom
I must with reason forever bless. He knew the beautiful
secrets of both languages and was able to judge
whether the son of Venus or the son of Thetis had
the better trumpet.[31] But at that time I did not care
to know of Hecuba's raging anger and how Ulysses
robbed Rhesus of his life together with his horses;[32]
for first I wished to understand how Aeneas so
offended Juno that she tried to deny him the beautiful
kingdom of Hesperia.[33] If first I do not understand
the language of my native Latins, knowledge of the
Achaean tongue can bring me no distinction. While

Mentre l'uno acquistando, e diferrendo
vo l'altro, l'Occasion fuggì sdegnata,
poi che mi porge il crine, et io nol prendo.

Mi fu Gregorio da la sfortunata
Duchessa tolto, e dato a quel figliuolo   185
a chi avea il zio la signoria levata.

Di che vendetta, ma con suo gran duolo,
vide ella tosto, ahimè!, perché del fallo
quel che peccò non fu punito solo.

Col zio il nipote (e fu poco intervallo)   190
del regno e de l'aver spogliati in tutto,
prigione andar sotto il dominio gallo.

Gregorio a' prieghi d'Isabella indutto
fu a seguir il discepolo, là dove
lasciò, morendo, i cari amici in lutto.   195

Questa iattura e l'altre cose nòve
che in quei tempi successeno, mi féro
scordar Talia et Euterpe e tutte nòve.

Mi more il padre, e da Maria il pensiero
drieto a Marta bisogna ch'io rivolga,   200
ch'io muti in squarci et in vacchette Omero;

truovi marito e modo che si tolga
di casa una sorella, e un'altra appresso,
e che l'eredità non se ne dolga;

coi piccioli fratelli, ai quai successo   205
ero in luogo di padre, far l'uffizio
che debito e pietà m'avea commesso;

a chi studio, a chi corte, a chi essercizio
altro proporre, e procurar non pieghi
da le virtudi il molle animo al vizio.   210

Né questo è sol che a li miei studii nieghi
di più avanzarsi, e basti che la barca,
perché non torni a dietro, al lito leghi;

ma si truovò di tanti affanni carca
allor la mente mia, ch'ebbi desire   215
che la cocca al mio fil fésse la Parca.

I was in the process of acquiring the first, deferring
the second, Occasion fled insulted; she had offered
me her forelock and I had not seized it. Gregorio
was taken from me by the unhappy Duchess[34] and
given to her son, whose uncle had usurped his dominion. She saw him soon revenged, but to her great
sorrow, alas, since he who sinned was not the only
one to be punished. Completely spoiled of sovereignty
and wealth, the nephew, after a short interval, was
taken with his uncle prisoner under Gallic rule. Isabella's prayers persuaded Gregorio to follow his pupil
to the land where he died and left his closest friends
in mourning.

This upheaval and other unexpected events that
followed in those days made me forget Thalia and
Euterpe[35] and all the nine. My father died, and I
was forced to turn my thoughts from Mary back to
Martha,[36] and to exchange Homer for account books
and ledgers, and find a husband and a dowry for
one sister, and then another,[37] and provide that the
inheritance should not suffer as a result. For my little
brothers, to whom I had taken the place of a father,
I had to perform the offices that duty and compassion
had assigned me, to propose study for one,[38] the court
for another,[39] and still another practice for a third,[40]
and to see that their pliable spirits did not incline
from virtue toward vice.

Nor is this all that prevented my studies from further
advancing and forced me to moor my ship so it might
not reverse its course. But I found my mind at that
time so loaded with anguish that I desired Atropos
to tie off my thread on the spindle. He whose sweet

Quel, la cui dolce compagnia nutrire
solea i miei studi, e stimulando inanzi
con dolce emulazion solea far ire,
 il mio parente, amico, fratello, anzi   220
l'anima mia, non mezza non, ma intiera,
senza ch'alcuna parte me ne avanzi,
 morì, Pandolfo, poco dopo: ah fera
scossa ch'avesti allor, stirpe Arïosta,
di ch'egli un ramo, e forse il più bello, era! 225
 In tanto onor, vivendo, t'avria posta,
ch'altra a quel né in Ferrara né in Bologna,
onde hai l'antiqua origine, s'accosta.
 Se la virtù dà onor, come vergogna
il vizio, si potea sperar da lui   230
tutto l'onor che buono animo agogna.
 Alla morte del padre e de li dui
sì cari amici, aggiunge che dal giogo
del Cardinal da Este oppresso fui;
 che da la creazione insino al rogo 235
di Iulio, e poi sette anni anco di Leo,
non mi lasciò fermar molto in un luogo,
 e di poeta cavallar mi feo:
vedi se per le balze e per le fosse
io potevo imparar greco o caldeo!   240
 Mi maraviglio che di me non fosse
come di quel filosofo, a chi il sasso
ciò che inanzi sapea dal capo scosse.
 Bembo, io ti prego insomma, pria che 'l passo
chiuso gli sia, che al mio Virginio porga 245
la tua prudenza guida, che in Parnasso,
 ove per tempo ir non seppi io, lo scorga.

company was wont to nourish my studies and to urge them forward in sweet emulation, my kinsman, my friend, my brother, nay my soul, not half, but all of it, with no part remaining to me, died soon after— Pandolfo. [41] Oh, what a savage blow you suffered then, stock of Ariosto, of which he was a branch and perhaps the most beautiful! Had he lived, he would have placed you in such high honor that no other family of Ferrara or Bologna, whence you derive your ancient origin, [42] could have approached it. If virtue gives honor, just as vice gives shame, there was to be hoped of him all the honor that a good spirit craves.

To the deaths of my father and two such dear friends, let it be added that I was oppressed by the yoke of the Cardinal of Este, who, from the accession to the funeral pyre of Julius, and afterwards for seven [43] more years of Leo, did not let me rest long in one place and from a poet made a horseman of me. Behold whether, dashing over cliffs and through ditches, I had the leisure to learn Greek or Chaldaic! I marvel that it was not with me as it was with that philosopher from whose head the stone knocked all he knew. [44]

Bembo, in a word, I beseech you to extend to my Virginio, before the pass is closed to him, your prudent escort, so that to Parnassus, where I could not go in time, you may show him the way.

NOTES

[1] Demetrius Chalcondyles (1424–1511), born in Athens, taught Greek in Perugia, Padua, Florence, and Milan. He established high standards of accuracy for the editing of Greek texts. Thomas Linacre was one of his pupils in Padua. Marcus Musurus (1470–1517) of Crete was a friend of Bembo and taught in Padua, Venice, and Rome. Leo X made him a cardinal. Ariosto remembered him in the *Orlando* Furioso, XLVI, 13.

[2] The original employs for the first time in Italian literature the word "umanista."

[3] The sin of unbelief. Ariosto is alluding to a popular anecdote about the Spaniard who, after he had just confessed himself, turned round to his confessor to say that he had forgotten one little sin: he did not believe in God. The anecdote refers to Spanish Moors and Jews who had been forced against their consciences to convert.

[4] Probably Nicoletto Vernia da Chieti, who taught philosophy in Padua, where he died in 1499. He was an Averroist and the ideal master of philosophy according to Pomponazzi. When threatened with excommunication, he returned to Thomist doctrine. However, this might also be Nicolò Lelio Cosmico.

[5] This is perhaps the first reference to Martin Luther in a literary work in Italian.

[6] Nicolò di Lello (1420?–1500) of Padua was a well-thought-of poet in Latin and the vernacular. Ariosto lamented his death in his *Lirica Latina*, XVI.

[7] Pomponius Laetus (1428–1498), whose real name we do not know, founded the Roman Academy. He lectured to large audiences on Latin authors and supervised productions of Plautus's plays every year at the anniversary of the founding of Rome. He was persecuted by Pope Paul II, but later gained the friendship and support of Paul's successors in the papacy.

[8] Giampietro Valeriano Bolzani (Pierius Valerianus, 1477–1558) of Belluno was an author of elegies, a teacher, and a servant of the Medici. Ariosto mentions him in the *Orlando Furioso* XLVI, 13.

[9] Giampaolo Parisio (Aulus Janus Parrasius, 1470–1534) of Cosenza was a poet in Latin and a professor of eloquence.

[10] The great poet Giovanni Pontano (Jovianus Pontanus, 1426–1503) of Umbria is held to have written the most living Latin of the Renaissance. He served as a secretary to King Ferrante, and developed, but did not found, the Neapolitan Academy of which Iacopo Sannazaro was a member.

[11] L1. 70–87 echo Horace's *Ars Poetica*, 11. 391–401.

[12] Antonio Cammelli (1436–1502), called Il Pistoia, was the author of humorous and satirical sonnets. See Satire III, n. 2.

[13] Pietro Aretino (1492–1556), notorious as a scandalmonger, lived in Rome during the papacy of Leo X and for the first ten years of Clement VII. After the Sack of Rome he moved to Venice. He was also notorious for his blackmailing letters. His *Giudizi*, annually issued prognostications of what would befall certain people in the year to come, circulated widely in Italy.

[14] The *improvisatore* Bernardo Accolti (1465–1536), who styled himself "l'Unico Aretino" because of his birth in Arezzo and his unequalled facility in impromptu music and poetry, is best known to students of Renaissance literature as one of the interlocutors in Castiglione's *Book of the Courtier*. Leo X rewarded him so richly that he was able to buy the small duchy of Nepi. He was nicknamed "il Biondo," the blond one. Ariosto remembered him in the *Orlando Furioso*, XLVI, 10. "*Aonius*" means "Boeotian" and by extension "poet," since Helicon

and the fountain Aganippe were held to be located in Boeotia. Hence, the Muses were referred to as "*Aoniae sorores.*" Ariosto uses the expression "*santo aonio coro*" in the *Orlando Furioso,* XLVI, 3.

[15] Pietro Accolti, a celebrated jurist and theologian, was made a cardinal by Julius II.

[16] An unknown person.

[17] Another unknown person.

[18] A poetaster who lived at the court of Leo X. He was called Pindarus. After having first spelled his name correctly in the manuscript, Ariosto, in a punning mood, then changed the "i" to an "a."

[19] Perhaps Celso Secondo Curione, who latinized his name to Curius. He was a latinist at the court of Leo X.

[20] Ludovico da Ponte, or Ponticus Virunnius, a Ferrarese humanist who was tried for heresy.

[21] According to Bertani, this might be the famous historian and topographer Flavio Biondo who graced the pontificate of Pius II. He had been dead, however, for more than half a century before Ariosto began to write the present satire.

[22] Amato Cusatro, a Mantuan judge, was tried in 1507 for extortion and incest.

[23] A reference to the Conspiracy of the Cardinals. See Satire III, n. 16, and Satire II, 11. 206–207. Cardinal Alfonso Petrucci of Siena bribed the surgeon Battista da Vercelli to mix poison with the medicinal hellebore Leo X used for the cure of his fistula.

[24] Again Pietro Accolti (see n. 15). He was in the habit of mixing his Tuscan with low dialectal expressions.

[25] Hesiod. In his *Theogony* (22–34), he describes his dream, to which Ariosto alludes in these lines.

[26] Theocritus. In his eleventh idyll, he tells of the love of Polyphemus for Galatea.

[27] Poetry. With a stamp of his hoof Pegasus, the winged horse, produced the fountain Hippocrene.

[28] See Satire III, n. 2.

[29] Phaedrus. Ariosto is exaggerating to say the least. By 1494 he was already writing Latin poetry.

[30] Little is known about the early life of Gregorio di Andrea d'Angelo except that he left the Augustinian friars in order to devote himself to humanist studies. He seems to have been befriended by a certain Pier Leoni, a physician and philosopher also of Spoleto, who may have introduced him at the court of Naples where he would certainly have met Isabella of Aragon. From 1485–1491, he served in Florence as preceptor to Franciotto Orsini and Giovanni de' Medici, the future Leo X. He may have left Florence as a result of the expulsion of the Medici in 1494, or earlier as a result of his protector Leoni's having been accused of hastening either intentionally or through negligence, the death of Lorenzo the Magnificent. Gregorio went to Ferrara where he served as tutor to the children of Rinaldo d'Este, and it was probably in Rinaldo's palace, called the *Paradiso,* that Ariosto first met him. After having spent several years buried in legal texts, Ludovico needed an experienced preceptor to guide him back to the study of Latin literature and the writing of poetry in Latin. Evidently, Gregorio was an excellent guide, for the poet remembered him with the greatest affection in his ode to Alberto Pio. In that ode, written after Gregorio had departed for France, Ariosto claims that he owes everything good in him to his tutor, and that Gregorio gave him his noble spirit, while his father only gave him his existence. But this beautiful student-teacher relationship came

to an abrupt end in 1497, when Isabella of Aragon, Duchess of Milan (see 1. 185), asked Gregorio to serve as her son Francesco Sforza's tutor.

[31] Through his knowledge of Greek, as well as Latin, Gregorio was able to tell whether Vergil or Homer was the better poet.

[32] Allusions to two episodes in *The Iliad*, in books XXII and X.

[33] Juno's wrath against the Trojans is the source of the adventures and delays Aeneas must undergo before he can establish his kingdom in Italy (Hesperia).

[34] Isabella of Aragon was indeed unhappy from the day she first set foot in Milan as wife of the rightful Duke Gian Galeazzo Sforza. Lodovico il Moro, the usurping uncle of 1. 186, had Gian Galeazzo poisoned, and took over the dukedom as regent for Isabella's son Francesco. Not only was Isabella's political authority removed from her, but in addition she was overshadowed socially by Lodovico's wife Beatrice d'Este. She saw her husband and her son revenged by the French, who twice in the years 1499-1500 expelled Lodovico from Milan, and finally took him into exile in France where he died in prison. However, with Lodovico's defeat, Isabella was forced to retire to Ischia with her daughter Bona, while her son was taken away from her by the French, in October 1499, and transported to Lyons. There he became a monk, and died a few years later from a riding accident. Isabella died in Ischia in 1524. Gregorio died in France where he had followed his pupil at her request.

[35] The muses of comedy and flute playing.

[36] Mary symbolized the contemplative life, and Martha the active. Luke 10:38-42.

[37] Laura Margherita and Taddea. See Satire I, n. 24.

[38] Gabriele. See Satire I, n. 23.

[39] Galasso or Alessandro. See Satire I, n. 20 preface.

[40] Carlo. See Satire I, n. 18.

[41] About Pandolfo Ariosto, Ludovico's distant cousin and the most cherished friend and confidant of his youth, we know almost nothing. He was several years older than Ludovico, and composed some Latin poetry. He served Ercole I and, from 1498-1505, Cardinal Ippolito, who greatly favored him, giving him the important post of chancellor. It is believed that Pandolfo may have been the one who managed to get Ludovico into the Cardinal's service. It is also believed that he was the one who finally persuaded the poet's father not to force him to study law. Two poems of the *Lirica Latina* (II and VI) are addressed to Pandolfo, in the second of which the poet informs Pandolfo that he will be unable to join him at his lovely villa in Copparo to write poetry because his love for a pretty girl is detaining him in Ferrara.

[42] With the marriage of "the beautiful Lippa" (*Orlando Furioso*, XIII, 73) to Obizzo III d'Este in 1347, the Ariosti moved from Bologna to Ferrara, where they were always to hold important posts at the Estensi court. Lippa, or Filippa Ariosto, had been Obizzo's concubine for more than twenty years prior to the marriage.

[43] Actually only five.

[44] An allusion to an anecdote narrated by Pliny the Elder in his *Naturalis Historia* (VII, 90). The name of the philosopher is not mentioned.

SATIRE VII

To Messer Bonaventura Pistofilo
Secretary to the Duke

On 14 September 1523 Pope Adrian VI died, bringing to a close his very brief and very unpopular papacy. Duke Alfonso, taking advantage of the vacancy, marched out at once to reconquer Reggio and Rubiera, Ferrarese domains that had been seized eleven years earlier by the troops of Pope Julius II. On 19 November 1523 the conclave elected Giulio de' Medici, who took the name Clement VII. Confronted with a papal opponent who was also the cousin of his former enemy Pope Leo X, Alfonso called an abrupt halt to his campaign of reconquest and dispatched three ambassadors extraordinary to the Vatican to negotiate peace. By the end of March 1524 a treaty had been signed, and it became necessary for the Duke to name a permanent ambassador to the papal court. Bonaventura Pistofilo,[1] the Duke's secretary and biographer, a very close friend of the poet, wrote to Ariosto, asking him if he would like the appointment. Pistofilo must have thought that after two years of misery in Garfagnana his friend would be easy to persuade.

Ariosto replied with the present satire, in which he thanks the secretary for trying to advance his interests but declares that he will accept the ambassadorship only if he must. He has honor and influence enough without the new appointment. As for wealth, he would indeed go to Rome if he thought Clement would reward him with the small sum of money he needed to free himself from the obligations of a public official. But there is no hope of that. Ever since the election of Leo X in 1512 he has had plenty of friends in Rome powerful enough to obtain for him the sinecure he has always wanted and deserved, but they have never condescended to do so. Even Leo X, with whom he had maintained friendly relations for years prior to his election, neglected him in favor of less deserving petitioners. What hope is there that Leo's cousin will be generous when Leo himself was not? The quest for wealth and prestige aside, he would be satisfied simply to escape from Garfagnana, but not in the direction of Rome. If Pistofilo wishes to do him a favor, he might better attempt to find for him a post in Ferrara, where he would be near his friends and near his Alessandra.

Satire VII should be read in conjunction with Satire III, its counterpart, dating from six years earlier. Ariosto recalls in both satires that time of disappointment in Rome when the new pope, Giovanni de' Medici, publicly displayed great friendliness towards him but gave him nothing, neither benefices nor a prelate's rank, in recognition of his merits as a poet.[2] Although Satire VII is the later work, the intensity of the attack against the Medici far surpasses that of Satire III, reaching a level of commination worthy of Dante.

It is appropriate that Satire VII should end the series of satires. Satire VI may have been written at a later date, but Satire VII presents in tone and content Ariosto's final renunciation of the life of ambitious striving after recognition, preferment, benefices and sinecures. It is his final statement of disgust with the patronage system. A year after he had composed Satire VII the poet ended his tenure in Garfagnana and returned to Ferrara, where after a short interval he bought and remodeled a small house on the Via Mirasole. Over the door he found inscribed the following distich:

Parva sed apta mihi sed nulli obnoxia sed non
Sordida parta meo sed tamen aere domus

A small house, but suitable for me; a burden to no one; Not mean; and purchased with my own earnings.

Ariosto bought the house in which he spent the last years of his life with money from his share of his father's and his cousin Alfonso's inheritances, with money painstakingly saved while he was Commissioner of Garfagnana, and with a remuneration from the Duke's eldest son Ercole II for his comedy the *Lena*, not with any rewards he had ever received from Cardinal Ippolito, Duke Alfonso, or Pope Leo X. It was Horace's good fortune and not his, to have had a liberal benefactor provide him with a home. Ironically, the only steady income ever to be his by way of patronage, Ariosto received too late in his life to enjoy, and, sad to say, not from an Italian. In 1531 Duke Alfonso sent him on a mission to one of Charles V's most famous captains, Alfonso d'Avalos, Marchese del Vasto, who was encamped with his army in Mantuan territory. After the mission was concluded successfully, d'Avalos, to show his admiration for the greatest poet of the age, granted Ariosto an annual pension of 100 gold ducats for life. Ariosto died less than a year and a half later.

Although in the present satire he fervently renounces any hope of preferment in public life, the poet was not in actuality to escape public prominence. Upon his return from Garfagnana he became a steady holder of administrative posts in the municipality of Ferrara. As the fame of the author of the *Orlando Furioso* spread throughout Italy, Duke Alfonso grew more and more to require his presence on occasions of state. He participated in the reception held in Modena in 1529 for Charles V, where Duke Alfonso was forced for the security of Ferrara to use all the diplomatic skill at his command to win the Emperor's favor. In 1531, the poet was in the Duke's entourage when he entered Bologna to be reinvested by Charles in the Duchies of Modena, Reggio, and Ferrara. Again in 1532, Ariosto found himself in the Emperor's presence when Alfonso went to Mantua where the Emperor and Clement VII were busy forming a league against France. On this occasion, Charles gave Ariosto an honorary diploma naming him poet laureate; but there is no record of a public ceremony and coronation in the tradition of Petrarch. After the publication of the third edition of his *Orlando Furioso*, the poet lived long enough to hear himself referred to as "*il divino Ariosto*"; "*il divino*" had till then been reserved almost exclusively for references to Dante.

Ariosto also found himself in the center of things in another department of court life. During his last years, he was the leading dramatist of Ferrara. The *Lena*, perhaps his most interesting comedy, was first performed during the carnival of 1528. Later in the same year, he became involved in preparations for the reception in Ferrara of Renée de France, the royal bride of Alfonso's eldest son Ercole II. Alfonso wished to give a performance in her honor of the *Menaechmi* in French. However, the French translator was not well enough acquainted with the style of Plautus to work directly from the Latin text. Ariosto was commissioned to provide for his guidance a faithful translation into Italian.[3] On 24 January 1529, just a few days prior to the performance of the *Menaechmi* in French, Ercole gave a banquet in honor of his father, his bride, and his aunt Isabella, at which the main entertainment consisted of a production of Ariosto's *Cassaria* in prose. Then within a matter of weeks, his *Negromante* received its second production, and the *Lena* was performed again but with a new concluding scene. The year 1531 saw the first performance of the *Cassaria* in verse, and also the construction of the first permanent stage in Ferrara. Ariosto designed it. It was believed by his contemporaries that he was first seized with fatal illness when he witnessed in December 1532 his beautiful creation destroyed by fire.[4] However, it was not destroyed before it could serve for performances of the *Lena* and the *Cassaria* during the carnival of 1532. Perhaps the best tribute to Ariosto's skill as a dramatist and as a supervisor of productions comes from Isabella d'Este. In a letter from Mantua thanking one of her correspondents for the account he gave her of the carnival of 1532 in Ferrara, she makes a very flattering reference to the poet:

> We too have produced two comedies, but they were not performed in as fine a manner as they deserved, nor as well as yours must have been, and with reason, since yours had the supervision of Messer Ludovico Ariosto, whose equal in such matters cannot be found today.[5]

Bonaventura Pistofilo may have been a good judge of how difficult it would be for the poet to avoid taking a prominent place in society; but for Ariosto in 1524, immersed in the drudgery of Garfagnana, his friend's offer of the ambassadorship to the Vatican could only have stirred up unpleasant memories. For all the attractions Rome had to offer, it would still be better to return to Ferrara and to a life free of any temptation to hope for the impossible. And besides, there was Alessandra, from whom any long absence meant suffering. After the long separation imposed by the commissariat, Ariosto must have been anxious to devote as much time as possible to his future wife. Pistofilo, related to Alessandra through marriage, understood full well the allusion to her in the closing lines of the epistle that lay before him.

NOTES

[1] Ariosto makes affectionate reference to him in the *Orlando Furioso* (XLVI, 10).

[2] Cf. Satire III, 11. 175-185, with Satire VII, 11. 55-69.

[3] The autograph of his translation of the *Menaechmi*, as well as of the *Aulularia*, is known to have existed at the beginning of the eighteenth century in Ferrara in the hands of the poet's descendants. Today there is no trace of it.

[4] Catalano, I, 594.

[5] Catalano, II, 321.

Pistofilo, tu scrivi che, se appresso
papa Clemente imbasciator del Duca
per uno anno o per dui voglio esser messo,
　　ch'io te ne avisi, acciò che tu conduca
la pratica; e proporre anco non resti　　　　　　　5
qualche viva cagion che me vi induca:
　　che lungamente sia stato de questi
Medici amico, e conversar con loro
con gran dimestichezza mi vedesti,
　　quando eran fuorusciti, e quando fòro　　　　10
rimessi in stato, e quando in su le rosse
scarpe Leone ebbe la croce d'oro;
　　che, oltre che a proposito assai fosse
del Duca, estimi che tirare a mio
utile e onor potrei gran pòste e grosse;　　　　15
　　che più da un fiume grande che da un rio
posso sperar di prendere, s'io pesco.
Or odi quanto acciò ti rispondo io.
　　Io te rengrazio prima, che più fresco
sia sempre il tuo desir in essaltarmi,　　　　20
e far di bue mi vogli un barbaresco;
　　poi dico che pel fuoco e che per l'armi
a servigio del Duca in Francia e in Spagna
e in India, non che a Roma, puoi mandarmi:
　　ma per dirmi ch'onor vi si guadagna　　　　25
e facultà, ritruova altro cimbello,
se vuoi che l'augel caschi ne la ragna.
　　Perché, quanto a l'onor, n'ho tutto quello
ch'io voglio: assai mi può parer ch'io veggio
a più di sei levarmisi il capello,　　　　30
　　perché san che talor col Duca seggio
a mensa, e ne riporto qualche grazia
se per me o per li amici gli la chieggio.
　　E se, come d'onor mi truovo sazia
la mente, avessi facultà a bastanza,　　　　35
il mio desir si fermeria, ch'or spazia.

Pistofilo, you write to me that if I care to be appointed Ducal Ambassador to the court of Clement for one or two years, I should let you know, so you can make the arrangements. And you do not hesitate to advance a few powerful reasons that should entice me there. For I have long been a friend of these Medici, and you yourself saw me move among them with great familiarity when they were exiles, and when they were restored, and when Leo wore the cross of gold on his scarlet shoes.[1] Besides the obvious advantage to the Duke, you think I should be able to rake in, to my profit and prestige, fast and ample winnings: I can hope to catch more in a big river than in a stream—if I fish. Now hearken to what I have to say in reply.

First I thank you, that your desire may be ever fresh to exalt me, and to transform me from an ox into a Barbary charger. Next I declare that you may send me through fire and through battle to France, Spain, and India, to say nothing of Rome, in the Duke's service. But instead of telling me that honor and wealth are to be earned there, go find another decoy if you want the bird to fall into your net. For I have all the honor that I want. It satisfies me quite enough if I see more than six doff their hats to me, because they know I sometimes dine at the Duke's table and bring a few tidbits back if I request them for myself or my friends. And if I had as much wealth as I have honor, my desire, which now casts about, would

Sol tanta ne vorrei, che viver sanza
chiederne altrui mi fésse in libertade,
il che ottener mai più non ho speranza,
    poi che tanti mie' amici podestade   40
hanno avuto di farlo, e pur rimaso
son sempre in servitude e in povertade.
    Non vuo' più che colei che fu del vaso
de l'incauto Epimeteo a fuggir lenta
mi tiri come un bufalo pel naso.   45
    Quella ruota dipinta mi sgomenta
ch'ogni mastro di carte a un modo finge:
tanta concordia non credo io che menta.
    Quel che le siede in cima si dipinge
uno asinello: ognun lo enigma intende,   50
senza che chiami a interpetrarlo Sfinge.
    Vi si vede anco che ciascun che ascende
comincia a inasinir le prime membre,
e resta umano quel che a dietro pende.
    Fin che de la speranza mi rimembre,   55
che coi fior venne e con le prime foglie,
e poi fuggì senza aspettar settembre
    (venne il dì che la Chiesa fu per moglie
data a Leone, e che alle nozze vidi
a tanti amici miei rosse le spoglie;   60
    venne a calende, e fuggì inanzi agli idi),
fin che me ne rimembre, esser non puote
che di promessa altrui mai più mi fidi.
    La sciocca speme a le contrade ignote
salì del ciel, quel dì che 'l Pastor santo   65
la man mi strinse, e mi baciò le gote;
    ma, fatte in pochi giorni poi di quanto
potea ottener le esperïenze prime,
quanto andò in alto, in giù tornò altrotanto.
    Fu già una zucca che montò sublime   70
in pochi giorni tanto, che coperse
a un pero suo vicin l'ultime cime.

come to rest. Only that much wealth would I desire as might enable me to live in freedom without asking others for money. But I no longer hope to obtain it, since so many of my friends have had the power to arrange it so, and nevertheless I have remained always in servitude and in poverty.

I no longer wish that she who was too slow in her flight from the vase of the imprudent Epimetheus[2] should lead me by the nose like a buffalo. I am dismayed by that painted wheel,[3] which every maker of playing cards designs in the same way: I do not see how such unanimity can lie. The top man on the wheel is portrayed as a donkey. Everyone understands the riddle without having to call on the Sphinx to resolve it. There one also sees all who ascend begin to grow donkey-like in their forward parts while what hangs behind remains human.

As long as I remember the hope that came with the flowers and with the early foliage and then fled without waiting for September (the hope that came on the day the Church was given to Leo as his wife, and I saw at the nuptials so many of my friends dressed in red garments;[4] the hope that came at the Kalends and fled before the Ides),[5] as long as I remember, it cannot be that I will ever trust again in the promises of others. My foolish hope flew up to the uncharted regions of heaven on that day when the holy Shepherd squeezed my hand and kissed me on the cheeks; but after I had made in few days time the first trials of how much I might obtain, just as far as it flew up, so far it fell back down again.

Once upon a time there was a gourd which in a few days climbed so high that it covered the highest branches of a neighboring pear tree. The pear tree

Il pero una mattina gli occhi aperse,
ch'avea dormito un lungo sonno, e visti
li nuovi frutti sul capo sederse,   75
    le disse: — Che sei tu? come salisti
qua su? dove eri dianzi, quando lasso
al sonno abandonai questi occhi tristi? —
    Ella gli disse il nome, e dove al basso
fu piantata mostrolli, e che in tre mesi   80
quivi era giunta accelerando il passo.
    — Et io — l'arbor soggiunse — a pena ascesi
a questa altezza, poi che al caldo e al gielo
con tutti i vènti trenta anni contesi.
    Ma tu che a un volger d'occhi arrivi in cielo,   85
rendite certa che, non meno in fretta
che sia cresciuto, mancherà il tuo stelo. —
    Così alla mia speranza, che a staffetta
mi trasse a Roma, potea dir chi avuto
pei Medici sul capo avea la cetta   90
    o ne l'essilio avea lor sovenuto,
o chi a riporlo in casa o chi a crearlo
leon d'umil agnel gli diede aiuto.
    Chi avesse avuto lo spirto di Carlo
Sosena allora, avria a Lorenzo forse   95
detto, quando sentì duca chiamarlo;
    et avria detto al duca di Namorse,
al cardinal de' Rossi et al Bibiena
(a cui meglio era esser rimaso a Torse),
    e detto a Contessina e a Madalena,   100
a la nora, a la socera, et a tutta
quella famiglia d'allegrezza piena:
    — Questa similitudine fia indutta
più propria a voi, che come vostra gioia
tosto montò, tosto sarà distrutta: 105
    tutti morrete, et è fatal che muoia
Leone appresso, prima che otto volte
torni in quel segno il fondator di Troia. —

opened its eyes one morning, for it had slept a long sleep, and seeing the new fruits sitting above its head, it asked them, "Who are you? How did you climb up there? Where were you before when, weary, I closed these wretched eyes of mine in sleep?" The gourd told its name and showed where its roots were planted and explained how in three months it had arrived there by quickening its step. "And I," replied the pear tree, "scarcely rose to this height after I had wrestled with all the winds in heat and frost for thirty years, but you who in the twinkling of an eye reach the clouds, make yourself certain that your stalk will decay no less hastily than it has grown."

And so might someone have admonished my hope, which sent me spurring to Rome, someone who had sensed the ax held over his neck for the sake of these Medici, or who had aided them in their exile, or had given their leader help to restore himself to his house, or to transform himself from a humble lamb into a lion.

One who had in those days possessed the familiar spirit of Carlo Sosena[6] would perhaps have prophesied to Lorenzo when he heard him called Duke,[7] and would have said to the Duke of Nemours,[8] to the Cardinal de' Rossi,[9] and to Bibbiena (for whom it had been better to stay in Tours),[10] and said to Contessina and to Madalena,[11] and to the daughter-in-law, and the mother-in-law,[12] and to that whole family full of joy, "This comparison may more appropriately be applied to you, for just as your joy swiftly mounted, so will it be destroyed. You will all die, and it is fated that Leo will die soon after, before the founder of Troy returns eight times to the sign of Leo."[13]

Ma per non far, se non bisognan, molte
parole, dico che fur sempre poi   110
l'avare spemi mie tutte sepolte.

    Se Leon non mi diè, che alcun de' suoi
mi dia, non spero; cerca pur questo amo
coprir d'altr'ésca, se pigliar me vuoi.

    Se pur ti par ch'io vi debbia ire, andiamo;   115
ma non già per onor né per ricchezza:
questa non spero, e quel di più non bramo.

    Più tosto di' ch'io lascierò l'asprezza
di questi sassi, e questa gente inculta,
simile al luogo ove ella è nata e avezza;   120

    e non avrò qual da punir con multa,
qual con minaccie, e da dolermi ogni ora
che qui la forza alla ragione insulta.

    Dimmi ch'io potrò aver ozio talora
di riveder le Muse, e con lor sotto   125
le sacre frondi ir poetando ancora.

    Dimmi che al Bembo, al Sadoletto, al dotto
Iovio, al Cavallo, a Blosio, al Molza, al Vida
potrò ogni giorno, e al Tibaldeo, far motto;

    tòr di essi or uno e quando uno altro guida   130
pei sette Colli, che, col libro in mano,
Roma in ogni sua parte mi divida.

    — Qui — dica — il Circo, qui il Foro romano,
qui fu Suburra, e questo è il sacro clivo;
qui Vesta il tempio e qui il solea aver Iano. —   135

    Dimmi ch'avrò, di ciò ch'io leggo o scrivo,
sempre consiglio, o da latin quel tòrre
voglia o da tósco, o da barbato argivo.

    Di libri antiqui anco mi puoi proporre
il numer grande, che per publico uso   140
Sisto da tutto il mondo fe' raccorre.

    Proponendo tu questo, s'io ricuso
l'andata, ben dirai che triste umore
abbia il discorso razional confuso.

But not to mince many words when they are not necessary, I declare that ever afterwards my greedy hopes were all buried. If Leo did not reward me, I do not hope that any of his relatives will. Bait your hook with something else if you wish to catch me.

If it is still your opinion that I should go there, I will go. But not for honor or wealth. I do not hope for the latter and no longer yearn for the former. Sooner say that I will leave the harshness of these rocks and of these people, wild as the place where they were born and became hardened, and that I will not have to punish someone with a fine and someone else with threats, and have cause to grieve every hour that force abuses reason.

Tell me that sometimes I shall have leisure to revisit the Muses and that with them beneath the sacred laurel I shall make poetry once more. Tell me that every day, to Bembo, to Sadoleto,[14] to the learned Giovio,[15] I shall be able to say a word, and to Cavallo,[16] Blosio,[17] Molza,[18] Vida,[19] and Tebaldeo.[20] Tell me that from time to time I shall choose from among them a guide over the seven hills, who book in hand will display Rome to me in her every part. "Here," let him say, "the Circus, here the Roman Forum, and Suburra was here, and this is the sacred hillock, here Vesta had her temple, and there was the shrine of Janus." Tell me that I shall always have advice concerning what I read or write, whether I wish to take it from a Latin, a Tuscan, or a bearded Argive. You can also remind me of the great number of ancient books that Sixtus harvested from all the world for public use.[21]

If you propose all these and I refuse the journey, you will indeed declare that a malicious humor has confounded my reasoning. And I in answer, like

Et io in risposta, come Emilio, fuore　　　　　145
porgerò il piè, e dirò: — Tu non sa' dove
questo calciar mi prema e dia dolore. —
　Da me stesso mi tol chi mi rimove
da la mia terra, e fuor non ne potrei
viver contento, ancor che in grembo a Iove.　　150
　E s'io non fossi d'ogni cinque o sei
mesi stato uno a passeggiar fra il Domo
e le due statue de' Marchesi miei;
　da sì noiosa lontananza domo
già sarei morto, o più di quelli macro　　　155
che stan bramando in purgatorio il pomo.
　Se pur ho da star fuor, mi fia nel sacro
campo di Marte senza dubbio meno
che in questa fossa abitar duro et acro.
　Ma se 'l signor vuol farmi grazia a pieno,　　160
a sé mi chiami, e mai più non mi mandi
più là d'Argenta, o più qua del Bondeno.
　Se perché amo sì il nido mi dimandi,
io non te lo dirò più volentieri
ch'io soglia al frate i falli miei nefandi;　　165
　che so ben che diresti: — Ecco pensieri
d'uom che quarantanove anni a le spalle
grossi e maturi si lasciò l'altro ieri! —
　Buon per me ch'io me ascondo in questa valle,
né l'occhio tuo può correr cento miglia　　　170
a scorger se le guancie ho rosse o gialle;
　che vedermi la faccia più vermiglia,
ben che io scriva da lunge, ti parrebbe,
che non ha madonna Ambra né la figlia,
　o che 'l padre canonico non ebbe　　　　175
quando il fiasco del vin gli cadde in piazza,
che rubò al frate, oltre li dui che bebbe.
　S'io ti fossi vicin, forse la mazza
per bastonarmi piglieresti, tosto
che m'udissi allegar che ragion pazza　　　180
　non mi lasci da voi viver discosto.

Aemilius, shall thrust my foot out and say, "You do not know where this shoe pinches me, where it gives me pain."[22]

He snatches me from myself who sends me far from home, and away I could not live happily even in the lap of Jove. And if I were unable to spend a month out of every five or six strolling around between the Duomo and the two statues of my lords,[23] I would certainly die, overcome by such a vexing absence, or I would grow thinner than those wretches who linger in Purgatory hungering for the apple.[24] But if I have to stay away, it would be far less harsh and exasperating in the sacred field of Mars than it is to inhabit this pit. But if my lord wishes to bestow upon me his fullest favors, let him summon me to him and nevermore send me farther East than Argenta or farther West than Bondeno.[25]

If you ask me why I love my nest so much, I shall tell you no more willingly than I am accustomed to tell the monk my most wicked sins; because I well know that you would gasp, "Are these the thoughts of a man who just the other day put behind his shoulders forty-nine years, long and ripe!" Good for me that I hide myself in this valley and that your eyes cannot see a hundred miles to discover whether my cheeks are red. For, although I write from afar, my face would seem redder to you than Madonna Ambra's[26] or her daughter's, or than the canonical father's when he dropped in the market place the bottle of Chianti he had stolen from the monk, beyond the two he had drunk. If you were within reach of me, perhaps you would take up a club to beat me the minute you heard me plead that a lunatic reason forbids me to live far away from you.

NOTES

[1] When he was elected pope.

[2] An allusion to the myth of Pandora's box. According to one version of the story, the gods filled a box with things harmful to mankind and gave the box to Pandora with orders never to open it. Then they sent her to Epimetheus, who had tricked Zeus into choosing for the gods' portion of every sacrifice the worst parts of the animal. In spite of his brother Prometheus's warnings, Epimetheus took Pandora into his house. In a short time, her curiosity caused her to forget the gods' orders, and she opened the box. Out flew plagues and miseries, but she clapped the lid down just in time to prevent hope from escaping.

[3] The Wheel of Fortune as depicted in the Tarot cards of the period.

[4] On 23 September 1513 Leo made his cousin Giulio de' Medici and his nephew Innocenzo Cybo cardinals along with Lorenzo Pucci and Bibbiena. On 26 June 1517 he created thirty-one cardinals all in one day.

[5] Ariosto is probably referring to early April in 1513 when he was in Rome awaiting Leo's coronation. His letter of 7 April 1513 (see Satire III, preface) records vividly his disappointment at Leo's hands.

[6] A cleric and astrologer of Ferrara who was much sought after by Duke Alfonso and others because of the enchantments and conjurations which he performed with the help of a spirit he said he held prisoner within his body.

[7] See Satire IV, n. 11.

[8] See Satire III, n. 9.

[9] Luigi de' Rossi, son of Maria, an illegitimate sister of Lorenzo the Magnificent, died on 19 August 1519. Leo, who had made him a cardinal in 1517, was grief stricken.

[10] See Satire III, n. 21. In 1518 Leo sent Bibbiena to the court of Francis I at Tours as papal legate. Soon after he returned to Rome in 1520 he died. Ariosto is alluding to a totally unfounded rumor that Leo, jealous of his friend's renown and influence, had him poisoned.

[11] Sisters of Leo who died in 1515 and 1519 respectively.

[12] Madeleine de la Tour d'Auvergne, wife of Lorenzo II de' Medici, is the daughter-in-law. She died in May of 1519. Alfonsina Orsini, mother of Lorenzo II, is the mother-in-law. She had urged upon Leo the seizure of the Duchy of Urbino for her son only to see her son die a few days after the death of his wife. She herself died in 1520.

[13] The founder of Troy was Apollo, or the Sun. Before the sun returns eight times to the sign of Leo (July–August), that is, from roughly the date of Giovanni de' Medici's election on 15 March 1513, Giovanni, Pope Leo X, will be dead. Leo died on 1 December 1521.

[14] Iacopo Sadoleto (1477–1552) of Modena served as a secretary first to Leo X and then to Clement VII. He was a distinguished latinist, and composed a widely admired ode on the discovery of the Laocoon. Ariosto remembered him in the *Orlando Furioso*, XLII, 86.

[15] Paolo Giovio (1483–1552), born at Como, served as a physician to Clement VII. He was noted as an historian, biographer, and collector of portraits. Thomas Linacre and Thomas More are eulogized in his *Elogia clarorum virorum.*

[16] Marco Cavallo of Ancona was a mediocre Latin poet whom Ariosto mentions in the *Orlando Furioso*, XLII, 91.

[17] Blosio Palladio, or Biagio Pallai, of Rome served as a secretary to Clement VII and Paul III. He was also a distinguished latinist.

[18] Francesco Maria Molza (1489-1544) of Modena was an extremely talented poet in Latin and the vernacular. He is the author of *"La ninfa Tiberina"* and of an esteemed collection of *Canzoni.* He migrated to Rome in hope of getting rich at Leo X's court. Ariosto remembered him in the *Orlando Furioso,* XXXVII, 12, and XLVI, 12.

[19] Marco Girolamo Vida (c. 1485-1566), born in Cremona, spent most of his active literary life in and near Rome where he served the Church in various capacities. In 1532 he was made Bishop of Alba. His reputation as a latin poet rests mainly upon three poems: *De ludo scacchorum; De arte poetica,* the first of the numerous sixteenth century treatises on poetry; and his most famous work, the *Christiad,* an epic in six books. Ariosto remembered him in the *Orlando Furioso,* XLVI, 13.

[20] Antonio Tebaldi (1463-1537), called Il Tebaldeo, of Ferrara was a very popular author of poetry in Latin and the vernacular. He is noted for his humorous excesses in the use of metaphor. In one of his poems, his lady's nose bleeds because Love, being blind, missed her heart. Ariosto remembered him in the *Orlando Furioso,* XLII, 83.

[21] A reference to the Vatican Library, founded by Nicholas V, and augmented and opened to the public by Sixtus IV.

[22] According to Plutarch (*Vita Aem. Pauli,* V) Aemilius Paulus answered those who rebuked him for having repudiated a beautiful, rich, and chaste wife by sticking out his foot and saying, "Look, this shoe is attractive, but it gives me pain."

[23] Opposite the cathedral of Ferrara in the major piazza of the city are an equestrian statue of Nicolo II and a statue of Borso d'Este seated.

[24] Dante's *Purgatorio,* XXIII, 11. 22-36.

[25] Two small towns on the borders of Ferrarese territory.

[26] The name indicates that she used much rouge.